HOW TO RESTORE YOUR COLLECTOR CAR

TOM BROWNELL

This book is dedicated to my dad
Wayne J. Brownell
whose love of cars inspired my own.

First published in 1984 by Motorbooks International Publishers & Wholesalers Inc, PO Box 2, 729 Prospect Avenue, Osceola, WI 54020 USA

Library of Congress Cataloging in Publication Data
Brownell, Tom
    How to restore your collector car.

    1. Automobiles—Conservation and restoration.
I. Title.
TL152.2.B76   1983   629.28′722   83-13348
ISBN 0-87938-174-4 (soft)

CONTENTS

SECTION I

SECTION II

PHOTO CREDITS

SECTION I

1

Restoration, A Learn As You Go Adventure

This book is designed to take you on a journey, an old-car journey, and when you've finished, you will have preserved more than a historic remnant; you will have visible proof of craftsmanship, a quality our society has nearly lost, on display in your garage. Before getting sidetracked by the end result let's talk about where you begin. Because of wear and decay, some cars have to be restored from the ground up. Others may need mechanical and cosmetic refurbishing. Still others may call for only selective repair. Determining your car's condition and deciding what work will be done is the first step. Disassembly comes next but before loosening the first bolt, it's important to familiarize yourself with your car's original appearance. That usually calls for research, a necessary first step because from it comes the knowledge to be sure that whatever work you do, be it restoration or repair, is done right.

Since the specific techniques for most mechanical repairs vary according to make and model, the hobbyist/mechanic needs to develop a knack for reading service manuals. A chapter in this introductory section explains the different types of service manuals and gives helpful tips for reading technical writing. To help new hobbyists get started, early chapters discuss setting up shop, list needed tools and give guidelines for shop safety.

Cleaning, degreasing, derusting and paint stripping are necessary first steps before restoring or refinishing most old car parts. There are several cleaning, degreasing and stripping methods that hobbyists can use. The one you choose depends on the condition of your parts and whether you want to do the work yourself or hire a commercial cleaning/stripping service.

The first workshop section of this book explains each method and describes the ones you can do yourself.

Service manuals seldom explain how to rebuild small mechanical parts, gauges and the like because these are items that mechanics typically replace rather than repair. Since hobbyists may find replacement parts unavailable or may desire to rebuild original parts in order to preserve their car's authenticity a later chapter shows how to repair and restore small parts.

Welding and metal repair are the two areas that most hobbyists fear most. The chapter dealing with welding technology describes different types of welding equipment and explains the welding technique in terms that readers who have never tried their hand with a torch or an arc will be able to understand. Other chapters explore methods for repairing the archenemy of all metal products—rust.

The remaining chapters of this book explain how to do body and trim work, jobs that are among the most rewarding areas of restoration.

The appendix contains a list of suppliers, sources helpful for research and plans for tools you can build yourself to save money and make difficult jobs easier.

My first car. When I was fourteen, my uncles gave me this Model A in runabout form to transport lawnmowers for my lawn-care business. Two decades later I gave the runabout a new lease on life by adding a "sportsman" body built from plans found in a 1950 *Mechanix Illustrated*. The magazine honored the project with its Golden Hammer award.

I grew up with cars. Dad was always buying, selling or trading them. In comparison with Dad's cars, contemporary vehicles seem to lack variety. At any rate they fail to rouse my enthusiasm. Other car buffs apparently feel as I do. This is no doubt one of the reasons the old car hobby has become so popular. For years Dad owned a roadster, backed up by a convertible, for fall and spring driving. His 1938 truck saw service hauling parts. His favorite, a 1949 Buick woody wagon, was a truly luxurious touring machine. Its departure after over 100,000 faithful miles was a sad event. Dad had a fondness for Buicks.

This is the stage at which a restoration project really becomes pleasurable. From this point on, the end is in sight. The woody in construction is a new reproduction, built by Victor Antique Auto, Victor, New York.

Dad's '58 Chevy convertible was the envy of my high school pals.

As a writer for *Hot Rod* magazine once put it, the true thrill of driving manifests itself in a roadster. Car collecting offers a return to full-flavored living.

My own interests have run the gamut from Model A Fords to sports cars, Corvettes and Porsches. Most recently I joined the special-interest crowd, purchasing a nimble Mustang convertible. It was a black day when the last American convertibles passed from production and though Chrysler and others are attempting a ragtop revival, it looks as though the convertible era has passed. It's up to collectors like us to jog the memories of those who watch us pass, and show kids hyped on two-wheel transportation that there was once a civilized way to enjoy fresh air.

Restoring an old car is a learn-as-you-go adventure. It's not necessary to know everything before loosening the first bolt. If you did, in some cases you probably wouldn't begin. Learning new skills can be frustrating. Those first passes with a spray gun may look like somebody took a mouthful of paint and blew it out through his teeth. It will indeed be humbling to see the effect of cool and damp or hot and dry weather on drying paint; and there will be other setbacks like those pesky bolts that strip on the last turn of the wrench. But, as with a journey, each experience brings you closer to the goal. Your accomplishments will make you justifiably proud. Soon you will understand why impatient restorers sometimes haul the chassis of their unfinished cars to shows for display. After lavishing hours of painstaking craftsmanship and attention to detail on mechanical parts that will be covered by the car's body and never seen again, you will want to show off your progress to neighbors at the very least. When the job is finally done you'll find a whole new avenue of enjoyment waiting. The shows, parades and family drives are just glimpses of the endless horizon of pleasure that comes from owning a distinctive bit of history called an "old car."

Good luck with your restoration and as the fuel company used to say, "Happy motoring."

Old car repair never fails to spring surprises. Here the puzzle is how to repair a broken carburetor casting.

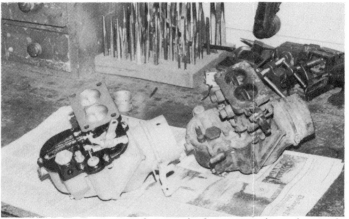
Before and after views show the work of craftsmanship that brings the joy of restoration.

2
The Search For A Collector Car

Not so long ago, premium specimens of what we now call antiques, classic and special-interest cars changed hands at garage sale prices. The junkyard variety cost even less. Early birds of the old car hobby were dyed-in-the-wool car buffs who saw potential in abandoned junkers and didn't care that the cars they drove weren't hot off the assembly line. In the years before interest shifted from new cars to distinctive cars, even the classics weren't hard to find. Stories from those gold rush days have an almost legendary ring. By the early fifties, members of the motoring gentry were sacking the Packards, Pierce-Arrows, Lincolns and Cadillacs they had driven through the war, turning from luxury to fashion. Drab colors and outmoded designs made prewar cars as salable as a hearse, unless they were Fords, and even then hot rodders didn't expect to pay more than $25 for a V-8 roadster.

During that early postwar period my cousin, Guy, shopped used car ads in the *New York Times.* Averaging less than $500 a car, Guy filled his two barns with some of the most spectacular cars ever built. Since my dad was a car buff, he and I spent many Sunday afternoons visiting Guy and admiring his cars. The autumn day Guy fired up his Cadillac four-door convertible is etched in my mind as vividly as if it happened yesterday. Eight spark plugs lined each cylinder bank. The engine cranked over so slowly, I wondered if the battery would expire after one revolution; but the brute caught and when it warmed up only gray smoke from the exhaust showed that the car was running. The German Horche in Guy's garage had been liberated from a Nazi general. It, too, was a convertible with chrome mounts on the front fenders for swastika parade flags and headlights blacked-out to cat's-eye slits. The car dated to 1937, but it had an overhead-cam engine, later made fashionable by the Jaguar, and a five-speed gearbox.

The search for collector cars today is every bit as challenging as it was three decades ago. Although inflation and the demand for old cars has driven up prices, more collector cars are available than ever before. Consider what gives a car collector status and you'll see what I mean. Antiques, of course, are obvious collector cars. While state license bureaus and insurance companies consider any vehicle twenty-five years old an antique, to car buffs the word "antique" generally has a pre-thirties ring. Model T Fords, for example, fit neatly into the antique bracket. They're cute, bizarre to drive and hardly designed for touring on today's highways. Though larger cars of antique vintage can sustain highway speeds, their two-wheel brakes, high-pressure tires, and "armstrong" steering also relegate their use to Sunday drives and club outings.

A true "Classic" is defined by the Classic Car Club of America (CCCA) as follows: fine or unusual foreign or domestic motor cars built between and including the years 1925 and 1948, distinguished for their respective fine design, high engineering standards and superior workmanship. Strictly speaking, classics are distinguished by special styling or mechanical features not found in run-of-the-mill cars. For these reasons, classics weren't high-production models. The term "classic" is widely abused, used in ads to refer not only to mundane business coupes, but even to fiberglass reproductions. True classics include the 1927 through 1933 LaSalle, Cadillac's low-priced sister noted for its innovative styling, and all Cords, distinguished by both outstanding styling and front-wheel drive. Classics are clearly among the most desirable collector cars and chances of finding a true

Nestled in the woods where their owners parked them years ago, these restorable vehicles are slowly settling into the earth. Both the Studebaker truck and early-fifties Packard deserve a better fate.

classic socked away in a barn are remote indeed. Today, classic cars are considered objects of art and are valued accordingly.

Collector interest is growing for late model cars set apart by their innovative features. Like classics, these "milestone cars" were trend setters. Loewy-designed Studebaker coupes with their stunning styling and Corvair Spyders with their turbocharged air-cooled engines exemplify cars granted milestone status.

Special-interest cars form a catch-all category that includes any car of special interest to its owner. In this guise, any vehicle from fire apparatus to chain-drive Mack trucks warrants collector status.

The list goes on. All woodies are collectables and convertibles are rapidly gaining the same status. Neither is produced anymore, at least not in volume; and both were supremely handsome body styles. Model A Fords are boosted by two national and numerous regional clubs. Ford V-8's, too, have a loyal following. Some cars, like the popular Mustang, are collector cars from several standpoints. In today's old car hobby, any car that attracts an owner's eye has merit, but clubs and shows do set restrictions. Cars built since 1967 aren't eligible for judging in my community's annual old car show. This means my '71 Mustang convertible can't compete. But nobody minds if its lines grace Mustang row; and it gathers as many admirers as legitimate entries four years its senior.

Having discussed what a collector car is, let's talk about buying one. As with any object that has had its value increased by collector status, two guidelines are essential: You have to be very careful to accurately appraise the car's condition and you have to be able to peg the price as close as possible to actual market value. The first requires careful shopping and knowing what to look for when buying what could be considered an expensive used car. The market value of collectables is always difficult to pin down since nostalgia and other emotional factors come into play. *Old Car Value Guide, The Gold Book* and *C.A.R. Values,* published price guides similar to a used car dealer's *NADA Blue Book,* are useful for making an initial judgment before price haggling. But the auction prices and variable condition guidelines that these books use to establish prices are subjective at best.

It takes a used car buyer's savvy to thoroughly check out a collector car. This isn't to say that sellers are crooks. To the contrary, most hobbyists are refreshingly honest, caring more that their cars have a good home than that they make a sale. But sometimes even an owner won't know a car's faults. Glaring problems stand out, of course, but mechanical troubles like cracked valve seats, worn or chipped transmission gears and structural damage like a rusted frame are the buyer's responsibility to detect.

There are several approaches to take when shopping for a collector car. One is to check out a collectable the same way you would a used car. Take it for a test drive that includes stopping at a service station to have the attendant raise the car on a lift. With the car elevated, inspect it carefully from underneath. Examine the frame and floor for rust. Check inside the wheel wells, along the frame arches and behind the rocker panels, areas especially vulnerable to corrosion. On Mustang convertibles and other unit-bodied cars be especially alert to rust holes along the edges of the floor pan, a sign of structural weakening of critical support members called "side rails." Shake the front wheels to test steering and suspension wear. Front tire wear along the inside edges of the tread indicates that at best the suspension needs alignment, and may need to be rebuilt. Inspect the engine pan, transmission and rear end for oil leaks. Check the exhaust system for rust. Hold a board against the exhaust outlet and listen for leaks.

With the car on the ground again, pull the dip stick and check the oil. Is it relatively clean showing that the owner gives the car regular maintenance, or is the oil black and looking like tar? Are there water droplets in the oil, indicating a leaking head gasket or, worse, a crack in the engine block? Start the engine, let it idle briefly then gun it. Does black smoke shoot out the tail pipe, a sign the engine is burning oil? As you drive the car check the gauges. Does the engine have good oil pressure? Does it run hot? Do the gauges work? Drive the car slowly over a stretch of dirt road to check for looseness that indicates high mileage. Verify the mileage shown on the odometer by noticing other, possibly contradictory, indicators. Are the springs well worn in the driver's seat? Does the driver's door sag slightly on its hinges when it is opened? Check wear on the brake and clutch pedals. If you have a companion, have him or her drive

When you are scouting cars you never know what will turn up. Ever seen a V-8 Model T? Don Snyder at Snyder's Antique Ford Parts pulled this engine from a dump truck. It packed plenty of power, he reports. Note the twin coils and slot in the left cylinder head for the steering column. It's not Ford built, but a very well-executed example of backyard engineering.

the prospective purchase while you follow. Does the car track straight or are the rear wheels askew from the front so that it angles sideways, the way a dog walks? Does the car bob over bumps indicating bad shock absorbers? These are all signs a wary buyer looks for when checking over a used car.

Evaluate cars that have been restored, either by the owner or professionally, as though you were a concours judge. Your inspection will include many of the mechanical areas that concern a used car buyer, but will concentrate on appearance and authenticity. The check list included at the end of this chapter is modeled after a judging sheet. It can serve as a helpful guide to use when you examine a restored car.

Basket cases, a term that describes cars that have been disassembled or are a collection of parts, and relics that require a frame up restoration call for a third set of standards. Remember that although the ability to see a car's potential is a worthy asset, a derelict vehicle is sure to look less inviting sitting in your driveway than it does in its rustic pasture or barn setting. (My dad once bought a car that was buried up to its windows in hay. When he went back the next day to bring the car home, he couldn't believe what he saw. The body was completely rusted from the tops of the fenders down.) Bring along a flashlight when you're looking at a car stored in a barn or, better yet, ask the owner to wheel the car outside.

The years of use and abuse that often precede a car's collector status leave their scars in vulnerable areas. Ads in *Hemmings Motor News, Cars & Parts* and other hobby magazines tell more than price and description. They identify cars' weak spots. Corvettes, for example, always look rust-free, thanks to their fiberglass bodies. But the nonmetallic exterior can disguise critical frame rust. Ads that stress the condition of the car's frame give collectors inexperienced with vintage Corvettes the clue that just because a plastic car looks rust-free doesn't mean it is.

Besides studying ads, visit restoration shops for an insight into the achilles heel of the types of cars you're interested in buying. Seeing the work that goes into restoration is an education in itself and shops are an ideal place to get an advance look at the types of problems you're likely to encounter. For example, the bodies on most cars built through the thirties and postwar MG's consist of metal skins tacked onto wooden frames. Replacing rotted body wood can be a major undertaking. Telltale signs of wood rot are easier to recognize when you've seen a disassembled body and spoken to the craftsman who is making the repairs. Talk, too, with collectors who have restored their own cars. They usually enjoy describing the condition the car was in when they started and will invariably mention the tough jobs they encountered along the way. When the owner of a 1934 Ford V-8 points with pride to the original aluminum heads on the engine, then tells how mechanics often had to break the heads with a sledge hammer to do a valve job, he is saying that finding a '34 Ford with original heads may be difficult.

Soon you'll be spotting subtle signs of deterioration like paint blisters that point to spongy metal underneath. The headlight "eyebrows" or mid- to late-fifties GM cars, for example, are especially rust prone. Front wheel wells weren't enclosed on most cars of that era, so road salt sprayed underneath the whole fender. Sand deposits accumulating on top of the headlight buckets eventually rot away the tops of fenders; and paint blisters over the headlights of a 1955 Chevy, for example, are a sure sign of trouble in that area.

While evaluating a car's condition, check for options that will make it desirable to own and add to its value. Overdrive was popular through the mid-fifties and cars equipped with that accessory are frugal on gas even by today's standards. Wire wheels, special trim, dressed-up interior decor and limited-production body styles, like woody station wagons, all warrant extra consideration.

Once you have narrowed the field of choice so that you know what type of car you want (maybe even a specific make and model) and have realistically based that choice on what you can afford, serious shopping begins. There are numerous ways to locate collector cars. Hobby magazines like *Hemmings Motor News, Old Cars Weekly* and *Cars & Parts* serve as an ad medium bringing together buyers and sellers nationwide. Club newsletters also carry cars-for-sale ads and since they circulate to a smaller, more specialized market, their offerings are more selective than those found in national magazines. Classified ads

When you are buying a unit-body convertible, such as the Mustang shown here, carefully inspect the door alignment. Sagging doors often mean a rusted unit-body frame. The doors should line up with body contours as they do here.

in Sunday editions of large metropolitan newspapers feature "antique and classic car" sections. Weekly advertisers are sources of ads for late model collectables. It is usually surprising to discover the variety of cars that exist in your own home town. Car shows and swap meets often feature cars for sale, but you have to beware of buyer's fever in that environment. Antique car dealers, restoration shops and auctions are good sources of rare models. Though they are rapidly disappearing, junkyards are still a treasure-trove of collector cars. But remember, cars in junkyards wound up there for a reason.

Part of the challenge of buying a collector car is figuring out how you're going to get your prize home. If the car is driveable, the owner may let you use his plates or you can license the car yourself. Either way, be sure to cover the car with your own insurance. Plan a leisurely drive and stop frequently, especially with cars that have been in storage or driven only short distances in recent years. Many dealers and some private owners will deliver cars that aren't driveable, at your expense. If you own a late model large-size car or pickup and are willing to travel secondary roads, you can stiff-hitch your purchase home. If you don't have a tow bar you can rent one from U-Haul or tool rental centers. Towing a car is tricky and hazardous, especially over long distances. An excellent article describing the circumstances that led to a collector's towing accident appeared in *Special-Interest Autos*, number 49, the February 1979 issue. Back copies of this magazine are kept in print and are available by writing *Special-Interest Autos*, Box 196, Bennington, Vermont, 05201. Hauling a car on a trailer is safer than towing, but requires a vehicle equipped for heavy-duty use and a rugged trailer. Commercial trucking is the safest method—and the most expensive. Clever hobbyists who have included a vintage truck in their collection are able to provide their own transportation. Of course, you'll find some cars that sounded promising but you won't want to bring them home.

One sunny spring day a few years ago, my old-car partner, John Nelson, and I set out on a fifty-mile drive to fetch a 1929 Ford roadster. The chassis was all restored, the owner had told us, and the rest of the car just needed finishing touches. Since the car had been evicted from its storage, $1,200 would make us the new owners. The directions were clear. We recognized the house as soon as we passed it. A pile of iron-oxide-colored metal rose out of a snowbank. "There it is," I pointed. Bright sunshine was turning the remnant of Vermont's thick winter snow cover into a mushy white lake. John had forgotten to bring his boots. Seeing his predicament, the owner let us short-cut through the living room to the back door, but hip-deep snowbanks still separated us from the roadster resting beside a fence fifty yards away. Patches of yellowed hay intertwined with the spokes of the car's wheels. Unworn tread showed that the tires were new, as the owner described them. At least they'd never seen the highway. The flat bulges on the ground showed cracks and rotting rubber.

To the owner of this car a restored chassis apparently meant a coat of black paint splashed over badly rusted, mud-caked metal. Few of the mechanical parts seemed to have originated from a common ancestor—the frame, engine, wheels and transmission had been gathered from the four winds of Model A manufacture. The body was not 1929 vintage as the owner had claimed, but from a 1931 model; and from its appearance the year could have been B.C. not A.D. Addition of a wooden frame and hinges would have easily converted the car's rear quarters into an airy screen door. Through the metal I could see steam rising from John's snow-soaked shoes.

John's casual comment that the car looked rather rough brought acknowledgment of our suspicions. The body had been dug out of a ravine where a farmer had buried it years back. In fact, the owner admitted that lack of success in finding a better body, not loss of storage, had prompted the offer to sell his roadster. John and I drove home that afternoon with our checkbooks still secure in our pockets, disappointed, wet and wary of cars being sold for lack of storage.

More than once I've asked myself what makes us old-car buffs scout back roads, rip our pants on barbed wire fences and tear our hands to scar tissue pawing through piles of rusting metal. Part of the reason, of course, is the possibility that a rumor of an old car stuffed away, forgotten in a barn could turn up an exotic prize—a rare Stutz Bearcat or an early MG, whatever

For $75 I bought this Model A roadster that a carpenter used to haul logs out of his woods.

your dream car might be. Discoveries like this have occurred. But in a larger sense, perhaps the real reason behind the search for old cars is that it leads back to a time when machines had character, where wood trim wasn't yellow plastic and leather wasn't vinyl—where what you saw was real, not phony.

Check List to Use in Appraising a Restored Car

Rate each item on a scale from 1 to 5, using 5 as the maximum value.

Exterior

1. *Body*

   Check for paint blisters, signs of rust.

   Sight along panels to check for waves or bulges, indications of inept body repair.

   Check the condition of running board covers, fender welting, rubber moldings, etc.

2. *Doors*

   Look for paint blisters indicating hidden rust along the bottom edges.

   Do the doors sag when they are opened? Check the driver's door particularly. Sagging doors are a sign of worn hinges and an indication that you are looking at a high-mileage car.

   Check weather seal around the doors and windows.

3. *Hood and Trunk*

   On older cars with center-hinge hoods, check for dents and tears in the metal around the hinge.

   Check inside the trunk and along the edge of the trunk panel for signs of rust, an indication of leaking weather seal.

   Do the hood and trunk close easily, showing proper alignment?

4. *Top*

   Is the convertible top made from original material? Vinyl tops appeared in the fifties. Cars built prior to 1950 should have canvas tops.

   Does the car have an original-style rear window? Many convertibles built from the mid-sixties to the seventies had glass rear windows. Convertibles built during the thirties had small glass windows set in metal frames.

   Inspect convertible top fabric for wear and discoloration.

   Check metal tops for dents.

   On cars with fabric inserts in metal tops, check the condition of the fabric and weather seal.

5. *Paint*

   If possible, check whether the car is painted an authentic color in lacquer or enamel, whichever was used originally.

Does the car have high-quality glossy paint or is the finish dull with an orange-peel texture?

6. *Trim*

Check the chrome plating on bumpers and diecast trim.

Is the chrome bright and lustrous or dull and worn so that base metal or nickel plate shows underneath?

Are plated diecast parts badly pitted?

Is plating authentic? Cars built prior to 1929 generally used nickel rather than chrome.

Is stainless steel trim dented?

Are trim pieces missing?

7. *Glass*

Check for cracked, broken or discolored glass.

Is all glass safety plate? This is important, especially on cars built in the twenties and thirties when side windows and, in many cases, even the windshields were plate glass.

Tinted glass is a desirable option that first appeared in the early fifties.

Interior

1. *Instrument Panel*

Are gauges original, intact and operating?

Are accessory gauges such as a motometer or tachometer included?

Appraise the general condition of the instrument panel.

2. *Upholstery*

Appraise the condition of door panels, seat covering and headliner.

Is the car upholstered in authentic materials?

Is the fabric soiled or torn?

3. *Floor Coverings*

Are the floor mats worn or missing?

Are step plates along the bottoms of the doors missing?

If possible, inspect the floors under the mats. Is the floor pan rusted?

4. *Interior Trim*

Are window moldings wood-grained, chromed or painted as original?

Is the interior trim complete and authentic? Check for missing door handles, window cranks, etc.

5. *Trunk and Tools*

Does rust damage show around insides of the wheel wells?

Is the trunk floor rusted?

Check the condition of the spare tire.

Is a trunk mat included (on cars that were equipped with trunk mats originally)?

Is a correct tool kit included with the car?

Engine and Chassis

1. *Engine Operation*

   Does the engine knock?

   Does it idle and run smoothly?

   Does it appear to burn oil?

2. *Engine Condition*

   Check the oil.

   Inspect the engine for leaks, either water or oil.

   Is the engine authentic?

3. *Belts and Hoses*

   Are radiator hoses and belts in good condition?

   Are hose clamps original style or replacements?

4. *Engine Compartment*

   Evaluate the general appearance of the engine compartment.

   Is the compartment clean, including the underside of the hood?

   Are the engine and accessories painted authentic color?

   Does the wiring appear to be original and in good condition?

5. *Undercarriage*

   Is the chassis clean and painted?

   Do the transmission and rear end appear to leak oil?

   Do springs have proper camber?

   Is the exhaust system original style and free from leaks?

   Chassis bolts were plated on many vintage cars. Are chassis bolts painted where they should be plated?

6. *Wheels and Tires*

   Check for matching tread on all wheels and for signs of uneven tread wear on front tires, especially.

   Check wheel condition. Are wire spokes tight?

   Is the car equipped with accessory wire or alloy wheels?

7. *Authenticity*

   Evaluate overall authenticity. Consider accessories that are included with the car as well as items already mentioned.

Add the points from all twenty categories. Compare the rating you have given the car to one hundred points maximum. This detailed evaluation should be helpful in determining whether you want to buy the car, and establishing its value.

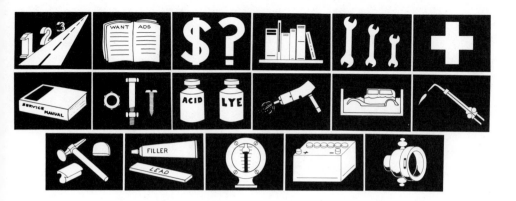

3

To Restore Or Not To Restore, That Is The Question

Whether you're considering refurbishing a collector car you've owned for several years or a new purchase, you should decide whether you're setting out to restore the car or just make repairs. The words "restore" and "repair" have entirely different meanings. When you restore something you take it completely apart then rebuild and refinish every component. Repair means to fix what's wrong without disturbing anything else, if possible. Before deciding on either approach, you should consider the car's condition, your budget and your plans for the car.

Some cars shouldn't be restored. Our European cousins have been wiser in this regard than we. Well-preserved cars may need only minor touch-ups to recapture their original appearance, yet these are the very cars collectors on this side of the pond lavish with frame-up restorations. The explanation for this difference is simple. In American show car competition winners have to be flawless and there is little hope of arriving at perfection when starting from a junker. This goal of perfection produces beautiful cars, but originality can be lost in a restorer's effort to create a museum piece.

Should a collector be lucky enough to find a vintage car tucked away in a barn still wearing its original finish and interior, is the car better preserved by restoration or by repairing the few areas suffering from age or wear? The choice is up to the owner, of course. Nonetheless, I caution collectors against assuming that all cars warrant or need full restoration.

What are the alternatives? First, original cars can be touched up or repaired just enough to preserve their appearance and assure safe, reliable operation. Polishing an old finish to restore its luster abrades an already thin layer of paint, but an original finish can be saved by overlaying it with a coat of clear lacquer or enamel, whichever was used by the manufacturer. Clean the engine compartment and overhaul worn components, check the steering and brakes. With little more than routine maintenance a well-preserved original car can be ready for touring, club events and shows.

Cars that are tattered, but intact, can be repaired as needed and restored later. This approach postpones the financial commitment required by restoration and allows you to enjoy the car. A fully restored car can't be driven casually about town and occasionally to work. If your pleasure in owning a vintage or special-interest car comes from driving it, the process of restoration will make your car inoperable for a year or more and that "downtime," plus the care required to preserve a restored car, may dampen the fun of having an old car.

Some cars that appear well preserved and seem candidates for an easy restoration may not be as solid as they look. If you are considering restoring your car, examine its condition before taking it apart so that you don't find yourself overextended financially or pressed beyond the limit of your skills.

My car pal, John, has owned a Model A phaeton that has served him as an ideal touring vehicle. Apart from a noisy transmission, the car runs smooth as silk. Though the paint isn't an authentic Ford color the car's appearance is presentable enough to capture trophies in local shows. Shortly after buying the car John tightened the front end by replacing the king pins. Later he added shocks, traded the nonstock klaxon horn for an original ooh-gah and replaced the speedometer with a restored unit. After improving the car gradually with a series of repairs, John decided that he would have the car restored. He had come to a point where he was willing to pass up the pleasure of driving the Model A through picturesque New Hampshire countryside for the satisfaction of seeing the car restored to top condition.

Though a Model T chassis looks spindly and naked without its body, an inexpensive and easy-to-install woody wagon or huckster kit would turn these bones into a prize.

While John was making this decision he collected missing parts that would be needed to make his A a show-quality vehicle. At one point he planned to restore the car himself, then, to hasten the job, he contacted a professional restorer. The craftsman's advice was sobering. After carefully inspecting the car he advised John against a frame-up restoration. The cost, he said, would be far in excess of visible improvements. Although the touring car's body looked rust free, the craftsman detected trouble. Once the car was disassembled, he advised that major metal work would be required. After adding expensive body work to the need for a complete mechanical overhaul, a new top and interior, replating plus other functionally unnecessary expenses like replacing all five tires just so the car would have a "new" look, John changed his mind about restoring the phaeton.

John's example and my arguments for repairing well-preserved cars aren't meant to suggest that restoration doesn't have a place; it does. Because of their deteriorated condition, many cars have to be fully restored just to preserve them. At other than local meets, cars competing for prizes have typically been restored. Restoration, then, is the ticket to success in show competition. Besides, repair work such as replacing rotted pieces of a wooden body frame or repairing rust-prone support members on unit-bodied cars require that the car be "gutted," and once disassembly has gone that far, it makes sense to proceed with a full-scale restoration.

By its nature, restoration requires complete disassembly before repair and refinishing can begin. Specifically, here's what is involved. Usually the car is taken apart so thoroughly that rebuilding starts, literally, from the frame up. But first the frame is stripped to bare metal then inspected for signs of metal fatigue and rust. After loose rivets, cracks and any rust damage are repaired by welding, the frame is primed and painted with a durable enamel or polyurethane finish. Then major suspension and drivetrain components, the front suspension, brakes, engine, transmission and rear end are each disassembled, inspected, repaired and refinished. Attention to detail determines the quality of a restoration. Chassis nuts and bolts were originally plated on many vintage cars. Dedicated restorers replate these nuts and bolts even though they can only be seen by crawling underneath the car.

Like the frame, the body on a restored car is stripped to bare metal, wood or fiberglass then repaired and refinished. Unless the interior is intact and well preserved, it too is scuttled and replaced. There's a note of caution here that should be heeded: Always try to remove an existing interior intact and never throw away the old fabric. The original headliner, door panels and seat coverings may have to serve as patterns and will definitely be needed to match new fabrics. While upholstery kits are available for popular makes, Fords and Chevrolets particularly, replacing the interior on other cars can be a challenge. Plated trim, instruments, even rubber moldings and running board coverings may all have to be rejuvenated or replaced.

Restoration demands keen attention to detail at every step. If window moldings were attached originally with phillips screws, slotted screws should not be substituted as replacements. Besides authenticity, the guiding principle of restoration is preventive repair. Components such as the steering mechanism may be rebuilt during restoration even if they show only slight wear. The rationale behind this extra effort is to produce a car that is as nearly "new" as possible and of course to ensure the car won't have to be taken apart again for repair.

To sum up this discussion, there are a number of reasons for performing a frame-up restoration as opposed to rejuvenating a car by repair. First, when a car is restored, all work is finished and the car is ready to be enjoyed. There are no patchwork repairs nagging to be done. Second, some cars require restoration. This is certain to be the case with dismantled antiques or cars that have weathered for years in outdoor storage. Third, major repair work like replacing a rusted floor is easier and more economical if the seats, floor mat and interior have already been stripped out during restoration than if the interior has to be gutted and replaced just to access the rusted panel. Sandblasting and chemical stripping to remove paint and rust are examples of processes that can be accomplished easily when a car is disassembled, but are difficult to couple with

Collector cars like this prize-winning 1914 Model T Ford owned by friend and fellow collector, John Nelson, preserve a slice of history.

repair. Fourth, although the skills required for restoration and repair are likely to be the same, there is a greater incentive to master new trades when rebuilding a car from the frame up. For one thing, you start with disassembly then work on rebuilding rugged chassis parts that even a novice can't damage and by the time you have progressed to finish work, time and toil are bound to have produced a certain finesse.

In weighing the decision whether to restore or repair, consider first your car's condition and your finances. Don't be put off by lack of experience or skills. You will learn along the way. Assess your plans for the car. If you are interested in competition, the car should be restored. If you are more interested in driving the car, repair and rejuvenation may be sufficient. Restoration requires a significant investment in time and money, so honestly evaluate your potential to endure a project that will take months, possibly years. Keep in mind, too, that unless your car is badly deteriorated, it can be driven now and restored later.

Whichever direction you take, you will invariably need to expand your knowledge of your car's original appearance and equipment, authentic accessories, perhaps even its history. This information will guide your efforts and investment. Ways to become better acquainted with your car are explored in the next chapter.

4
A Practical Guide To Old Car Research

Newcomers to the old car hobby and seasoned veterans alike should acquire a knowing eye before purchasing, restoring or sprucing up a collector car with repairs. Seemingly minor items like missing trim, an engine swapped from another year or model, incorrect paint or upholstery schemes easily go unnoticed in the enthusiasm of a new purchase and can even be overlooked when a car is refurbished if the owner takes a casual attitude toward authenticity.

Hobbyists face a unique challenge in this age of specialization. Car repair and refinishing put us in the position of having to become mechanics, bodymen, upholsterers, jacks of all trades; learning new skills as we go along. In order to do each job right we have to know more than how to rebuild a transmission or how to spray a glossy coat of paint. Each of us needs to know our car with the authority of an expert so that we can spot factory color and trim schemes, recognize standard equipment that belongs on the car and note options that have been added, either at the factory or by previous owners. We need to know what the car's interior should look like, what tire size should be on the car to match original equipment and dozens of other details.

Much of this information is found on the manufacturer's data plate, usually located on the firewall or driver's door pillar of cars built since the thirties. The data plate identifies the car's original color, engine type, interior trim scheme, the model, transmission type and rear axle ratio, often the assembly plant, even date of manufacture. Once acquainted with the car's background, this information can be used to determine the car's originality and to guide repairs or restoration so that the work will preserve and enhance its authenticity. The question, of course, is how to decode the data. Dealer service manuals carry translation charts for the vehicle identification plates and the information is also contained in facts books and other reference publications such as Grace Brigham's *The Serial Number Book for US Cars 1900–1975*.

Research and authenticity are important for many reasons. Rehabilitating a collector car without concern for originality decreases the car's value. Then, too, restoring a car is a project of sufficient complexity so that most hobbyists only want one pass through one cycle per car. Nothing is more discouraging than overhearing an expert point out the flaws in your work. Furthermore, locating replacements for incorrect parts and reworking errors wastes time and money that could have been spent productively.

Memories fade quickly, so hobbyists need to gather data in order to return their cars to original standards. Wooden wheels used into the thirties were sometimes painted, sometimes varnished, occasionally highlighted with a color stripe. Which style did Buick use, for example, on its Master series in 1926? Where does a restorer find patterns to accurately reconstruct a missing wooden cab on an antique truck, or engineering specs detailing the distinctions between Crosley's diminutive Hot Shot sports car and its sister model the Supersport? What are the differences between a "pony" model and a standard Mustang? How many units of your car's make and model were originally produced? Many hobbyists are interested in production figures because the numbers give an indication of their car's rarity. Answers to questions like these lie scattered in the pages of automotive history.

Where research begins depends to some extent on each hobbyist's interests, but probably the most enjoyable place to start becoming acquainted with your car's features and background is to read a book that includes your make and model. The catalog pages of Classic Motorbooks and other vendors of old car lore contain a wide range of books describing virtually all cars. Spotter's guides give a thorough explanation of annual styling changes and trim features that distinguish different models year to year.

Books are an ideal starting place to thoroughly familiarize yourself with your car and its distinct features. For instance, the Mustang was introduced mid-year 1964. The 1964½ models, as the first cars are called, are rare and command a premium price. If you are shopping for a Mustang, how do you tell whether or not the car you are looking at is one of the first production models? To learn the answer read the *Mustang Recognition Guide* by the folks at *Mustang Monthly*.

Automotive histories have been written for nearly every popular make, including Buick, Chevrolet, Dodge, Porsche and Jaguar, to name but a few. Other books explore major events of the automotive era such as the demise of Packard and Kaiser's challenge of Detroit. Besides histories, the list of automotive topics ranges from biographies of automotive greats, to reprints of service bulletins, owners manuals and the like.

For limited-production models and other unique antiques research can resemble a history mystery. Automotive encyclopedias, *The Complete Encyclopedia of Motor Cars 1885 to Present* and *The Complete Encyclopedia of Commercial Vehicles*, both by G. N. Georgano, and Richard Langworth's *Encyclopedia of American Cars: 1940–1970* are good places to start. These references contain comprehensive data including manufacturing history and production figures for virtually all U.S. and foreign-made cars and trucks. Although all makes are not documented with photos, a number of cars are pictured.

The rich collection of artfully produced old car literature is a tempting parking place, but hobbyists who are serious about their research homework should explore further. Display ads can often be found in older magazines. Dealer brochures, service and parts manuals are sold by literature vendors at flea markets or through ads in hobby magazines like *Hemmings Motor News*. Established dealerships that have occupied the same premises for many years may have copies of obsolete manuals and sales brochures packed away in storage.

The National Automotive History collection at the Detroit Public Library is a rich repository of automotive lore. The collection houses over one million cataloged items, or 200 tons of automotive information. At present, another 60 tons await cataloging. Over 300 cases of photographs, containing some 300,000 photos, are included in the collection. Margaret Butzu, senior clerk for the National Automotive History Collection, presents several views of the library.

Besides service manuals, original dealer literature includes body repair manuals and parts lists. The three together give comprehensive coverage of a car's mechanical and structural makeup. Body repair manuals are especially helpful in showing how panels, window glass, doors, tailgates on a station wagon and other components are removed, replaced and adjusted. Parts lists contain more than just a series of numbers. The exploded drawings included in many parts listings can be used as visual aids to accompany the repair instructions in a service manual.

Since parts books commonly list all vehicles using a particular part, they are also excellent sources of interchange information. To illustrate the importance of being able to reference interchange data, Robert Gottlieb, "Classics Comments" editor for *Motor Trend,* once wrote that he was able to replace the worn-out differential in his Chrysler LeBaron phaeton with an identical unit from a Dodge truck. Besides manufacturer's parts lists, this extremely useful reference data is found in Hollander interchange manuals. Original Hollander manuals are sold at flea markets and reprints are available from Hollander Publishing Company, Minneapolis, Minnesota. The Hollander reprints include parts interchange listings for U.S.-built cars and trucks from the twenties through 1974.

Sales brochures show the different models and distinguishing features of each. Manufacturers typically marketed their cars in at least two series, standard and deluxe. Restorers often blur this distinction by dressing up the plain cars with deluxe trim. Dealer sales literature can serve as a helpful guide to determine whether a car should be preserved as a standard or deluxe model.

For the past quarter-century enthusiast magazines have blanketed the hobby with old car lore. The great drawback to fine out-of-print articles, whether they are the *Cars & Parts* custom coachwork series written by Hugo Pfau or Tom McCahill's feisty road tests in *Mechanix Illustrated,* is the difficulty that comes in locating the issue you want. Literature peddlers list random back issues in their ads and include random magazines in their flea market displays; but to shop with success you should know which issue contains the article you're looking for. *Special-Interest Autos* and *Cars & Parts,* two of the leading hobby magazines, maintain listings of all the articles that have appeared since their first issues (*Special-Interest Autos* also reprints back issues). Several of the other hobby magazines include an index for the year in their December issues.

While popular automotive magazines aren't indexed in *Reader's Guide,* they are listed in the *Automotive Literature Index,* edited and marketed by Angelo Wallace, 2307 Shoreland, Toledo, Ohio. Wallace's *Index* is bound in two volumes. The first lists articles published between 1947 and 1976. The second covers 1977 to 1981. These two volumes contain 56,000 entries from sixteen automotive journals. Besides Wallace's publication, partial listings of automotive literature can be found through the major automotive history collections.

Gloria Francis, curator for the world famous National Automotive History Collection at the Detroit Public Library, and her counterpart, Louis Halverson, at the Philadelphia Public Library, both stress that while they help restorers in specific research needs, they cannot do a hobbyist's legwork. Their rich collections of automotive lore include literally tons of material. In addition to issues from nearly all current car magazines, the Philadelphia Public Library holds a complete bound set of *Cycle and Auto Trade Journal,* beginning in 1899. This early publication is rich in technical information, ads and contemporary comments on vintage cars. The National Automotive History Collection holdings range from parts manuals to over 300,000 photographs.

Before mailing a request to the Detroit or Philadelphia automotive collections, make a thorough attempt to locate the information you're seeking through available sources. Halverson says that he would answer a letter requesting information on Corvettes by mailing an ad on Corvette literature clipped from a book publisher's circular. But for requests fitting the scope of the Detroit and Philadelphia holdings, both libraries offer hard-to-match service. Both will copy pages from original brochures or manuals at a nominal fee. Make your request as specific as possible and enclose a courtesy SASE. User hours for automotive history collections may vary from the library itself. To avoid the frustrating experience of arriving from out of town, only to find the history collection closed, make arrangements with the curators in advance.

Restoration of a limited-production gem, like this 1932 Plymouth convertible sedan, requires careful research to determine authentic color options and whether the headlights, taillights and other accessories are the correct items for this car. In this case they're not, unless Plymouth supplied a rear light assembly that reads Buick.

Research departments connected with private museums like the Pate Museum of Transportation in Fort Worth and the Automotive Hall of Fame in Midland, Michigan, also hold treasures of automotive lore. These collections have individual policies for public use, so anyone seeking permission to use these resources should phone or write the directors for guidelines. Corporate archives are another source of old car research. These collections contain abundant photos and original documentation. Addresses of companies and museums with holdings of interest to automotive hobbyists are listed in the appendix.

It goes without saying that car enthusiasts benefit by joining a club representing their chosen marque. The chance to chat with other members, the informative newsletters and membership rosters that often list owners of similar cars all give a personal dimension to old car research. Seasoned hobbyists can help guide newcomers through the sandtraps of automotive history. With this in mind, plus the pleasure of enjoying each other's company, prominent figures in the old car ranks banded together in the early seventies to establish a Society of Automotive Historians. In this short time the society has grown from a handful to a group with international membership and chapter offshoots. The organization has made its mark as a recognized sponsor of scholarly automotive research and serves as a clearinghouse where members can exchange and request information. The Society's address appears with the listing of automotive archives in the appendix.

When car buffs start exchanging information, the results can be surprising, as the following incident attests. One of the surviving examples of the early Cameron car is owned by a hobbyist of the same name. Think what it must be like to have a car as your namesake, then consider the difficulty of locating the information to document restoration of a nearly unique automobile—to say nothing of the virtually hopeless search for spare parts. In collector Cameron's pursuit for information, he

The Western New York Model A club assembled around my Model A roadster one bitter March day. The "deuce" coupe, belonged to another member.

stumbled on a dated boarding house address of the car's inventor. Realizing that the chance of a response was slim, he wrote the inventor. Months passed. Finally inventor Cameron's landlady answered collector Cameron's letter saying that though her boarder had once been a wealthy industrialist, he had died penniless a few years earlier leaving behind only a carton of papers. If collector Cameron wished, she would send him the contents. Of course it was impossible to guess what the box might contain, but naturally an ardent car buff would prize the chance to possess even a shadow of the inventor's archives. More letters were exchanged and eventually the carton arrived. It contained all that remained of the Cameron venture, correspondence and sales brochures of the early cars, including collector Cameron's model. By a quirk of fate, the inventor's legacy had fallen into respectful hands.

Delving into old car research assures that a hobbyist's labor of love will carry the stamp of authenticity; but even more rewarding, it offers rich contacts among fellow collectors along the way.

Old car memorabilia have become popular collector items. This old-time gas station at the Lancaster, Ohio, fairgrounds serves as a reminder of by-gone days.

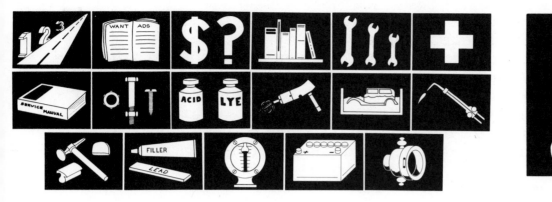

5
Setting Up Shop

Restoring an old car doesn't require a heated or air-conditioned shop with multiple bays, cement floor, fluorescent lighting, spray booth, stationary air compressor and the like. Facilities of this nature are probably every hobbyist's dream, but reality for only a few. Cars have been restored out-of-doors, in the cellar, practically every place but under the bedsheets—although an acquaintance who rebuilt his Model A in a milk house did keep its engine under his bed! Naturally a workshop of some form is desirable, and the family garage will be adequate if bikes can be stored in another quarter and the everyday car is parked outside. A basic shop should include a sturdy workbench with machinist's vise, shelves to store parts and tools and a locking cabinet for paints, solvents and chemical supplies. Additional equipment and facilities can be added as they're needed.

Acquisition of a hobby car, a parts car, then a second hobby car at a price too good to pass up, has driven collectors to build bigger barns in which to store and restore their prizes. But for some hobbyists the problem is more basic, namely the lack of a garage or any suitable workshop facility. Although there is no simple solution some suggestions may be helpful. Storage can usually be rented, either in the form of a vacant garage or, for country dwellers, unused barn space. Be sure to carry insurance coverage on cars or parts that are placed in rented storage.

One way to gain access to workshop facilities and tools, along with valuable training, is to enroll in an adult education auto shop class. These are commonly taught in the evening at vocational high schools or technical colleges where tuition costs are nominal. The instructors are usually cooperative in allowing their students to work on personal projects.

One of the beneficial features of restoration is the fact that the process doesn't happen overnight. Working through a car from the ground up takes most hobbyists a couple of years, sometimes longer when patience wears thin, or missing parts and a disrupted cash flow hold things up. This prolonged pace is helpful in the sense that it isn't necessary to possess all the tools, equipment, even the facilities that may be needed for restoration when the project is begun. Since restoration or major repair work occurs in stages, it is possible to start out with a modest investment in tools and a minimal work area—a rented garage or working out-of-doors while the car is disassembled—then build from there.

Here is a recommended tool list for getting started in restoration or repair work. The cost of purchasing the tools on this list may appear to represent a sizable investment for beginners who are setting up shop, but nearly the whole list is included in modestly priced tool sets sold by Sears, Penneys and Wards. Handymen and seasoned restorers will find they have most if not all these items in their tool kits already. A hobbyist's basic tool kit should contain:

A socket set—preferably ½-inch drive

    Make sure the set matches the measuring system used on your car. The alternatives are metric, standard and Whitworth. The socket set should include both ratchet and straight-drive handles and extension bars.

The key to a workable shop is orderly arrangement of tools and ample working space.

Small items are easier to find if they are organized in small drawers or jars.

A set of open-end wrenches

These are needed to loosen bolts inaccessible to sockets or box wrenches.

A large adjustable wrench for wheel bearing, rear axle and other nuts that may exceed socket and open-end wrench sizes.

Allen wrenches (also called ignition wrenches)

These are used to tighten set screws found on ignition and other mechanical parts.

Assorted screwdrivers with both phillips and slotted blades

The slotted type should include long and short shanks with narrow and wide, thin and thick blades.

Assorted pliers

Visegrips or channel locks to hold rusted screws and bolts. Needle-nose pliers to hold tiny parts, crimp wire connectors, attach and remove small springs and the like. Standard and cutter nose pliers. Note: Never use pliers as substitutes for a wrench.

A hacksaw and supply of fresh blades

This tool has multiple uses and is essential for disassembling rusted parts.

A metal file

This tool also has numerous uses ranging from fitting parts to restoring stainless steel trim.

An electric drill—preferably a heavier-duty unit with a ⅜-inch chuck.

Be sure to include a set of sharp, assorted drill bits. A small wire brush that fits in the drill chuck is an optional, but highly useful, accessory for cleaning small parts.

These tools are needed to free rusted parts:

A set of sharp metal chisels, punches and a hefty hammer to drive them.

Hammer weight of three to five pounds is recommended.

Spare parts can be stored on simply constructed wooden shelving nailed to the shop walls.

A set of taps and dies to restore banged over, rusted threads.

Assorted size Easy-outs.

This tool is a four-sided, hardened steel wedge that is used to remove shafts of bolts which have broken off inside engine castings. When a bolt breaks off leaving its shank inside a casting, drill a hole into the center of the bolt stub, then drive an Easy-out into the hole. Grip the Easy-out with an adjustable wrench. Turn the wrench counterclockwise. As the Easy-out turns it will bite into the bolt forcing it out of the casting.

·Optional but very useful tools:

Impact screwdriver/wrench

Available either as a screwdriver or wrench, this tool is driven by hammer blows and offers the advantage of applying very high torque to free rust-frozen screws or bolts.

Jack stands

Since the car will be off its tires during most of the restoration, four sturdy jack stands make a safer set of props than sections of timber or cement blocks. They move about easier too.

As you get more involved you will encounter other tool needs; but starting out, the only other basic item you'll need is a set of spare knuckles. A friend once asked, "When you work on cars do you get skinned knuckles?"

"Sure I do," I answered. "I think I'll have to settle for a skin transplant when this restoration is finished."

Turns out he wasn't talking about my hands, but a hobby publication by the same name. Whether or not that particular *magazine* comes to your address, you're sure to get skinned knuckles restoring an old car.

Surprisingly, an assortment of rather ordinary hand tools is usually sufficient to take a car apart but restoring parts and putting things back together gets a bit more complicated. This follows from a basic lesson we learned when we were kids. A crude tool like a rock will shatter a toy in one blow, but making it work again—that's another matter.

Car restoration divides into four stages: mechanical, sheet metal, trim and refinishing. With the possible exception of trim work where prestitched upholstery kits are marketed ready to install for some cars, each of these areas requires special tools to do the job right.

While tools on the initial list are adequate for repair work, a few additional items are suggested for those undertaking a major mechanical overhaul. A torque wrench is needed to properly tighten engine bolts. Heavy-duty torque wrenches fit half-inch drive sockets, a point to keep in mind when you purchase a socket set. In a number of disassembly and overhaul applications you will find a puller essential. A universal puller that can be adjusted to accommodate parts such as gear sets which may be six inches or more in diameter is recommended. For electrical trouble-shooting and repair you will need a test light and soldering gun. As you are setting up your work area, include a bench grinder with a wire wheel mounted on one end of the shaft. The wire wheel is useful for cleaning rust from small parts.

You can build a number of useful tools yourself. For example, a buffing wheel can be made using an electric motor salvaged from a discarded washer, refrigerator or dryer and a buffing kit available from Sears for a few dollars. Renewing brightwork and restoring stainless steel trim are just two applications for a buffing wheel. Plans for a parts washer and hydraulic press are included in the appendix. The parts washer makes a safe, effective tool for cleaning grease-caked parts. A hydraulic press is needed to remove or replace bushings and gears when rebuilding a transmission, for example.

An air compressor with sufficient capacity to power air tools along with a sandblaster and spray gun may be a hobbyist's largest single tool investment. A compressor is a highly versatile tool and one that you really can't do without if you plan to refinish the car yourself. Units that produce an adequate air supply, at least eight cubic-feet-per-minute, operate on 230-volt current which may necessitate running a heavy-duty circuit to your workshop. The largest-capacity portable air compressors—three to four horsepower with twenty- to thirty-gallon storage tanks—are adequate for most hobbyists. The sale catalogs of Sears, Wards and Penneys regularly feature these tools at substantial savings over the normal retail price. A compressor's versatility comes from its ability to power tools, spray guns and sandblasters; it'll do practically everything but join metal. Air tools are cheaper than their electrically powered counterparts, so the dollars saved in purchasing an air grinder and other accessories compared to electric units helps offset the cost of the compressor.

Probably the biggest incentive for purchasing an air compressor is the tool's ability to supply air for spray painting. There isn't any practical alternative to spray painting a car's finish. The job can be hired out to a bodyshop but refinishing small parts that need repeated painting to fill pits and assure overall coverage, plus the difficulty of keeping quality control on these items, makes it more practical to spray the parts yourself. Besides, to most bodymen painting a batch of individual parts is a nuisance. The only other options are to apply a baked enamel finish or spray small parts with an aerosol can. Both methods have limitations. Baking is slow and aerosol painting in volume is expensive. Painting small parts with a brush is seldom satisfactory.

Besides a portable air compressor, other major tool investments depend on how self-sufficient you intend to be. If your shop has a cement floor, your other major investment may be a welding torch. This tool can apply heat not just to weld metal, but to free rusted parts. It is as essential to metal repair as a spray outfit is to refinishing. Advantages and drawbacks of the various types of welding equipment are discussed in the welding chapter.

At various stages of restoration you may need additional, special-purpose tools. Body hammers and dollies are required, for example, to straighten dented metal. If you plan to finish body repairs with lead filler, you will need hardwood paddles and a vixen file. Upholstery work will require hog ring pliers and a tack hammer. These tools are relatively inexpensive items that can be purchased later as they are needed. In the chapters that follow, useful or required special-purpose tools are mentioned as they are needed.

Tool quality is measured by how well a wrench grips rusted bolts and the "feel" it has in your hand. My tools are mostly Craftsman. I also purchase Sears premium brand because of the lifetime guarantee and attractive sale prices. These and a number of comparable brands are handyman tools, well suited to a hobbyist's use. Professional tools made by Snap-on, for example, are sold directly to mechanics by sales representa-

A portable cart, mounted on castors, is a handy way to keep needed parts nearby.

A pit, sunken in the floor of a shop, makes an inexpensive alternative to a hydraulic lift for working on the underside of a car.

tives who make the rounds of repair shops and auto dealerships in their territory on a weekly basis. Hobbyists, too, can purchase Snap-on, or other professional tool brands, by contacting the sales representative. Although these tools are more expensive than the handyman variety, they carry a similar guarantee. The major difference between the two grades of tools can be seen when they're put to work.

I discovered something of the difference in tool quality several years ago when I was having difficulty disassembling a batch of Model A carburetors (a situation made all the more frustrating by the fact that Model A carbs are held together by a single bolt). The area Snap-on dealer, also a car enthusiast, seized the opportunity to demonstrate the effectiveness of his tools. Where my wrenches slipped, his gripped. As to the claim that professional tools are easier to grip and have a better "feel," I can only cite the testimony of mechanics who hold them in their hands day in and day out. Generally speaking, this factor would not be a major concern to most hobbyists.

Tools that are used once or twice during a restoration, such as a portable hoist for engine removal, can often be rented. Hobbyists can also share their tool resources to lighten each other's burden. A neighbor and I have worked together in this way to our mutual benefit despite Benjamin Franklin's counsel, "Neither a borrower nor a lender be."

Whatever investment you make in tools and equipment will actually represent a savings by allowing you to do expensive restoration work yourself. And of course, as with any capital investment, when the restoration is finished you will have your tools for future use.

6

Make Shop Safety A Habit

Taking the necessary precautions to ensure shop safety is about the last thing an eager hobbyist thinks about as he starts out to restore or fix up an old car. Safety consciousness is important precisely for this reason. Restorers, car buffs generally, putter about blithely in a lethal environment and call working on cars "recreation." Consider the risks: Many modern paints contain highly toxic chemicals. Gasoline, which should never be used to clean parts—but often is—and of course is stored in the car's gas tank, packs enormous explosive power. Electrical hazards include the possibility of fire from shorted wiring and shocks. Welding torches expose hobbyists who use them carelessly to the danger of burns, or worse calamities, if welding near the gas tank ignites fuel fumes. Using power tools also carries a risk, though more to limbs than life. Naturally, each of these presents a greater danger to children who may play in the shop or enjoy watching the work.

Before starting to work on your car consider the attitudes that are most conducive to safety, then inspect your shop following the safety guidelines contained in this chapter. An accident prevented is worth all the time spent making sure that your shop is a safe place to work. Shop safety results from carefully cultivated habits and a frame of mind that says "quit" when frustration builds. A hobby, be it car restoration or any other, should provide a change of pace and in that sense offer relaxation. Even so, there are bound to be times when everything seems to go wrong. When you feel trouble brewing, step back and reflect on the progress you have made thus far. Don't let anger or anxiety distort your thinking. If you are still pent up, quit while you're ahead. Things will look brighter from a fresh start.

Frustration and anger aren't the only mental states that threaten shop safety. Carelessness can be equally hazardous.

Hobbyists need to develop a cautious attitude about using power tools such as grinders, and when welding or working with chemicals including paint products, rust and degreasing agents, even fiberglass resin. Shop accidents occur most often when hobbyists neglect warnings and precautions. In sections of this book where safety measures are called for that go beyond what an average hobbyist would recognize from common sense, recommended safety procedures will be spelled out. Keep in mind that the presence of children always dictates greater caution.

Use the advice on this list as a guide to shop safety. If you notice other potential hazards correct them as you prepare your shop.

1. Avoid a messy shop. Grease and oil spills are potential fire hazards, especially in combination with power tools or a welding torch.
2. Keep parts and tools on shelves where they can be found easily and won't be objects to kick out of the way.
3. Maintain sharp cutting edges on tools such as chisels and drill bits.
4. Store paints, solvents, rust remover—any toxic chemicals—in locked cabinets where they will be kept safely out of children's reach.

Painting supplies, stored here on open shelves, should be kept in cabinets that can be locked to prevent their access by children, and as a fire-prevention measure.

Every shop should be equipped with a fire extinguisher. The unit should have a sizeable capacity and should be located in a prominent spot within easy reach.

5. Always read health warnings. A label that states, "Danger, this product could be harmful or fatal," means just that. Warning labels often list emergency antidotes such as washing the exposed area. If you are using a mildly toxic lye solution to degrease parts, for example, keep a supply of water handy to rinse exposed skin.

6. Install a first aid kit in your shop where it can be reached quickly.

7. If you are spray painting, install a ventilation system and wear a charcoal-activated painter's mask. Professional painters work in spray booths where powerful ventilation fans remove toxic fumes. Hobbyists sometimes spray paints that can irritate respiratory tissue so severely that Accute Respiratory Distress Syndrome—ARDS, a cardiac-like condition—can result from failure to take the precaution to wear a respirator or use an exhaust fan. Never spray paint near an open flame or hot electrical connections.

8. Never work underneath a car that is raised off its tires unless it is supported by sturdy jack stands or blocked securely under the axles.

9. Double up for safety. If you are working on an engine mounted in an engine stand, it is wise to take the precaution of supporting the engine's weight with a chain or cable suspended from an overhead support.

10. Wear safety glasses and protective clothing—when welding, grinding or cutting metal, sandblasting and similar activities; and when pouring, to prevent the fluid from splashing into your eyes possibly causing blindness.

11. Equip your shop with fire extinguishers. Make sure the extinguishers are easily reached and their location is clearly visible.

12. Use parts cleaning fluid and, preferably, a parts washer for degreasing parts. Avoid cleaning parts in gasoline.

13. Be alert to the danger of shorts in old wiring. Remove or disconnect the battery if your car's wiring needs replacing. Make sure your shop wiring will support the current load of your tools.

14. Develop the habit of anticipating the possible consequences of your actions. For example, never weld near a gas line or the car's gas tank. Remember that fenders and other body panels may be backed with undercoating or upholstery. Welding these panels can cause the car to catch on fire.

Safety is a product of caution, precaution and mind over mood. No hobby, however rewarding, is worth jeopardizing your health.

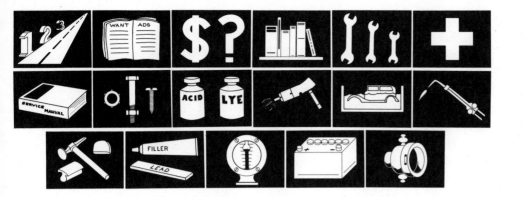

Service Manuals—A Hobbyist's Guide To Taking A Car Apart And Putting It Back Together Again

Reading a service manual to set ignition timing or rebuild a carburetor isn't like skimming *The Book Of Lists* or an Ellery Queen who-dun-it. Technical writing takes technical reading. The simplest way to explain how to read and understand technical writing is to call to mind high school or college science texts, preferably the ones in chemistry and physics. The problem wasn't the paragraphs or even the sentences; it was the words. Technical and scientific words have specific meanings, sometimes applied in a particular context. Technical writing isn't intentionally obscure, even though the following example from an Austin-Healey manual makes it seem that way.

> First fit the screwed fulcrum pin into the lower trunnion at the bottom end of the swivel pin, ensuring that it is centralized and secured by means of the cycle type cotter. Fit a cork ring into the recess provided at each end of the lower trunnion and introduce the lower wishbone arms into position. Ensure that the half-moon cotters are positioned to receive the steel bushes which should now be greased and screwed partially home.

How would you like to take a comprehension test on that fact-filled bit of garble? At this point the service manual is describing how to reassemble the front suspension. When the reader understands what the key words—fulcrum pin, lower trunnion, swivel pin and lower wishbone arms—refer to, the process becomes clear. Illustrations help and the Healey manual devotes nearly half a page to both exploded and assembled views of the front suspension, with key parts labeled. But since the Healey manual is written in the peculiar vocabulary of British English it presents additional hurdles by calling wheel pullers "extractors," wrenches "spanners," and telling the reader to "centralize" the swivel pin where American manuals would probably say "center." "Home" is a common word that takes on a special meaning in a technical context. Screwing the steel bushes partially home means tightening the parts until they are snug.

Why don't service manuals give straightforward explanations? Some do, but keep in mind that most are written for mechanics who are already at least partially familiar with the process the service manual is describing. If you're an amateur, study the manual by reading through the relevant section a few times before heading out to the garage with toolbox in one hand, service manual in the other. Take the time to familiarize yourself with the key words by identifying them on the illustrations and looking for the parts on the car itself. If the manual still doesn't make sense, ask a mechanic or a fellow restorer with mechanical background to explain the process.

The first step, of course, is to obtain a service manual (or better yet, manuals) for your car. There are several types available from a variety of sources. The most detailed are shop manuals distributed to dealers by manufacturers. These contain mechanical overhaul instructions as well as body repair information. Some manuals include sections on bodywork along with mechanical service information. In other cases, manufacturers issue separate body and chassis shop manuals. Dealers are sometimes willing to sell old manuals, but literature vendors

How do you replace the windshield glass in a 1936 Chevy pickup? You start by reading a vintage Chevy manual for instructions on how to take the windshield frame apart.

are the most reliable source of manufacturers' shop manuals. Their display booths can be found at flea markets, car shows and swap meets and their ads appear regularly in the literature-for-sale sections of prominent hobby magazines such as *Hemmings Motor News*, *Cars & Parts* and *Old Cars Weekly*. A number of older shop manuals have been reprinted and are available from dealers such as Classic Motorbooks. In cases where a shop manual isn't available, the automotive collections mentioned in the research chapter may photocopy an original or hobyists can sometimes obtain permission from a private collector who has the needed manual to make a copy.

General service manuals (Motor, Chilton, Clymer, Haynes and Bentley to name the most popular editions) are useful supplements to dealer shop manuals or can be used as a primary shop reference when manufacturer's manuals aren't available. These general service manuals are valuable as sources of tune-up specifications and for a mechanical overview. Since they attempt to provide repair instructions for all domestic or foreign makes of cars or trucks manufactured over a multi-year period, service manuals forego preliminary details and start right in with the repair process. Like shop manuals, general service manuals are written for seasoned mechanics. The problem with this orientation is that amateurs are often skeptical of their mechanical skills to begin with and need to be told what they can botch up by taking the car apart.

Both shop and general service manuals depart from a hobbyist's point of view in another important respect. They assume that replacement parts are readily available. For vintage cars, replacements often have to be mail-ordered or may not be

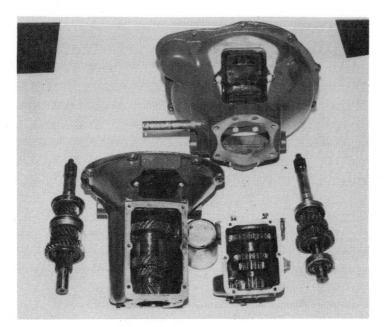

Vintage Ford parts, especially, have a straightforward design that makes them relatively easy to rebuild. Although a manual was used to overhaul the Model A transmission seen on the right, a parts diagram provided the only instruction needed to rebuild the Ford V-8 transmission on the left.

available, in which case repairs will have to be made using salvaged parts.

Shop and service manuals neglect to mention that while new cars come apart easily, worn out, rusty wrecks that are often the candidates of restoration more often than not require severe surgery, a torch and sledge even, in order to pry loose their innards. Manuals describe the easy way; presuming, perhaps, that mechanics have learned how to do tough jobs by doing them. For example, according to the manuals, replacing the king pins on a Model A Ford front end is a simple process. Remove the brake drum, brake shoes and backing plates, unscrew the locking pin and the king pins will pull free. The job can be that straightforward, but Model A's are now a half-century old and some have seen enough abuse to freeze the king pins solid to the front axle. Old-time mechanics, especially those who worked on beam-axle trucks, know that the only way to free rusted king pins is to heat the axle, and drive the pins loose, but manuals don't mention that trick.

Restoration manuals, a new category of service literature written by hobbyists for hobbyists, are oriented toward amateur mechanics. These manuals include mechanical theory and tips for coping with rust and wear—steps shop and service manuals leave out. But even more important, their instructions are written in everyday language to guide hobbyists through mechanical jobs one might think only an expert would tackle. The section of *Rick's Model A Shop Manual,* written by hobbyist and parts dealer Rick Freeman, that introduces transmission overhaul reads as follows:

> *The Model A transmission is without doubt one of the most simple transmissions ever used. Many restorers fear the transmission; however there are only 11 or 12 moving parts and shafts and no alignment of gears is necessary.*

Plain talk gets a hobbyist going. Model A Ford transmissions really aren't complicated. That's the beauty of restoring vintage, or even late model, special-interest cars. In contrast with modern automobiles, complete with on-board computers and enough hosing to outfit a hook-and-ladder truck, working on collector cars provides hobbyists with a chance to become master mechanics on the job. Besides restoration manuals for popular makes like Mustangs, Corvettes and early Fords, there are also mini-manuals such as the fine handbook by Paul Moller that explains the principles of carburetion while describing how to rebuild the classically simple Model A Ford carburetor. Restoration manuals are advertised in the literature sections of hobby magazines and listed in the catalogs of automotive book publishers.

Copies of older service literature, popular repair manuals like Victor Page's *Model A Service Manual and Handbook* first published in 1929, or Morris A. Hall's *Automobile Construction and Repair* published in 1920, may be available from a nearby public library. These books are sometimes found, too, at auctions or garage sales. When they aren't, check publishers' catalogs. Page's Model A manual is still available in a reprinted edition.

In some cases manufacturers present dealer service information in the form of periodic bulletins rather than comprehensive manuals. These bulletins can be extremely useful and although a complete series of Ford service bulletins covering Model A years has been reprinted, owners of other makes will have to rely on literature peddlers or club libraries for access to original copies. The Crosley club is reported to have collected a complete set of dealer service bulletins so that the valuable information it contains can be distributed to club members. Woody wagon owners have been responsible for printing blueprints and instructions to aid complicated wooden body restoration in their National Woody Club newsletter. Makes that never made it to the top of the popularity charts have their own hide-bound following and the best advice for restorers tackling what are sometimes called "orphan" cars is to join a club dedicated to preserving that marque.

Hobby magazines provide a steady stream of how-to articles explaining such practical projects as straightening trim pieces, re-arching springs, restoring gauge faces, the art of pinstriping, and numerous other topics. These articles are written by hobbyists so they include all the steps that a novice needs to know and call for tools that hobbyists are most likely to use. Prominent for their how-to features are *Cars & Parts, Special-Interest Autos, Old Cars Weekly* and *Car Collector*. A hobby publication appropriately called *Skinned Knuckles* devotes itself exclusively to repair and restoration articles. Rather than wait for a magazine to present needed how-to information, check to see whether this material has already appeared in a

Painting instructions are rarely included in repair manuals; probably because mechanics are usually more interested in making the car run than how the repair looks. Even so, hobbyists will want to repaint mechanical parts. Machined surfaces should be masked to prevent a paint build up.

back issue. Car magazines aren't listed in *Reader's Guide* or similar library indexes, but most publications print annual indexes in their end-of-year issues. *Old Cars Weekly* has compiled many of its restoration features into several "Best Of" editions. Reprints and back issues are available for many of the magazines directly from the publishers. As mentioned earlier, out-of-print back issues may be available from literature dealers or veteran collectors who have retained back issues of their magazines and are willing to help by photocopying needed articles.

Parts catalogs are useful for more than placing orders. Their illustrations can be helpful assembly guides, sometimes showing parts missing due to wear or earlier repairs. Parts catalogs are basic items that belong in every hobbyist's library. In most cases they are enclosed free with an order or may cost a nominal price if requested without an accompanying purchase. Besides current parts catalogs from hobby suppliers, dealer parts lists also provide valuable service information. Parts lists provide a means to correctly reference parts numbers that may be needed for a mail order. Dealer parts lists may also give interchange information showing multiple applications for a given part. Late model collectors will have little trouble turning up dealer parts lists at flea markets or literature-for-sale ads in hobby publications.

Like any other course of study, reading manuals and technical articles builds confidence and expertise so that complex

Friends who work together on restoration projects can pool knowledge and talent. Here Model A restorers have laid out steering column parts in an assembly-line fashion. Teamwork gets the job done faster.

jobs eventually become ho-hum. This book encourages its readers to tackle major restoration projects themselves. Let's remember that good mechanics used to be able to set timing by ear and they didn't need an electronic diagnosis to tell when a car had a skip. The old-timers were't any smarter than today's mechanics, it's just that the cars were simpler.

This view isn't confined to Model T Fords either, it includes a wide spectrum of collector cars including the popular Mustangs and late model hot ones like Corvettes. After all, Corvette suspension up to 1963 was nothing more complex than a warmed-over 1953 Chevy. Reading manuals and developing mechanical skills assure progress from the simple jobs to the more complex ones.

This book is written for hobbyists. The do-it-yourself operations it describes are within the grasp of anyone who can repair a bicycle and some who haven't tried that yet.

8
How And When To Take The Car Apart

There's nothing easier than taking something apart if you don't care what you break in the process. Observe, for example, that demolition experts can drop a skyscraper into its own foundation hole in a matter of seconds. Just because something comes apart quickly doesn't necessarily mean it will go back together. In fact, as much damage can be done to a car by inept disassembly as by the ravages of time, weather and high mileage.

Before approaching your car, tools in hand, you should decide what repair or restoration work you want to accomplish. For bodywork and refinishing you will probably remove the bumpers and trim, perhaps even some of the upholstery if you have to weld where the heat could ignite the interior. Once you have begun the job you may find further disassembly is necessary; but start conservatively so that you don't find yourself overextended financially and beyond the level of your skills. Mechanical repair should follow the same precaution. Engine overhaul, for example, will require disconnecting wires, hoses and carburetor linkage plus removing the radiator and hood. While working on the engine, you could decide to rebuild the water pump, carburetor and fuel pump, in which case these units, too, would have to be disassembled.

The point is, whether you are doing repair work or embarking on a frame-up restoration, you should take apart only those components that you will be working on, and remember to approach each disassembly step with the realization that you will have to put everything back together sooner or later. When you are unhooking wiring in preparation to lift out the engine, be sure to tag each lead with its proper connection.

Before removing the hood, mark the bolt positions so that you can easily align the hinges when you replace it.

Disassembling a vehicle for a frame-up restoration may appear to be a simple operation. Just take everything apart until the car is stripped bare to its frame or unit body. But here, especially, you should proceed with caution. Start by photographing the car from every angle, including the interior. Use color film to capture trim schemes, and a quality camera for clear prints that show detail. If you have a friend who is a camera bug he or she may be willing to take the photos for you. Collect copies of dealer literature, magazine ads or articles showing pictures of your make and model in its original condition. Compare them to your car and note any discrepancies. For example, dressing up a used car by swapping wheels has been popular since Model A days. On Model A's the lanky twenty-one and nineteen-inch rims and high-pressure tires were usually replaced by sixteen-inch V-8 wheels and smoother-riding balloon tires. Late model fifties and sixties cars are prone to lose their stamped steel wheels to chrome rims and custom mag wheels. If the fancy wheels are factory accessories you're ahead of the game but if they are speed shop specials you may want to locate stock rims and hubcaps. The latter will probably present the greater challenge.

To illustrate the disassembly process, Dan Colombo of Victor Antique Auto offered to take apart a newly constructed Model A woody wagon. Key to proper disassembly is reversing the sequence by which the car was put together. The doors were removed first.

With the roof and doors removed, the cowl was unbolted and lifted free.

Check the information on the manufacturer's data plate to determine whether your car has its original engine and drive-line configuration. You may have to study illustrations in a service manual or ask an experienced mechanic to point out the subtle features that identify different models in a family of engines. Small-block Chevrolet V-8's are a prime example. It takes a trained eye to spot the difference between an early 265-cid engine, its 283-cid successor and a later 327-cid mill. Data plates also list color and interior schemes. If the paint code listed on the data plate refers to a color that appears to match the present finish you can usually determine whether the car has been repainted by looking at the underside of the hood, trunk, firewall or dash. You can also take a look at door jams and underneath the weatherstripping around doors for traces of the original paint. These areas are seldom repainted. Note your discoveries in a journal. The more thoroughly you document your car's condition, the more accurately you will be able to list needed parts and supplies and construct a tentative work schedule.

From the list you can draw up a preliminary cost estimate of the supplies, parts and services you will need for your car's restoration. Your next concern could be to plot the major expenses on your work schedule. Apart from investments in tools, beginning restoration steps usually require a greater expenditure of labor than capital. As a result, you may decide the disassembly stage is an opportune time to absorb plating expenses, for example. After all, the car's brightwork can be sent away for replating at any time, once the parts are removed.

This metal wheel well is the main structural member supporting one side of the woody body. Removing a few more bolts detached the wheel wells and body subframe, exposing the chassis and running gear.

Restorers sometimes make the mistake of waiting until they are working on a particular area to purchase the parts and supplies that will be needed. While your "shopping list" will surely grow as the restoration progresses, you should start scouting hard-to-get items early. Even reproduction parts are sometimes in sporadic supply or may involve long delivery delays. Shopping for vintage car parts is like trading a volatile commodity. In many cases you should buy when opportunity strikes because the chance may not present itself again.

After photographing your car's present condition and appraising its originality, you should determine the degree to which the car will have to be taken apart to accomplish necessary repair and refinishing work. If your car's condition (or your desire to produce a showpiece) dictates a frame-up restoration, log each disassembly step in your journal and record the process with photographs. In effect, you will be writing an assembly manual in reverse. Your notes and photos will provide an invaluable aid when you begin to put the pieces together again.

Although the procedures for disassembling a car for restoration will vary depending on the car's vintage and whether it has unit-body or frame construction, typically you begin by removing the bumpers, headlights (if they are detachable), mirrors and any extraneous trim that could be damaged if left attached to larger assemblies. Next take off the nose (front fenders, hood and grille), then remove the rear fenders if they are the bolt-on type. If the body is mounted on a frame, it can be unbolted and lifted off with a hoist or a half-dozen strong friends. Body mounts are cushioned either with rubber or wood. If wooden blocks are used on your car, label their location as they're removed. Before attempting to detach the body, make sure that all wiring, cables, clutch, brake, carburetor or steering linkages are disconnected. Once the body is removed from the

Many modern cars, such as the Mustang convertible shown here resting on its side, must be worked on intact due to the unit frame and body construction.

frame, engine and driveline components are easily accessed. With unit-body construction, chassis components are unbolted from their mountings on the body/frame assembly. Wiring may have to be disconnected at each step.

Save nuts, bolts and other small parts in labeled jars and tag each component. Leave assemblies such as the seats, engine and drivetrain components intact. These units can be disassembled and rebuilt later. Even badly deteriorated parts, rotted upholstery for example, should be saved. They may be needed for patterns. Store parts in an area where they won't deteriorate or be damaged. If space limitations force you to stack parts or hang them from the walls or ceiling, make sure that they are placed securely so that they can't fall.

Recommended tools for the various stages of restoration are listed in an earlier chapter. Disassembly requires mostly common tools, starting with a socket set or box wrenches matching your car's measuring system, which may be metric, Whitworth or standard U.S. dimensions. Don't try to take a car apart with channel-locks, visegrips, pipe or adjustable wrenches—you will round the bolt heads so that they may have to be chiseled off, and damaged beyond reuse. It is important to note that vintage bolts have larger heads than modern replacements, so if you are aiming at authenticity you will want to save the old bolts.

Besides wrenches you will need a set of sharp chisels and a heavy hammer. A chisel's effectiveness is directly proportional to its sharpness and the weight of the hammer that drives it. You will also need a variety of screwdrivers and a hacksaw with sharp blades. Depending on the extent to which you are taking the car apart, you may need to rent or borrow heavy-duty tools like a chain hoist, transmission or floor jack. You will find a welding torch an indispensable tool for disassembling

In order to replace sections of the floor and front fenders on this early Thunderbird, the owner has stripped out the upholstery, removed the wiring, windshield glass, rubber moldings and all trim.

rusted parts. Torches and how to use them are discussed in the welding chapter.

For all his genius of standardization, Henry Ford sprinkled his cars with 1/16- and 1/32-inch bolt sizes. His thinking, no doubt, was that when owners found that their wrenches wouldn't fit the odd-ball bolts, they would take their cars to Ford dealers for repair. The more common outcome was that Ford owners knurled-over the bolts, giving restorers of Ford cars an added challenge. If you find you need a special tool such as a square socket to remove main bearing caps on a Model A or an impact wrench to loosen frozen bolts, buy the tool rather than risk damaging the parts. In some cases you may have to make the tools you need.

Canadian-built Model A Fords, for example, feature screws with a unique square slot, much like the inset found on allen-head screws. Since no standard screwdriver or allen wrench fits this unusual design, the only alternative to drilling out these screws is to make a tool that will fit into the special head. With ingenuity you can turn scrap into useful tools. For example, discarded spring leaves can be used as body tools to straighten fender beads and lips on body panels. Thirty-gallon oil drums make effective jack stands to support a car body at working height.

If you are inexperienced with mechanics and uncertain about taking your car apart, you will need to refer to service manuals for disassembly instructions. Some manuals contain mechanical and body repair information, but in most cases the two areas are covered in separate manuals. Even though the manuals are extremely useful, you will soon discover that when you are working on an older car their instructions don't always apply. For example, fenders are often bolted to hidden nuts that have been welded inside the body. If these nuts break loose as they are prone to when they're rusted, the bolts will

This Model A Ford sport coupe has simply shed its hood, providing open access to the engine compartment for minor mechanical repair.

turn freely and you will have to cut them with a torch or chisel, or hold the nuts from inside the body to prevent them from turning.

When you've reached the limit of your resources and can't figure out how an assembly comes apart, ask a seasoned restorer or an experienced mechanic for advice. If you're embarking on a restoration adventure without mechanical training, the experience you gain taking the car apart will pay off when you begin rebuilding and putting the components back together. The key, of course, is not to destroy what you're learning on as you take the car apart.

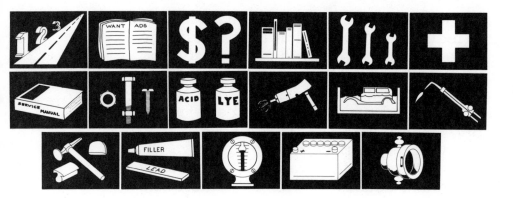

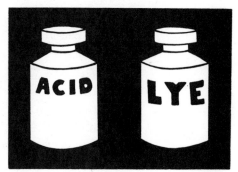

9

Derusting And Degreasing Techniques That Work

So you've bought an old car, and now that you've got it home, looked it all over, even crawled underneath, it's probably not as substantial as it appeared when it belonged to someone else. You can have the engine rebuilt and buy new tires, but what about the rust? It gnaws at your confidence. Paint won't bond over rust, nor will body repairs, so what do you do?

Corrosion is insidious. Moisture, alone, sets off the oxygen-absorption cycle that turns steel to rust. Once established, the electro-chemical rusting mechanism proceeds without interruption until all that remains of an old car is a small mound of iron oxide. Consequently, sheet metal and chassis parts that show signs of decay have to be cleaned to bare steel before repairs or refinishing can begin. Light surface rust will scour clean with steel wool, sandpaper or a wire brush, but serious rust that has eaten holes or pits in the metal doesn't vanish as easily.

As metal rusts, pits and crevices develop on the surface. That is why wire brushing corroded metal or attempting to remove rust with a grinding wheel really doesn't work. Specks of rust in the deeper pits that haven't been reached will continue to fester under the refinished surface. Even tiny traces of rust can eventually blister paint loose from restored parts.

Signs of rust are easy to detect when you know the clues. Apart from obvious gaping holes, paint blisters covering pin holes or specks of rust showing through metal appear most frequently on the lower edges of doors, fender panels and surfaces where paint has worn thin. Coatings of surface rust are often found inside door and body panels though these areas are hidden from view until the upholstery is removed. In order to appraise the full extent of corrosion damage, parts should be stripped of paint, grease and other coatings. In most cases disassembly will be required first. Doors showing rust damage along the lower edges should be removed from the car and window glass, upholstery, door handles and trim, plus weather seal will have to be removed from the doors leaving just a metal shell. Fenders, hood, and trunk lid should all be detached unless the entire body is going to be stripped and derusted. In that case, upholstery, window glass, accessories and trim will all have to be removed first. Details of required disassembly will be discussed in greater detail with each of the derusting and stripping processes.

Derusting Methods And Parts Best Stripped By Each

Restorers can pick from three alternative methods for removing rust: acid pickling, sandblasting, and a commercial alkaline electrolytic derusting process. Each has advantages and drawbacks.

Soaking parts in a mild acid bath is a simple, cheap way to quickly clean surface rust or remove deeply pitted rust coatings from small parts such as castings, valve covers and other accessories. When I was restoring my Model A Ford, I found a number of uses for acid derusting ranging from cleaning trunk rack brackets, the steering box and transmission case to hinges and interior trim pieces. Fifty-year-old antiques, especially those that have seen outdoor storage, require extensive derusting. Acid pickling, as this method is called, is impractical to use with large parts such as fender panels and dangerous to use with mechanical parts such as steering arms that are subject to stress. The cause of concern, here, is a condition called hydrogen embrittlement which occurs when metal immersed in an acid solution absorbs extra hydrogen atoms, significantly reducing the metal's strength.

Sandblasting is the most commonly used derusting method. Besides the convenience of being able to do your own sandblasting using a portable air compressor and hobby-size sandblaster, this method that uses a high-pressure abrasive spray to penetrate pits cleans metal to a satin finish and assures a good paint bond. Sandblasting offers the advantage of cleaning paint and rust from fenders or frames, an entire car or truck body, wheels, brake drums, all types of parts, large or small.

Sandblasting does have drawbacks, though. Carelessly using the high-pressure sand blast can stretch and distort sheet metal parts. The problem occurs most frequently when restorers arrange to have commercial sandblasters, who are experienced mainly in polishing tombstones and cleaning buildings, strip a car body. The results can be disheartening, to say the least.

Chassis parts such as transmission housings, rear end assemblies, suspension or steering must never be sandblasted unless they have been completely disassembled with all gears, bearings and bushings removed. Even in this condition, an empty transmission housing, rear axle housing or steering box is better cleaned with one of the two other derusting methods. Beam front axles used on vintage cars through the mid-thirties and on Fords until 1949, can be safely sandblasted when king pins and wheel spindles are removed, as can the more modern A-arm assemblies. These parts should not be derusted by acid pickling. Frames can be cleaned by sandblasting only after springs, drivetrain and all mechanical assemblies are removed. Otherwise sand will penetrate into bearings and gear housings causing rapid wear when the vehicle is driven. Although sandblasting will strip paint, it won't touch grease or undercoating and should not be used on wood. Abrasive derusting works well in most applications when properly used, but it does have limitations.

If you live near one of the two-dozen facilities that specializes in stripping and derusting car parts, your major rust worries are over. Using an alkaline electrolytic bath, these commercial "metal laundries" are able to safely clean parts, large or small, regardless of their coating or rusted condition. Sheet metal, wheels, mechanical parts, even entire car bodies with suspension parts intact can be dipped in the commercial stripper's tanks. At the end of the stripping-derusting process the parts are cleaned to bare metal and treated with a protective coating to deter rerusting. Using a commercial derusting ser-

Restoring weathered chassis parts begins with derusting and degreasing.

vice also has drawbacks, however. The facilities are located primarily in major cities, making their geographic distribution spotty. Although the results are impressive, the service is generally more expensive than either acid pickling or sandblasting.

Preparing Parts For Derusting

In order for derusting to work effectively grease, dirt and undercoating (also paint for the acid pickling and chemical electrolysis methods) have to be stripped from the metal first. Stripping and derusting methods can also be used to clean mechanical parts such as a brake master cylinder that have been removed for rebuilding.

There are several degreasing methods that hobbyists can use to strip accumulated grease and grime from mechanical parts. One of the simplest is to spray a commercial degreasing solvent, such as Gunk, on the parts and wash them with a garden hose. Gunk works well to remove light coatings of grease and grime. But engine and chassis parts that are often covered with thick layers of oil, grease and road dust should be scraped with a putty knife first, then sprayed with Gunk and scrubbed with a parts cleaning brush before they can be washed completely clean. As an alternative to Gunk, you can also clean mechanical parts, such as carburetors or master cylinders, whatever you are working on, in a parts washer using kerosene as a degreasing solvent. Plans for a parts washer are included in the appendix. Thick grease and oil coatings should also be scraped off parts that are cleaned in a parts washer.

The chemical stripping method described below removes stubborn coatings of grease, oil and road grime without hours of tedious scraping. It also strips paint and undercoating from body parts. Chemical stripping is cheap and effective but requires safety precautions. Safety reminders are not intended to discourage you from using the chemical stripping method, but to assure its safe, effective use.

Chemical Stripping And Degreasing

Chemical stripping and degreasing is a relatively inexpensive one-step process you can set up in your own shop, providing you recognize the danger of working with sharply caustic chemicals and take appropriate safety precautions. Lye and trisodium phosphate are two easily obtainable alkaline chemicals that can be used to strip paint, heavy coatings of grease and undercoating from ferrous metal parts. Caustic soda, as lye is often called, is the active ingredient in Drano, a common inexpensive household product used to clear clogged drains. It is sold in nearly any grocery store. When working with lye (purchased generically or under the Drano name), heed the warning on the can. The chemical is corrosive and can cause severe skin or eye damage. Always wear rubber gloves and a protective face shield when cleaning parts with lye and be careful to ensure that children do not have access to the lye solution.

Any size metal container from a pail to an oil drum or stock-watering trough makes a suitable vat for mixing the lye solution. To prepare the stripping and degreasing bath, simply fill the container three-quarters full of water and add lye. Half of a thirteen-ounce plastic jar of lye added to two gallons of water in a ten-quart pail makes an effective degreasing solution. Applying this same ratio to larger containers, you would add eight to ten cans of lye to forty gallons of water in a fifty-five-gallon drum. Fenders, wheels, engine oil pans—mechanical, chassis and body parts of nearly any description—can be stripped of paint and grease quickly and inexpensively by immersing them in a lye bath contained in a large metal barrel. A dip tank of this size will easily clean a number of parts at the same time.

Lye works best when heated. If the container is elevated on cement blocks, a small wood or propane fire can be lit underneath to heat the lye. A solution of hot lye will completely strip thick, caked-on grease and layers of paint in less than an hour. Since heated lye is more corrosive, always wear safety garb—rubber gloves, a face shield, full covering of old clothes, including a plastic or rubber apron—when working near the

A concentrated lye solution in a metal pail quickly cleans mechanical parts such as these assorted Model A carburetor castings.

chemical. Keep a supply of fresh water nearby to wash off any lye that does come in contact with your skin.

Trisodium phosphate is a less corrosive, yet an equally effective, degreasing agent. The chemical is the active cleaning agent in heavy-duty cleaners such as TSP, a Savogran product, sold by discount department and hardware stores. The TSP label identifies that the cleaner contains trisodium phosphate. If TSP is not available in your area, look for trisodium phosphate in the list of ingredients on the labels of other heavy-duty cleaning products. Trisodium phosphate in concentrated form, as found in heavy-duty cleaners, is added to water in the same proportion as lye. As with lye, heating the solution improves its degreasing action. While trisodium phosphate is safer to use than lye, it does not remove paint as effectively.

Both lye and trisodium phosphate degreasing baths will collect a layer of grease on the surface after heavily coated parts have been cleaned. Adding detergent helps dissolve grease, but the film should be skimmed off periodically, otherwise the parts will pick up a thin grease coating as they are removed from the cleaning tank. Even a slight grease coating prevents effective derusting and raises havoc with painting. Parts that are contaminated with the grease film should be washed with a solvent such as Gunk before derusting or painting.

Bathing parts in trisodium phosphate is an alternative to using lye. Care should be taken not to dunk brass parts or other soft metal parts in a caustic solution.

Nathan's assistance isn't meant to suggest that chemical cleaning is child's play, but to illustrate that hosing the cleaned parts with water is all that is necessary to clean off the chemical residue.

As the alkaline cleaning solution is used it will gradually lose its strength. This does not occur rapidly. I have cleaned parts in my lye barrel for several days before noticing an appreciable loss in potency. The solution can be restored to full strength by adding more lye or trisodium phosphate. Eventually the cleaning bath will become contaminated with sludge and have to be disposed of and refilled. A recommended procedure for disposing of the spent degreasing chemical is described at the end of this chapter.

After parts have been cleaned, they must be washed thoroughly. A garden hose works well to rinse off the slimy film left on the naked steel. Cleaned metal is rust prone and even a slight alkaline film left on the surface after washing leaves the metal with poor "wetting" or paint-bonding properties. Unless parts that have been stripped and degreased also need to be derusted, they should be wiped with an etching solution. A product containing dilute phosphoric acid that etches metal to assure good paint adhesion is sold by auto supply stores under brand names like Chem-Grip and Metal Prep. (In addition to etching the metal for good paint adhesion, these products will also combine with any iron oxide particles (clearly visible or microscopic) and turn iron oxide into a more stable compound, either slowing or stopping the chemical reaction that forms rust.) Directions for using the acid-etch solution are written on the container. Proper application leaves a slightly yellowish film on the metal. Parts that have been treated with a mild acid solution will stay free of surface rust if they are stored in a dry area. It is still advisable to prime and paint stripped and derusted metal parts as soon as possible.

After degreasing, mechanical assemblies such as water pumps, old cast iron carburetors found on Model A Fords and other cars of twenties vintage—whatever components you have immersed in the stripping tank—should be taken completely apart for rebuilding or derusting if necessary. Parts that are rust-frozen can often be freed by heating them with a torch. Note that applying heat to loosen an assembly containing soft pot metal or brass parts is risky. A better method to use when dissimilar metals have bonded together, as is often the case with Model A carburetors where a diecast venturi straddles both halves of the cast iron housing, is to heat the assembly in a kitchen oven at 350–400°, then place it in the refrigerator freezer compartment for a few hours. Differences in expansion and contraction rates between the dissimilar metals should help free the parts.

Acid Derusting

The next step, acid derusting, is also a simple chemical process. Since acid will attack metal, a plastic or hard rubber container must be used to hold the acid bath. Plastic garbage cans with snap-on lids work well since acid derusting solutions have a distinct "garlic and onions" odor. Acid will not penetrate paint or grease so parts must be thoroughly stripped before entering the derusting bath.

While many acids are effective derusting agents, phosphoric acid, sold by auto supply stores as Rust Remover—American Parts brand name for this product—is a readily available, safe and effective rust removing chemical. Recommended dilution is a 2:1 mixture of water to Rust Remover. The diluted acid solution is relatively harmless but you should wear a face shield or glasses and rubber gloves to protect your eyes and hands.

When you prepare the derusting bath you should use a container large enough to immerse the parts. I have found that a five-gallon plastic trash container is ample to hold parts as large as fender brackets from my Model A Ford. I fill the container with 1½ gallons of acid and three gallons of water. I use the same proportions with larger or smaller containers. Small parts, such as door hinges, usually need only a few minutes immersion in the acid solution. Larger or more deeply corroded parts may need to soak several hours, possibly as long as several days in the phosphoric acid solution. Check the derusting progress on thin metal parts every few minutes because acid attacks metal as soon as it finishes eating rust. Springs and tempered steel parts should not be derusted in an acid solution. A reaction called hydrogen embrittlement occurs that weakens springs, wheel spindles and other high-stress parts. Nonferrous

Acid derusting is a chemical process that hobbyists can also do themselves. Because acids eat metal, the solution must be kept in a plastic pail, preferably one with a tight-sealing lid. Rusted parts may have to soak for several days for thorough cleaning, but should be inspected daily to make sure that the acid doesn't eat the metal. Fresh acid works faster than a solution that has been used to strip several batches of parts.

parts should not be placed in an acid bath either. They will be consumed by the acid. Components that contain springs or nonferrous parts should always be disassembled before de-rusting. Hood clamps found on cars (through the early thirties) and Jeeps are an example. The springs located inside the clamp would be destroyed by acid derusting.

When all traces of rust are gone the parts can be removed from the acid bath. The metal will be coated with a yellowish-gray film left on the metal by the phosphoric acid. This residue will retard rerusting but the parts should be painted for lasting protection. The phosphoric acid treatment provides wetting properties that assure good paint adhesion.

The following suggestions will improve the effectiveness of chemical cleaning and derusting solutions: Small items can be placed in a plastic kitchen colander and suspended in the vat, to save fishing for lost pieces in the bottom of the container. Rust remover accumulates a grayish sludge. The chemical's working life will be prolonged if you dispose of this residue. The easiest way to do this is to slowly pour the acid from one container into another, taking care not to agitate the sediment. After most of the acid has been transferred, pour the sludge into a gallon milk bottle or similar container that can be disposed of in a safe manner.

Chemical cleaning and derusting baths can be easily set up not only during the on-going stages of restoration, but also as a profitable wintertime activity for flea market vendors. Cleaned, rebuilt, repainted parts and accessories make a nicer display and command a higher price than rusty stock that looks salvaged from a scrap yard. Antique tools purchased at garage sales, for example, clean up to look like new with simple de-rusting and painting.

The acid bath is brewed from dilute phosphoric acid, sold commercially as Rust Remover.

A User's Response

The chemical degreasing, derusting procedure just described appeared originally in *Cars & Parts.* Among those who applied these cleaning methods was William T. Cameron, a reader who was having difficulty stripping heavy caked-on paint and surface rust from his rare 1908 Cameron car. He had contacted a commercial stripping/derusting service, but, fearing damage to the car's wooden frame, the company refused to undertake the work. Following the guidelines that you have just read, Cameron set up his own stripping facility. He was completely successful in stripping the car's frame, engine, suspension, running gear and wheels. The wooden parts suffered no damage whatsoever. Cameron reported his experience in a letter. Excerpts follow.

"First off, I bought a ninety-six gallon galvanized stock watering trough from a farm supply agency for the stripping tank. It is oval shaped, four feet long, two feet wide and two feet deep. I mounted it on cement blocks over a converted laundry stove set up to use propane gas, the tank of which is mounted outside my garage. I filled the stripping tank with eighty gallons of water and ten cans of lye, which is about the same proportion recommended in the article.

"The heat from the stove was never enough to bring the solution to the boiling point but I found that I got excellent results with a temperature somewhere between 100 to 120 degrees F. There were a number of occasions when I didn't even turn on the heat and found that I got fairly good results with just the plain cold solution, except that it takes somewhat longer to do the job.

Bill Cameron used the lye stripping solution on his 1908 Cameron car. Note the safety garb, including rubber gloves, plastic face shield and rubber apron. Here Bill washes the air-cooled Cameron engine after removing it from the lye bath.

"I would strongly recommend that parts be thoroughly degreased before immersing in the tank. The solution does remove some grease which then floats on the top of the solution and leaves a greasy residue on some parts, especially wood parts as they are withdrawn from the tank. I find that if I use water soluble degreasers like Gunk in advance of dipping, the solution remains fairly clear and gives much better results. (It should be noted that Mr. Cameron used his lye tank primarily for paint stripping.)

"My 1908 Cameron chassis had three or four coats of paint over a considerable amount of surface rust and I am glad to say that the hot lye treatment did an excellent job of removing both. The before and after pictures of the Cameron wheels show how well it worked.

"I immersed the entire engine in the solution and, as the pictures show, washed off the solution with a garden hose while the engine was still suspended over the tank. These pictures also show the safety equipment I wore during the process.

"My stripping equipment has become so popular with other club members that it has been in almost constant use for the last three months. I have now reached the point where the solution is as thick as molasses and will have to be disposed of. To do this I propose using a small marine bilge pump attached to the faucet installed at the bottom of the tank and will pump the solution into a fifty-five gallon drum mounted on the back of a pickup truck. I will then take it to our Sanitary Land Fill facility where it will go into a deep trench far from anyone's water supply.

"I cannot stress too strongly the importance of not immersing aluminum, brass or pot metal parts in this solution and that any doubtful parts be checked with a magnet to be sure they are made of iron or steel before dipping.

This lye tank came from a feed store. Note the marks on the side of the tank showing the ratio of lye to water.

"I have used various phosphoric acid solutions on very badly rusted parts and prefer a somewhat stronger solution than that recommended by the Rust-remover people. I have been using a two-to-one or even a one-to-one phosphoric acid bath with good results.

"The advocates of sandblasting would lead you to believe that this is the ultimate way to remove paint and rust. However, I think it should be pointed out that sandblasting tends to peen over deep pits and crevices which eventually will continue to corrode and bleed through the paint. If sandblasting is utilized to achieve a smoother finish on metal parts, I would still recommend chemical rust removal prior to the blasting.

"I neglected to mention that a good steel bristled brush is needed to get the softened paint and rust off many parts. Also not shown in the pictures is a plywood cover for the tank which cuts down heat loss.

"My setup, including the tank, cement blocks, second hand gas stove, a twenty pound tank of LP gas, copper tubing, etc. cost less than $100, which is certainly a lot cheaper than using one of the commercial paint stripping and rust removal concerns."

Wooden wheels that a chemical stripper wouldn't clean for fear of damaging them cleaned up perfectly in the lye solution.

The finished wheels mounted on the restored car show the effectiveness of alkaline cleaning.

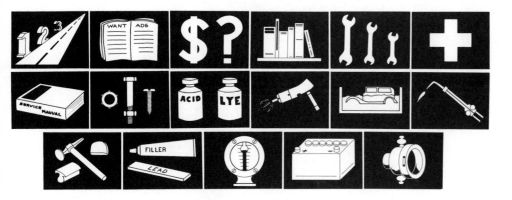

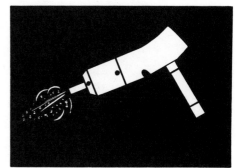

10

Hobby-Size Sandblasters—A Second Solution To The Stripping And Derusting Problem

Investing in tools you can use for stripping and derusting parts on a current project and others that may follow, rather than paying someone else for a one-time service, makes sense. When the job at hand is finished, the tools can be put to a number of uses. Both a sandblaster and an air compressor needed to power it are versatile additions to any shop. Metal, masonry and some wood products can be cleaned by sandblasting. Besides providing air for a sandblaster, a compressor will power air tools and is essential for quality painting.

A sandblaster is an extremely simple tool, both in function and design. Sandblasting removes rust or other surface coverings, usually paint, using an abrasive suspended in a flow of compressed air. The force of the abrasive strips the surface clean. Sand is the most commonly used abrasive, though glass beads and ground-up corn cobs are better suited for cleaning soft metals and wood. Specially sifted abrasive silica is sold through builders supply stores and auto parts outlets, but common sand can be shoveled free from a beach or sand pit and after thorough drying and sifting through a screen, the native product cuts with nearly the same effectiveness as commercial sand.

Ads in hobby magazines display two types of sandblasting equipment: relatively inexpensive siphon-fed models that sell for under $100 and the more expensive ($200 and up) pressure-fed sandblasters. Basic differences in design and capacity distinguish the two models. Siphon-fed sandblasters operate by directing a stream of compressed air past a hose connected to a supply of dry sand. As the compressed air rushes past the hose opening, it creates a partial vacuum, drawing sand into the air blast. The sand can be drawn from an attached container or the sand hose can simply be inserted into an open bag or mound of dry sand. The sand hose and air supply converge in a gun-shaped nozzle. Squeezing the trigger opens the air valve and activates the sandblaster.

The siphon unit's low cost is offset by limitations in capacity and durability for large projects such as stripping or derusting an entire car body. Siphon sandblasters will not generate as powerful an abrasive blast as the pressurized models. Then, too, the steel nozzles that are generally supplied with siphon units wear rapidly, resulting in an ineffectual blast that wastes both sand and air. Some manufacturers offer optional ceramic or carbon-steel nozzles to solve rapid nozzle wear on their deluxe units, but the more durable nozzles are not commonly available with spray-gun-style and other inexpensive siphon sandblasters.

On the plus side, siphon sandblasters don't require time-consuming refilling. They are adaptable, too, for use as a liquid

Sandblasting is one of the least expensive stripping methods. The prime ingredient, sand, can often be shoveled free, as helpers John Shulman and John Edgar demonstrate. This "generic" sand has to dry thoroughly before it can be used.

Protected by a sandblasting hood, I look more like a moon man or a radiation inspector.

blaster. Filling the sand canister or a separate container with a degreasing solvent like Gunk, turns a siphon blaster into a high-pressure spray washer that can be used to clean an engine compartment or chassis.

Stripping layers of paint and deeply embedded rust from an entire car body and frame calls for sandblasting efficiency exceeding that of siphon units. Pressure-fed sandblasters have greater capacity because the sand is held in a rugged steel container that is sealed and pressurized. Sand is forced out of pressure-fed sandblasters, not sucked out, as with siphon-fed models. Pressure-fed sandblasters use less air and sand than the siphon sandblasters and apply the abrasive with greater impact. By using small 3/32-inch-orifice nozzles and nozzle shut-offs that allow the air supply to catch up, hobby-size sandblasters can be operated on relatively low-volume, seven-cubic-foot-per-minute air supplies. This means that two- and three-horsepower portable air compressors can be used to power small pressure-fed sandblasters. The quarter-inch air hose normally supplied with these compressors will have to be replaced

This TIP hobby-sized sandblaster, made by Truman's Inc., features a moisture filter on the air inlet and an air shutoff valve at the spray nozzle. The shutoff allows the blaster to be used with a small-capacity air compressor. Sandblasting equipment varies in size and capacity but the essential design stays the same.

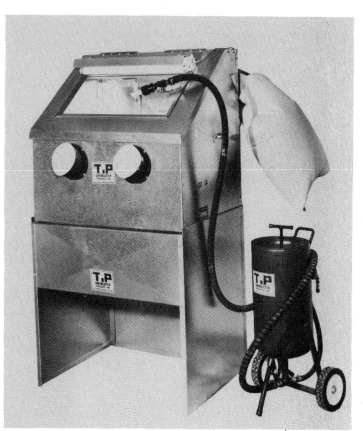

Sandblasting cabinets are used for cleaning small parts indoors.

with three-eighths hose for sandblasting. Attempting to use quarter-inch hose will starve the sandblaster for air giving the impression that the compressor is not delivering a sufficient volume of air. Nozzle shutoffs are intended to be used only to allow a compressor to build up its air reserve. A nozzle shutoff should never be used in place of an air shutoff valve to turn off the blaster. Closing the nozzle shutoff and allowing the compressor to build up pressure in the sand container could explode the sandblaster should the pressure release valve at the compressor fail to work. For this reason sandblasters designed for larger-capacity air compressors do not feature nozzle shutoffs.

Sandblasting is not a stripping/derusting technique that can be used indiscriminately. Sand grit will penetrate the smallest crevices, so mechanical assemblies such as front suspensions, transmission, rear axles and other driveline parts have to be removed before a frame can be safely sandblasted. Sandblasting gives an attractive frosted appearance to decorative glass. Blasting a car body with uncovered window glass will produce the same effect. Sandblasting equipment suppliers sell high-strength reinforced tape to protect parts from the sand's abrasive force; but it is wise to remove window glass, trim parts such as door handles, decorative moldings and the like, even wooden tack rails and of course the interior if you are sandblasting the entire body. Usually it is advisable to remove doors and fenders in order to sandblast the inside of these panels. Small rust areas on the lower body panels can be safely sand-

Two compressors can be connected in tandem to supply additional air pressure as shown.

Air Requirement Chart

Nozzle Size (Orifice)	Air Required (In H.P.)	CFM Required (@ 80 PSI)	Abrasive Used Per Hour	Cleaned Per Minute
3/32"	2-3 HP	7 CFM	100 Lbs.	1/2 Sq.Ft.
1/8"	3-5 HP	15 CFM	150 Lbs.	1 Sq. Ft.
5/32"	5-10 HP	25 CFM	200 Lbs.	2 Sq. Ft.
3/16"	10-15 HP	40 CFM	300 Lbs.	3 Sq. Ft.

VALVE
OPERATION

1. Open 2. Closed
NOZZLE-END VALVE

3. Throttled
Mixing Valve Only

PROBLEM	CAUSE	CORRECTIVE ACTION
Leakage of Abrasive through the Nozzle-End Shut Off Valve *Note- Premature leakage of this valve is due to improper use. See instructions	A. Valve has worn seals (if slight leak only) B. Valve has worn seals, ball & hex nut C. Valve is worn out D. Improper Use	A. Replace Seals (Part No. SK12 (1/2" Service Kit) B. Replace Seals (Part No. SK 12), Steel Ball (Part No. SCB12) and Valve Hex Nut (Part No. SHN12). C. Replace Valve (Part No. 106SV), Nipple (Part No. 104N) and Sand Hose Adapter (Part No. CHA1212). D. Quick On & Off for maximum life- See Valve Operation above Turn ALL THE WAY ON & ALL THE WAY OFF QUICKLY
Air, but no sand coming out of the nozzle	A. Moist Abrasive B. Moisture in the incoming air supply C. Abrasive blockage at bottom of unit. D. High Humidity in the surrounding air	A. Abrasive can contain considerable amounts of moisture, even though it appears dry. Always purchase abrasive in sealed bags. Spread out in the sun on cement driveway to dry if necessary (Strain before use). B. Many compressors (especially if working hard under heavy load) put out moisture in a vapor form which can easily pass through standard moisture traps. We recommend a Coalescing Air Filter at sandblaster. C. Stop, shut off Nozzle-end Valve and remove the Nozzle Cap and the Ceramic Nozzle & Gasket. Then TURN ON the Nozzle End Valve all the way, allowing moist sand and air to blow out for 1-2 minutes. In most cases you will be able to blow out the obstruction in this way. If not, it will be necessary to dis-assemble the bottom end of the unit and clean out thoroughly with clean, dry air. Re-assemble unit & resume. D. Same as "C" above. *Note- in high humidity areas, we recommend adding a 4 way cross and plug in place of the tee at the bottom of the unit (Part No. 4WC12 & 4WP12) for ease in cleaning bottom end. Insert steel rod up through 4 way cross or can insert air line at this point and blow out the obstruction. After cleaning, replace plug & resume.
Surging or Sputtering of the sand flow at the nozzle	A. Mixing Valve is too far open B. Incoming Air Hose from your compressor is too small C. Nozzle "Worn Out" D. Restriction in your incoming air supply E. Air Compressor is too small for the job F. Moist Abrasive or moist air supply	A. Re-adjust Mixing Valve located on bottom of unit. Best method is to close the valve all the way, then GRADUALLY open valve until sand is just slightly visible. Should be in Throttled position. B. Incoming air hose should be Minimum of 3/8"I.D. up to 25 ft. & 1/2"I.D. up to 50 ft. Ordinary 1/4" or 5/16" hose will not work. This is the chief cause of "Surging" or poor operation of the flow. C. Replace Nozzle (Ceramic Nozzles wear to next size in 6-8 hours) D. Check for clogged airline filters, clogged or improperly sized air regulators, undersized valves, fittings, strainers, etc. For sandblasting you need a MINIMUM of 1/2"I.D. air lines, hose & fittings. E. See "Nozzle Selection Chart" on top of this chart. Match nozzle size to your air compressor. If necessary, add to your air supply. F. See Items A,B,C,D in 2nd Section (above) of this chart
No Air or Abrasive coming out of the Ceramic Nozzle	A. Clogged Nozzle	A. Stop, shut off Nozzle End Valve and remove the Ceramic Nozzle. Clean out Nozzle Orifice with a fine wire and re-assemble. *Note - Clogging at the nozzle is due to the use of improperly graded abrasive or re-use of abrasive without straining (Use finer grade).

* PLEASE NOTE - 99% of the problems encountered with sandblasting are due to moisture, such as damp abrasive, moisture in your incoming air supply, and high humidity in the surrounding air. There are no moving parts and nothing to break (other than valves) in your sandblaster. If your air supply is reasonably dry and your abrasive kept dry and properly strained, you will have little trouble with sandblasting. Important also is that the proper size hose or piping from your air compressor be used along with suitable moisture removing equipment.

This chart provides a guide to efficient use of sandblasting equipment.

blasted if you remove nearby trim, roll up and cover the windows and are careful to concentrate the sandblast on the target area. In the event that you are sandblasting a gas tank, be sure to cover the inlet and drain holes. Otherwise you will be able to hear sand sifting around inside the tank when you are finished and later the tiny sand grains will wash into the gas line, continually plugging the fuel filter and causing untold carburetion problems.

The two factors that assure successful sandblasting are a sufficient air supply and dry sand. The smaller nozzles and shutoff valves which enable small portable compressors to power hobby-size sandblasters do so at the penalty of slower operation than commercial-capacity equipment. Attempting to sandblast an entire car in one day with a hobby-size sandblaster is an unrealistic goal. There is no reason, of course, why you shouldn't take your time, particularly with your first project; but methods that can be used to increase the air supply and sandblasting efficiency are worth considering.

Since portable air compressors are popular tools with hobbyists, it is often possible to make sandblasting a joint venture by borrowing a friend's compressor and hooking two units in tandem. Connecting a pair of compressors through a T coupling increases both the air output and reserve. Renting a large compressor is another option. Hobbyists have been known to wrangle the use of commercial-size compressors from their place of

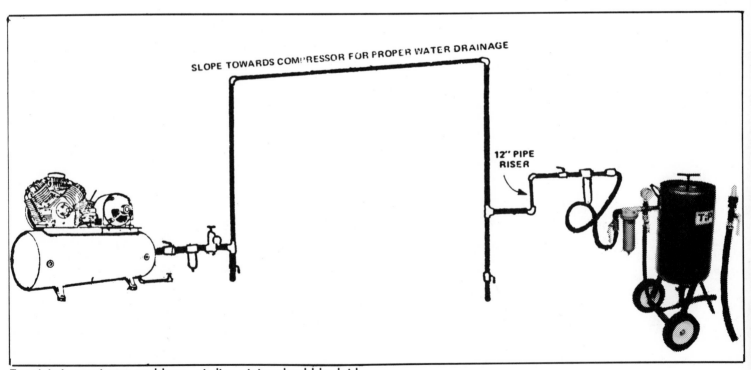

To minimize moisture problems, air-line piping should be laid out according to this diagram.

work or the neighborhood gas station, especially when the sandblasting session also includes services for the compressor's owner.

Sandblasting equipment is highly vulnerable to moisture. In humid weather, moisture that condenses in the compressor tank and air lines is then pumped into the sandblaster where

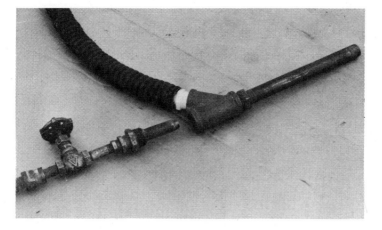

The protruding "venturi pipe" must seat deeply enough into the Y fitting to draw sand into the airstream. This simple homemade sandblaster works as well as commercial products.

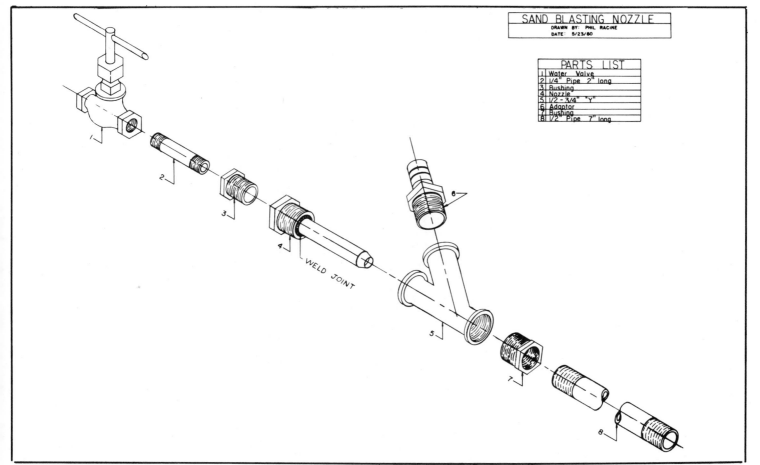

SAND BLASTING NOZZLE
DRAWN BY: PHIL RACINE
DATE: 5/23/80

PARTS LIST

1	Water Valve
2	1/4" Pipe 2" long
3	Bushing
4	Nozzle
5	1/2 - 3/4" "Y"
6	Adaptor
7	Bushing
8	1/2" Pipe 7" long

WELD JOINT

An exploded view of the homebuilt sandblasting nozzle shows the parts and assembly pattern. Galvanized Y fittings can be purchased from a large plumbing supply house.

it soaks into the sand and gums up the works. Trying to sandblast with wet sand is a frustrating experience, to say the least. To assure trouble-free operation, you should locate the air compressor in a cool, dry, well-ventilated area of your shop. Before sandblasting, make sure that the sand itself is thoroughly dry. To test the sand, squeeze a handful from the bottom of the supply.

Moist sand will dry out gradually if it is stored in a low-humidity area. Wet sand dries quickly if it is spread in the sun on a tarp or driveway apron. When the sand is powder dry, it can be shoveled into the sandblaster for use or into an open-top oil drum for storage. Sand should never be stored in the sandblaster because it will absorb moisture and clog the machine at the outset of the next work session.

Moisture pumped from the compressor can be controlled by routing the air line through a length of iron pipe. Humid air will condense as it comes in contact with the pipe. The water can be trapped at the sandblaster-end of the pipe and drained from the trap periodically. Installing condensers at the air outlet from the compressor and at the sandblaster will also help cure moisture problems originating at the compressor. Note the illustration showing a suggested air line hookup. Even with these precautions, attempting to sandblast in highly humid weather is neither sensible nor feasible.

You must wear protective clothing when using a sandblaster. The most important piece of sandblasting garb is a heavy canvas hood worn to cover your face and head. The hood has a front viewing lens and screened ventilation openings. Although the hood protects your eyes from sand spray,

The shaved top on the spigot projecting from the five-gallon bucket is the other critical feature of this homemade design. Without the opening, a vacuum develops in the sand hose.

you will inhale sand dust unless you also wear a dust mask. Heavy leather gloves, such as those welders wear, leather work shoes, a long-sleeved shirt and work pants complete the sandblasting outfit. Even if you are sandblasting on a hot day, you should not expose bare skin to the abrasive blast. Some operators slip rubber bands around their shirt cuffs and pant legs to cut down the dust that blows into these openings.

At best, sandblasting is a noisy, dirty outside job. Spraying a jet of sand with an air line pressure of 60 to 125 psi against a metal surface pulverizes the silica granules into a fine dust which sifts through clothing fibers coating every inch of skin, from nose to toes. The air compressor must be separated from the sandblasting area since tiny dust particles created by the sandblasting action will clog the compressor's filters and could ruin the motor bearings. Sandblasting should never be done inside your shop unless you use a special cabinet designed to contain the abrasive. These cabinets are becoming increasingly popular with restorers since they spare the mess of outdoor sandblasting and can be used where sand dust would bother neighbors. Although sandblasting cabinets are designed primarily for cleaning parts the size of automobile wheels or smaller, they do conserve sand and are ideal for use with more costly

The design of a sandblaster is simple enough so that homebuilt models can be assembled by clever craftsmen. Craig Brownell, a cousin, built this large pressurized sandblaster for use on the family farm.

Craig's sandblaster was fabricated from a discarded glue pot. Note the heavy-duty clamps that hold the lid in place.

abrasives like glass beads. Commercial shops that regularly blast large parts often construct sandblasting pens outside their shops to confine the dust and sand spray.

Operating a sandblaster is as simple as the machine itself. First, attach the unit to a source of compressed air, and fill the canister with dry, sifted sand. If you are operating a siphon sandblaster you may simply need to insert the sand hose into the sand supply. Pressure-fed sandblasters have a mixing valve mounted at the bottom of the tank which has to be closed as does the lid that seals the canister. The sandblaster is then pressurized by opening the inlet air valve. After you have donned the protective hood, gloves and dust mask, the sandblasting session can begin. If you are using a siphon sandblaster, simply point the nozzle at the workpiece and press the trigger. With pressure-fed models, open the nozzle shutoff all the way, then open the mixing valve in a gradual motion. Deflect the sand spray so that it strikes the workpiece at a forty-five-degree angle. Paint and rust will spray off the metal surface much like hosing off dirt. When the tank is drained or the sand mound is consumed, shut off the air supply. On pressure-fed models you must also close the mixing valve. After the dust settles you can take off your hood and refill the sandblaster. If you are frugal you can sweep up the used sand and add it to the fresh sand. Refill the tank and repeat the process until the parts are stripped clean.

Sandblasting penetrates rust pits and cleans metal to a satin finish that assures a good paint bond. Raw metal must be washed promptly with a dilute phosphoric acid solution sold by auto supply shops under brand names like Chem-Grip and Metal Prep to retard rerusting. Parts that need straightening, welding or filling should be worked at this stage, then primed and painted without delay.

Unless you are prepared to reverse the inevitable corrosion damage found on most old cars, you will be virtually hamstrung at the first stage of restoration. Because of its simplicity, both in design and operation, sandblasting equipment is relatively inexpensive and its use reqires no special skill. All it takes is sand and air to have a blast!

Frame cleaning is one of the most popular uses for sandblasting. Chassis parts are too large and cumbersome for most other stripping methods.

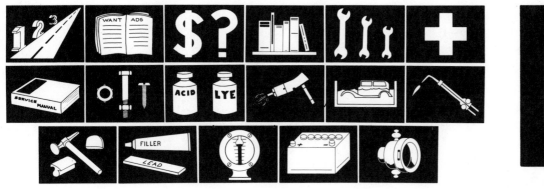

11

Metal Laundries End Rust

The fact that we live in an era of high technology gives us reason to suspect that someone has developed a harmless, yet sure, method of derusting metal parts. Somebody has, actually there are several companies engaged in metal laundering. Redi-Strip, the General Motors of the alkaline electrolytic derusters, opened its first stripping facility in California three decades ago. Today, Bob and Paul Deringer, the Redi-Strip founders, have perfected chemical formulas for stripping off practically any manmade coating and chemical electrolysis solutions that float off rust without harming or changing in any way the chemical properties of the sound metal underneath. Redi-Strip franchises operate in major U.S. and Canadian cities. Competitors also serve the larger population centers with their versions of the alkaline electrolytic process. Chemical strippers, as these firms call themselves, advertise in hobby publications like *Hemmings Motor News* and in telephone-book yellow pages.

For dramatic effect, Redi-Strip ads have shown whole cars, complete with tires, being dunked in the stripping tanks. These ad photos were intended to demonstrate that alkaline electrolysis won't destroy delicate parts but were not intended to be taken as a guide to properly preparing a car for stripping and derusting. A sure sign that the ads weren't meant to be taken seriously is that they show cars with tires left on the rims. Dunking a car with tires attached would make the chassis buoyant, and of course the tires would block the derusting solution from cleaning inside the rims.

Having a commercial stripper tackle the dirty work of cleaning off caked-on mud, layers of paint and rust saves time, but metal laundering isn't a drive-through process. Parts that are candidates for the stripper's bath have to be disassembled as completely as possible. Chemical immersion will strip off tar, caulking, bondo—virtually all applied coatings—but it won't penetrate beneath covered surfaces. This means you should remove door handles, rubber moldings, trim pieces, everything that will keep the stripping and derusting chemicals from cleaning the metal underneath.

Door handles are usually held in place by screws or bolts. Trim moldings are fastened by clips or screws. Rubber moldings that seal doors and trunk openings are glued in place so removing them is more of a challenge, unless you know the secret. Trying to pry rubber moldings loose with a putty knife or screwdriver usually results in tearing the rubber. Unless the rubber is badly deteriorated you will probably want to reuse it—especially since finding replacement rubber moldings is not always possible.

There is an easy way to remove weatherseal that should leave the rubber undamaged. Simply ignite a propane torch, the type with a wide tip used for soldering works well, and apply the torch's heat to the back side of the metal to which the rubber is glued. (The heat melts the glue and loosens the rubber.) On trunk moldings, the underside of the weatherseal lip is generally easily accessible. This isn't true for door weatherseal. With the upholstery panels removed you may be able to reach the torch inside the door panels and apply heat to the metal behind the weatherseal. Otherwise you will have to play the torch against the metal beside the weatherseal, being very careful not to burn the rubber.

Metal laundries can safely strip nonferrous parts; however, brass, aluminum and pot metal items must be separated from steel parts at the derusting stage. Some commercial strippers

Anthony and Nathan, my two sons, hold a rusted Model A roadster cowl in preparation for commercial stripping.

are hesitant to dip wood. This means that wooden wheels and car bodies built before the mid-thirties (and the bodies of post-war MG and Morgan sports cars) that are constructed of metal sheets tacked to a wooden frame probably shouldn't be stripped and derusted chemically. Wood isn't dissolved by chemical cleaning but after soaking up to twenty-four hours in a heated caustic solution, followed by a high-pressure rinse, wooden body framing and wheel spokes look like pieces of waterlogged driftwood.

Any steel component—doors, fenders, the frame, an entire body, even an engine block—is a candidate for metal laundering. Sheet metal parts usually need paint stripping and de-rusting prior to straightening and metal repair, but engine blocks, too, are prime candidates for derusting. You will find that if you have the engine block stripped clean of rust, grease and accumulated sediment prior to rebuilding, the engine will operate at peak lubricating and cooling efficiency. Commercial strippers claim that their alkaline electrolytic process carries none of the disadvantages for cleaning mechanical parts such as engine castings that occur with sandblasting and chemical de-rusting. They back this assertion with testimonials from their industrial clients who use the alkaline deruster to strip costly tooling and other precision parts.

Of course before you can have your car's sheet metal, wheels and any mechanical castings stripped and derusted you have to transport them to the stripper. The wheels and smaller sheet metal parts, the doors perhaps, even the castings may fit in the trunk of the car you use for everyday transportation. If you own a pickup you will be able to transport all the components easily, though you may need to make more than one trip. Otherwise you may need to rent a trailer or even a small van to transport

A pair of 20-foot tanks are the heart of a chemical stripping operation.

The tanks will hold a full frame such as the one shown here, even an entire car.

parts that need derusting. If you are having the body derusted intact (with upholstery, instruments and wiring and all mechanical components removed) you will probably need to rent, borrow or hire a truck or trailer large enough to transport a car.

Commercial stripping and derusting solutions aren't alchemists' brews but they do contain special chemical blends that are carefully guarded company secrets. Most stripping facilities feature giant twenty-foot-long by eight-foot-wide immersion tanks, big enough to dip a full-sized car. The first tank holds a heated alkaline and detergent bath that strips parts down to bare metal and rust. Parts are soaked in this tank first to loosen paint and other coatings, then they are hoisted out and rinsed with a high-pressure hot-water spray. Stubborn coatings such as epoxy finishes, thick layers of paint and undercoating are attacked by hand with a putty knife. A second immersion in the alkaline bath usually strips off even the toughest coatings. Parts are washed again to prevent the stripping chemicals from contaminating the derusting solution.

An overhead hoist is used to lift large parts into and out of the tanks. The alkaline electrolytic derusting process is activated by an electrical current that causes the chemical solution to float rust off metal. Every crevice, seam, even the inside surfaces of door and hood panels emerge as clean as new stampings. After a final rinsing the metal is ready for another alkaline

The stripper removes all traces of rust, preparing the metal for repair and painting.

After stripping, parts are treated to prevent rerusting.

dip that coats the parts with a rust-inhibiting film. This coating must be washed off the parts with water before painting. Many of the commercial stripping facilities offer an extra-cost phosphate dip that both protects against rust and leaves the parts ready for painting.

Paint doesn't glue itself to metal, rather it adheres to surface irregularities. Consequently, a coat of paint sprayed over smooth metal is likely to chip and peel unless the surface is scuffed-up some to aid bonding. One reason sandblasting assures good paint adhesion is that it abrades the metal. Since commercial chemical derusting attacks rust only, not the metal surface, sheet metal parts should be treated with a phosphate coating or etched with metal prep before priming and painting. Many restorers don't realize that a primer coat alone offers little protection against rerusting. Sheet metal parts are actually better left unprimed and treated with a rust inhibitor than if they are primed only. Body parts such as fenders, doors, hoods or splash shields that will be stored for some length of time while mechanical repair and body work are completed, should be primed and finish-painted before they are put away. They may need to be painted again when they are installed on the car but the initial paint covering will give long lasting protection against rerusting.

Since chemical stripping and derusting cleans all exposed metal surfaces, the insides of doors, hoods and trunk panels, even body pillars must also be treated against rerusting. On doors, hoods and trunk lids, an effective way to coat hidden inside surfaces is to pour rust-inhibiting primer through holes in the stiffening panel that covers the backside of these parts, then rock the panel back and forth until the primer coats the metal. Repeat this process with paint after the primer coat dries. Body pillars can be treated against rust by spraying grease or wax-

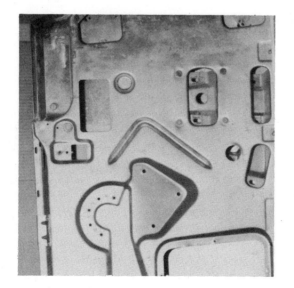

With the protective coating washed off, as shown on this inner door panel, the metal is as bright and shiny as a fresh steel stamping.

based rustproofing into them. You can buy rustproofing kits and spray the panels yourself with aerosol cans or you can have a commercial rustproofing business do the job for you.

Cleaned and derusted parts show all their flaws. Holes in sheet metal parts that are plainly visible now may have appeared only as tiny paint blisters before stripping. Leaded fillings survive chemical derusting, but bondo and fiberglass patches will dissolve in the tanks. With the full effect of corrosion damage plainly visible you should carefully inspect the stripped and derusted parts to determine needed repairs. Frames that have been stripped should be examined both for signs of corrosion damage and for cracked welds. If frame channels have been weakened, reinforcing plates will have to be welded to the rust damaged sections. Sheet metal parts can be repaired by welding patches in the corroded areas. Welding and leading repairs are likely to be stronger and are much easier to make when you're working with clean metal.

Commercial strippers will usually give a cost estimate over the phone, but to do so they will need a detailed description of the parts. Their rates are calculated on a time-in-the-tanks and labor basis, so batches of small parts can often be stripped for the same price as an individual item. The cost of commercial stripping is generally higher than commercial sandblasting and the service is located primarily in large cities, at some distance from restorers living in the hinterland. These two factors are commercial stripping's major drawbacks. Even so, alkaline electrolysis produces unmatched results on rusted, heavily grease- or paint-coated parts. Commercially stripped parts come out of the tanks looking like new metal, and that's what restoration is all about.

Before and after view of this demonstration fender shows the effectiveness of the commercial stripping process.

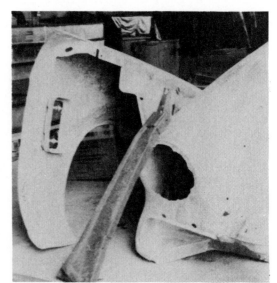

The Model A roadster cowl section rests against a modern-era fender, waiting its turn in the derusting bath.

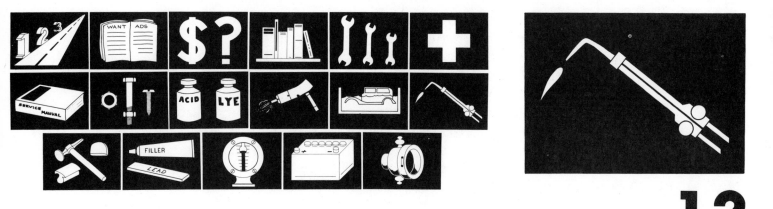

12

Welding For Beginners

Welding is one of the major technological discoveries of this century. Although very early cars reflect prewelding construction methods—body metal is screwed to wooden frameworks and chassis frames are largely riveted together—automobile manufacturers soon discovered that welding increased assembly speed and resulted in stronger, more durable vehicles. As a result, whether you are working on an early or late model, your chances of restoring or repairing a car without welding are slim. Mending rust damage is only one of a number of applications for a welder's skills. Besides sheet metal repair, other uses for a tool that concentrates several-thousand-degree heat on a workpiece include cutting away rusted floor pans or rocker panels, freeing rust-frozen bolts or tapered fittings that have become tightly embedded . . . the examples are endless. While rust-frozen or tapered parts that have been force-fit together may appear permanently wedded, a torch's heat will loosen their bond as surely as soap eases a tight-fitting ring off a finger. For both body surgery and mechanical repairs, access to welding equipment is simply indispensable.

While welding requires skill, learning to use a welding torch or an arc welder isn't beyond a handyman's ability. There are two distinct welding processes hobbyists are likely to use: gas welding, where a fuel such as acetylene or MAPP (short for stabilized methylacetylene-propradiene) is burned in the presence of pressurized oxygen; and electric arc welding, which is generally easier for beginners to learn. Following a brief period of instruction, most novices should be able to arc weld with at least moderate proficiency. However, hobbyists are more likely to need gas than arc welding skills. Arc welding is suited primarily for heavier-gauge metal. Applications include repairing cracks in a car's frame, constructing shop tools such as the hydraulic press and parts washer described in the appendix and for handyman repairs, mending a cracked lawnmower housing, for example. Arc welding is not well suited for light-gauge sheet metal repair and unless an adapter is used an electric arc can't be used to heat rust-frozen parts.

Gas welding is better suited to car repair or restoration because this method is more versatile than electric arc. A gas cutting torch can be used to cut out sections of rust-damaged body metal and a welding torch can be used to repair rust by welding in new panels. Since the temperature of the gas welding torch can be controlled by varying the flow of fuel and oxygen this method can be used for brazing, where low heat is required, or for applying a great deal of heat to free rusted parts such as an exhaust pipe that has joined itself to a muffler outlet. Gas welding does have several drawbacks for the beginner. The equipment costs from two to five times as much as handyman-capacity arc welders (primarily because of rental and refilling costs for the fuel and oxygen cylinders). In addi-

Hobbyists find welding equipment useful but may not have enough need for a full-sized welding outfit to justify the expense. This scaled-down gas welding unit called the Toteweld is ideally suited for hobby use.

tion, gas welding is potentially more hazardous than arc welding and many novice welders find they need a longer period of instruction and practice before feeling comfortable using gas welding equipment than they do to achieve a comparable skill level with arc welding.

Examining The Welding Process

To see why gas and electric arc welding have different applications, let's look at what happens in the two welding methods. With arc welding a pool of molten metal is formed in the very intense 6500–7000°F heat generated by an electric arc. After the arc is withdrawn, the molten metal fuses, creating the weld. The electric arc occurs between two conductors, the workpiece and an electrode. Electrodes used in arc welding are coated with flux that floats impurities out of the weld and releases inert gas to prevent the weld from oxidizing. The flux forms a brittle coating that can be chipped off after the weld has cooled. Small particles of slag, as this coating is called, may also be embedded in the weld.

Although striking an arc and drawing a weld are relatively simple processes, arc welding does have drawbacks. Since slag impurities are usually trapped in the seam of an arc weld, beginners aren't able to rework improperly made welds with

Exhaust system repair can be a nightmare without a torch but with the simple addition of heat, rusted metal separates as easily as new parts.

success. Even though arc temperature can be controlled by varying the thickness of the electrode (welding rod) and the amperage setting on the welder, it is difficult to limit the heat generated by a standard arc welder to the range required for welding thin-gauge sheet metal. A special arc welding technique, called MIG welding, shields the weld with inert gas rather than flux and automatically feeds the welding electrode at the same rate that the rod is melted into the weld. This is an ideal method for welding sheet metal. Unfortunately, the expense of MIG welding equipment makes this method impractical for most hobbyists.

Gas welding also melts and fuses metal by applying an intense, concentrated heat that is generated when a fuel gas, commonly acetylene, burns in a stream of pure oxygen. Filler metal from a welding rod is melted into the molten puddle created by the welding torch, giving strength to the weld. One of the skills required for gas welding is the ability to control the flame so that enough heat is generated to puddle the metal,

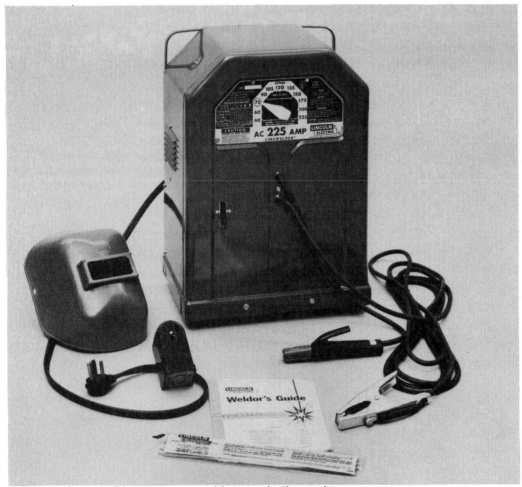

Shop-sized arc welders are reasonably priced. This tool is used to repair car frames and other heavy-gauge metal parts.

but not so much that the molten pool burns through the seam you are trying to weld. Flame temperatures are determined by the amount of gas being burned and the oxygen flow. Besides adjusting the fuel flow and the flame, a gas welder learns to select the proper torch tip with large or small orifices depending on the thickness and type of metal.

Whether you decide to develop your skills as a gas or electric arc welder, it is important to remember that rigorous safety precautions apply to both methods and that welding isn't learned by "dubbing around."

Selecting Equipment

Arc welders range from AC and DC utility models to portable generator-powered commercial units. If you are shopping for arc equipment, avoid the inexpensive 110-volt units because of their limited capacity. AC welders that operate on 220-volt current and are rated at around 230 amps have adequate capacity for a hobbyist's use. These units are frequently featured in Sears, Wards and Penneys sales catalogs and are sold by professional welding shops as well.

If you compare the cost of arc and gas welding equipment, the latter may appear less expensive. Usually, though, when

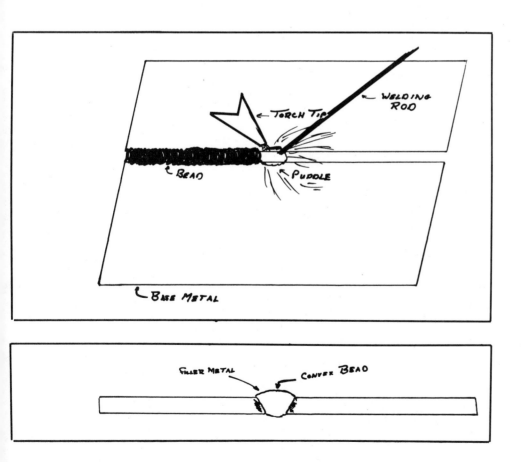

With gas welding, molten metal flows behind the welding (filler) rod in a puddle. Welders develop the skill to control this puddle with practice.

Welds should thoroughly penetrate the base metal.

you buy a gas welding outfit you get only the torch tip, hoses and valves that attach to fuel and oxygen cylinders. Cylinder rental or purchase and the cost of periodically refilling the cylinders are expensive extras. In recent years small-capacity gas welding outfits that use solid oxygen pellets and burn propane gas have appeared on the tool shelves of discount marts and home improvement stores. These units are intended for brazing and light welding, filling pinholes and patching small rust holes on sheet metal, but are not suited to replacing larger panels, such as floor sections.

For hobbyists who are not ready to invest in a full-size gas welding outfit, but require greater welding capacity than the small oxygen-pellet models provide, MAPP Products markets a portable gas welding outfit called the Toteweld. MAPP distributors sell this compact unit complete with welding and cutting tips, gauges, hoses, a twenty-cubic-foot refillable oxygen cylinder and a one-pound disposable cylinder of MAPP gas all contained in a handy plastic carrier. The Toteweld retails in the $200 range, making its price comparable to a utility-size arc welder and about one-third the cost of a full-size gas welding outfit. Mapp gas used as a fuel by the Toteweld (and in many full-size gas welding outfits as well) produces about twice as much heat per cubic foot of fuel as acetylene. Consequently, the heat range and welding duration offered by the Toteweld is sufficient for most restoration or repair welding and cutting applications. MAPP gas is better suited than acetylene for brazing, a factor especially important to hobbyists who may be concerned with making low-heat auto body repair. Using MAPP carries a safety bonus, too. The gas has a heavy garlic-and-onions smell that is noticeable in a miniscule 100-parts-per-million concentration. You are not likely to leave the MAPP gas valve open. Leaking acetylene is not detected as easily.

Learning To Weld

Practice makes perfect, but it takes instruction to become a skilled welder. Learning how to light a torch or strike an arc and melt filler rod in a smooth bead are only two steps in welding instruction. Developing safety consciousness when working with gas or arc welding equipment and becoming acquainted with welding techniques that apply to metals of different thickness and composition are equally important. The best way to master welding fundamentals while learning important safety habits and to be able to draw on an expert when you need assistance is to enroll in a welding course offered through the adult education branch of a nearby technical college or a vocational high school. Classes meet evenings or Saturdays, times convenient for working adults.

Safety instruction is not the kind of information that most people pick up when they're trying to teach themselves a skill. In a welding class you will learn that ultra-violet rays from an arc flash can cause retina damage, consequently, you will be told that you must wear a helmet specially designed to shield your eyes whenever you are arc welding. You will also be instructed to develop the habit of warning bystanders when you are about to strike an arc. Since a child's curious eyes are drawn to the welding action, you must be careful not to weld when children are around.

Welding requires protective clothing similar to that worn during sandblasting. Heavy leather gloves, work clothes, leather shoes, welding goggles (for gas welding) or a helmet (for arc welding) and a cap will protect your eyes and keep sparks and hot metal from burning your hair or skin.

When you are working with equipment that produces several-thousand-degree temperatures you have to think of the possible consequences of seemingly harmless habits. Carrying a butane lighter in your pants or jacket pocket, for example, invites disaster. If a spark from the welding operation were to ignite a butane canister the tiny lighter could explode with deadly force.

Some other good safety tips include: Make sure you are not standing on damp ground when arc welding. And when gas welding, never put oil on regulators, hoses, torches, fittings. The combination of oil and oxygen makes a violent explosion. Always remember that acetylene pressure should not exceed 15 psi—the pressure at which it will explode—so avoid "crimping" hoses.

The most effective way to become a proficient welder is to enroll in an evening class at a nearby trade school. Here, Glen Goodrich, welding instructor at St. Johnsbury Academy, St. Johnsbury, Vermont, points to the tell-tale signs of a weak weld.

Besides the benefit of thorough instruction, welding classes usually give students the opportunity to practice newly learned skills on projects they choose. If you decide to learn welding in order to repair rust damage on your car a welding class may be an ideal opportunity to get acquainted with different types of welding equipment before purchasing your own, to learn welding basics and to call on an expert for help when you have difficulty.

If you want to learn how to weld but don't have time or access to a class you can teach yourself the skill by carefully

1 Keep equipment in good working condition.

2 Light torch with friction lighter or stationary pilot flame.

3 Point away from persons and combustibles when lighting torch.

4 Keep oxygen away from combustibles; don't use oxygen for compressed air; never allow oxygen jet to strike oily or greasy surfaces; don't use oxygen to blow away dust.

5 Store and use acetylene and LP gas cylinders with valve end up.

6 Store oxygen cylinders apart from fuel gas cylinders.

7 Store cylinders in protected place.

8 Handle cylinders with care, to avoid damage to valves, safety devices, or the cylinder itself.

9 Use valve protection caps on cylinders that will accept them.

10 Secure or wedge cylinders into position when transporting by motor vehicle.

11 Only the cylinder owner, or persons authorized by him, shall refill a cylinder.

12 Use a pressure regulator!

13 Secure cylinders, to keep them from being knocked over while in use.

14 When a cylinder is empty, close its valve and mark it "EMPTY".

15 Replace or repair damaged hose.

16 Use the proper regulator for each gas and pressure range.

17 Never force connections that do not fit. Watch out for connectors with faulty seats; get rid of them.

18 Weld or cut only in a nonflammable atmosphere.

19 Take steps to prevent sparks from falling through floor cracks, etc. Remove or protect combustible materials in "falling spark" zones.

20 Keep suitable fire extinguishing equipment close at hand.

21 Before cutting or welding on an "empty" container, be sure it does not contain flammable vapors or any residues that might burn or give off flammable or toxic vapors.

22 Keep flame and hot slag off of concrete; intense heat may cause flying fragments.

23 Wear gloves and goggles or other suitable eye protection

24 Keep sleeves and collars buttoned. *Pants uncuffed.*

25 Choose protective clothing to suit the work to be done.

26 Provide adequate ventilation whenever welding or cutting around cadmium, zinc, lead, fluorine compounds, or other toxic materials.

27 Protect stored gasoline, oil, grease, etc. from sparks and slag.

28 Store reserve oxygen and fuel gas cylinders away from sparks and slag.

29 Wear a safety hat in designated areas.

30 Check connections for gastightness. Use soapy water or its equivalent — never a flame.

31 Post a warning near a leaking fuel-gas cylinder and promptly notify the supplier.

32 Don't tamper with or attempt to repair cylinder valves. Notify supplier.

33 Never leave a lighted torch unattended.

34 Place cylinders in a cradle or on a suitable platform for lifting. Don't use slings or electromagnets.

35 Keep hoses, cable, and other equipment clear of passageways, stairs, ladders, etc.

36 Use only approved manifolds.

37 Call fuel gases by their proper names.

Welding safety is no joke. If you can match the photo errors with this chart you're on your way to safe welding.

following written instructions. Remember to be alert for safety tips. Let's assume that your interest in welding is motivated by the desire to repair rust damage and to be able to heat rust-frozen parts as needed during repair or restoration. These are among the most common uses a hobbyist has for gas welding equipment.

Rather than invest in a full-size gas welding outfit before you've learned to weld, I recommend that you purchase the MAPP product Toteweld, mentioned earlier, to learn on. The Toteweld operates just like full-size gas welding equipment and unless you plan to do extensive welding, you will probably find the Toteweld fully adequate for all your repair or restoration needs. When you purchase a Toteweld you will receive a small instruction booklet that explains how to set up and use the welding outfit. These instructions apply specifically to the Toteweld and generally to any gas welding application.

The first step after you purchase any gas welding outfit is to anchor both cylinders vertically, making sure the fuel and oxygen valves point away from each other. Crack each cylinder's valve for a second to blow out any dirt in the outlet. Then connect the regulators to the oxygen and fuel cylinders. The important caution in this step is to make sure that each regulator seats properly on the cylinder outlet threads so that oxygen or fuel does not leak from the cylinders. Next, connect the hose lines to the regulators and attach the torch tip to the torch handle. After installing and tightening the regulators, hose and torch tip, check the oxygen line for leaks by first opening the oxygen valve and screwing-in the T handle on the oxygen regulator until oxygen flows from the torch. Now shut off the oxygen flow by closing the torch valve for the oxygen hose. Brush soap-and-water solution around the hose connections. If bubbles appear, shut the oxygen valve, disconnect the hose, clean and retighten the connection. Follow the same procedure to check the fuel line for leaks.

With the regulators, hoses and torch all properly connected you are ready for the next step—lighting the torch. When you begin this step the valves on both cylinders should be closed and both regulator screws should be loosened, turned counterclockwise. Both valves on the torch handle should be closed. Open the valve on the oxygen cylinder—slowly at first until the regulator pressure gauge reaches its maximum reading—then turn the valve all the way open. The Toteweld does not have a valve on the MAPP cylinder, but if you are using a full-size welding outfit the next step will be to open the fuel-cylinder valve. The fuel valve should only be opened a quarter-turn so that the cylinder can be shut off quickly in an emergency. Next, adjust the oxygen pressure at the torch by opening the torch valve on the oxygen line and turning-in the regulator handle until oxygen flows from the torch. Close the torch valve and turn in the regulator handle one more turn. If you are using a full-size welding outfit you will adjust the oxygen regulator so that the low-pressure gauge registering the flow of oxygen to the torch reads between 8 and 20 psi (for welding sheet metal). Now adjust the fuel pressure by repeating these steps with the

After opening the valves on the fuel and oxygen cylinders to the proper setting, slightly open the fuel valve on the torch. Ignite the torch using a striker. The fuel gas will burn with a yellow, sooty flame.

Adjust the torch by slowly opening the oxygen valve. It may be necessary to alternately open the fuel and oxygen valves until a proper neutral flame appears with a smooth rounded inner cone.

Skill in welding or brazing is largely a matter of practice that can be gained working on marginally usable parts.

fuel line. The fuel regulator setting depends on the thickness of the metal, welding rod diameter and tip size. Recommended settings are listed below.

Metal Thickness	Welding Rod Diameter	Welding Tip	Acetylene Pressure
1/16–1/8	1/16–1/8	small to medium	4–5 psi
1/4–3/8	5/32–1/4	medium to large	8–9 psi

To make sure that the hoses are not contaminated with a mixture of gasses, purge the lines before lighting. Open both torch valves briefly to allow fresh gas to flow through the lines. When both lines are purged, close the torch valves. Now light the torch by opening the torch fuel valve slightly (approximately ½ turn) and immediately striking a spark at the torch tip with a torch lighter. If you have opened the valve too far the flame will light, then blow out. Otherwise, a sooty yellowish flame will lick out of the torch tip. Open the torch oxygen valve slowly and gently. As you do so the flame will change in shape and color. If you open the oxygen valve too far or too fast the flame will blow out with a pop. Don't be alarmed if this happens. Close the oxygen valve and relight the flame.

You are now ready to adjust the flame so that gas and oxygen are mixed in correct proportions. You should be wearing welder's goggles at this point because you will be looking at the flame while you adjust it. As you open the oxygen valve you will see the flame separate into three distinct parts. A small light-colored cone will emerge close to the tip, surrounded by a darker-colored cone and the flame's outer halo. A flame with a large outer cone has too much fuel and too little oxygen. It is called a carburizing flame and will produce a sooty burned-looking effect on metal. Continue to open the oxygen valve until the outer cone disappears and the inner cone has a smooth, round shape. This neutral flame contains an even mixture of oxygen and fuel. If you open the oxygen valve too far, you may hear the torch hiss. A flame that has too much oxygen is called an oxidizing flame. The inner cone of an oxidizing flame is smaller than a neutral flame and has a sharp point. When you have adjusted the torch for a neutral flame you may need to increase the fuel and oxygen until you have a large enough flame for the metal you are welding. As you open the fuel valve to get a larger flame you will also have to open the oxygen valve until the inner cone has the round shape of a neutral flame.

With the torch lit and the flame properly adjusted you are ready to weld. The surface you are welding must be stripped clean of paint, rust, grease or other coatings. Practice first on a scrap part such as a fender and position it so that the section you are welding is horizontal. When you are welding, the molten metal will solidify as soon as you remove the flame so it is possible to weld vertically, even overhead, but at the beginning you will find it easier to weld on a flat horizontal surface. You should start by welding over an unbroken surface. After you have learned to control the angle and movement of the torch you can practice making actual welds either along a tear in the metal or by welding patches over rust damage that you have cut out. The welding technique will be essentially the same in either case. If you are applying a patch, you will have to clamp the patch in place with visegrips and tack the edges in several spots before welding the seam. A tack weld is made the same way as a seam weld; the tack is simply shorter.

Welding is done by heating the metal until it forms a molten puddle. Practice heating and puddling the metal by holding the torch tip at a 30–45-degree angle nearly touching the metal surface. Keep the torch tip about ⅛-inch from the metal; don't let it actually touch the puddle. Work the torch over the metal in a circular motion, moving the torch ahead slowly as the puddle forms. After you have practiced welding on a solid surface until you can make welds that are straight, even in width and are able to weld without burning holes in the metal, you are ready to practice welding a seam using filler rod. The welding motions are the same but you should hold the filler rod ahead of the torch, letting the puddle—not the torch—melt the filler rod. Lighting and controlling the torch are the keys to gas welding. With practice you will become proficient in both. After you have finished welding you will have to shut off the torch. Always close the fuel valve first, then shut the oxygen valve at the torch. With both torch valves closed, shut the cyl-

Building shop tools provides a practical way to build welding skills. Heavy steel pieces are usually arc welded.

inder valves. Now open the torch valves to purge the hoses. When the pressure gauges on both cylinders read zero, open the regulator screws and close the torch valves.

When you feel comfortable with your welding skills, there are other uses for a gas welder that you will want to learn. Where the heat required for welding might warp the metal, you can install patches and fill small cracks or tiny rust holes by brazing. In braze-welding you use a bronze filler rod either coated or dipped in flux to bond the edges of a seam or fill small holes in the metal. For brazing you should adjust the flame so that it has a slight excess of fuel, rather than the neutral flame used for welding. Besides brazing you will want to use the torch as a source of heat to free rusted bolts. The technique, here, is not to heat the bolt, but the metal around it. If the bolt is screwed into a nut, heat the nut red hot. The heat will cause the nut to swell, freeing the rust-frozen bolt. If rusted bolts are fastened to a housing, such as studs that screw into exhaust manifolds, heat the casting around the bolt. There may also be times when you will want to use the torch to cut metal. A cutting tip is ignited and the flame is adjusted similar to a welding tip. There is, however, a basic difference between the two tips. A cutting tip has a third valve that is used to shoot a blast of oxygen against a preheated metal surface. This oxygen blast burns through metal with the ease of a hot knife slicing through butter.

If you choose arc, rather than gas, welding you will learn to set the amperage on the welder and strike an arc instead of adjusting and lighting a torch. The principles are similar, but the actual welding steps are different. With arc welding the procedures that make strong welds are:

1. Select a dial setting that will match the welding amperage to the thickness of the base metal.
2. Choose an electrode that matches the thickness, type of metal and the welding position; be it vertical, horizontal or overhead.
3. Hold the electrode at the correct arc length, usually equal to the diameter of the rod but also determined by the sound of the arc.
4. Move the electrode across the base metal at a steady speed to assure proper penetration and a smooth weld.

Remember that slag from the electrode flows into the weld, requiring that arc welds be made correctly on the first pass.

With practice it is possible to become an accomplished welder and the abilities associated with this skill are those restorers covet most. The next two chapters describe how to use welding skills to repair rust damage and finish the repair by the time-tested art of leading.

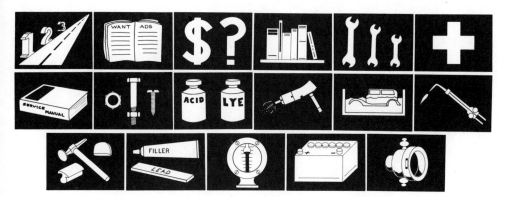

13

A Hobbyist's Guide To Metal Repair

Before describing methods you can use to repair damaged metal, we will review ways to recognize the telltale signs of rust and poorly made body repairs. Serious rust where metal is missing is obvious and so are dents. But, unless you have carefully inspected the car or have disassembled and stripped the doors, fenders and other body parts you may have overlooked hidden damage. Further, if you haven't looked carefully underneath the car you may not have spotted frame or floor pan rust.

Briefly, because we're reviewing points made in the early chapters, here's what to look for: Paint blisters are a sure sign of trouble underneath. The blisters can be caused by tiny rust holes in the metal, a rusted seam, fiberglass filler that has absorbed moisture or brazing flux that has seeped out of an earlier repair. To check for rust, push a jackknife blade into the blisters or poke them with a small, sharp screwdriver. If the blade penetrates the metal, you know there's rust underneath. Running a magnet across the panel is a sure way to check for fiberglass filler. The magnetic pull will cease when the magnet passes over fiberglass. Filler can absorb moisture if it is wet-sanded before painting or if it is used to plug holes. In both cases, as moisture works out of the filler, it will blister the paint. Blisters can also be traced to flux that was not properly cleaned off a braze-welded repair. If yellowish metal appears when you scrape through the paint there's a good chance that brazing flux has caused the blisters.

Earlier rust or dent repairs that were poorly done are noticeable if you sight along the fenders, doors and quarter panels after you have washed the car and parked it in the sun. Check above the wheel wells, the front fender panels just behind the front wheels, and rear fender panels ahead and behind the rear wheels. These areas are especially prone to rust. Waves, bulges or low spots and slight depressions over rivet heads are all telltale signs of clumsy repairs. Although you may not care to disturb earlier repairs if you are using the car for pleasure driving, recognizing their presence gives you an accurate appraisal of the car's condition. If your goal is restoration, you should replace patches that have been attached with sheet metal screws, pop rivets or fiberglass and replace them with welded panels.

After you have inspected the exterior, check inside the wheel wells, edges of the trunk, floor panels (lift up the floor mats or look the car over carefully from underneath). Unless the car is disassembled for restoration, frame rust may be difficult to detect. Check inside the frame channels, especially where the frame curves to form the rear wheel arches. Use a long-bladed screwdriver to probe the metal for signs of rust.

Once you have located areas needing metal repair, determine whether a large section or whole panel (in the case of fenders or doors) needs to be replaced or if the rust is limited to a small area. When a front fender, for example, shows rust

Although the Mustang door looked solid, it really wasn't. Jabbing the door skin with a screwdriver showed that the metal had rotted underneath a cover-up paint job.

Once rust gets a hold, it will continue to spread.

on both the front and rear quarters, with a string of holes or paint blisters speckling the wheel well to boot, the entire panel should be replaced. But if the damage is limited to one of the quarters, as on the 1971 Mustang convertible shown in the photos, then replacing the whole fender wastes parts and labor to say nothing of having to remove rear seat upholstery and unfasten the top. Patching the quarter panel will sufficiently repair the damage, particularly in a case where rust hasn't spread to inner wheel wells or the trunk.

Small rust areas, visible either in the form of pinholes or actual rust damage, can be repaired by first cutting away the spongy metal then covering or filling the hole with a handmade patch. Covering a hole takes less skill than filling one so if you are a beginner, you may want to try this approach.

Before you can patch rust damage, you have to cut away the rusted metal, leaving a hole with fairly straight edges. Next, strip the paint and any surface rust from the sound metal that surrounds the hole. An abrasive wheel mounted on an air or electric grinder or an electric drill will quickly strip the finish to bare metal. Extend the bare metal surface several inches from the edge of the hole. Now cut a patch to match the contours of the hole, but make it slightly larger so that it overlaps the surrounding metal by about an inch. Sheet metal for patches can be purchased from steel yards or you can use metal cut from a junked late-model hood panel. Hoods have large flat areas that will usually provide ample metal for patches even if they've been removed from a wreck. You should be able to purchase a scrap hood at a junkyard for a few dollars. When you are cutting patches be sure to wear heavy gloves since raw metal edges are sharp. Remember that if you are cutting patches from painted metal you also have to grind the paint off the patch.

 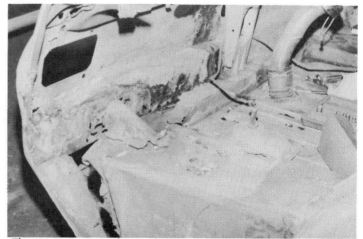

These airy views of a Mustang trunk floor and wheel housing show that where corrosion is extensive, major body panels may have to be replaced.

If the hole you are patching is located near the edge of a panel, you can clamp the patch in place with C clamps or visegrips. In other locations you may need to attach the patch temporarily with metal screws or have an assistant hold the patch while you tack weld it in place. The assistant should not touch the patch, but press it against the panel with a screwdriver or other metal tool.

To control heat build-up and prevent the panel from warping, tack weld the patch first on one side then another. Make sure that the edges of the patch are flush with the surrounding metal as you tack the patch in place. Now the seam between the patch and the panel has to be welded or brazed to lock out moisture. Brazing requires less heat than welding and reduces the risk of metal distortion; but remember that flux used with brazing can seep out of the seam and blister the paint. If you decide to weld the seam, you can control heat build-up by filling the gaps between the tack welds, first on one side of the patch, then another. You can also have assistants hold wet rags on the panel side of the seams as you weld. The rags will act as a heat-dam to minimize warping. As you are welding or brazing the seam, tap the edges with a body hammer to lower the patch so that it is flush with the contours of the panel.

After you have welded the patch in place, smooth the seams with a grinder or file. Slight irregularities in the surface can be

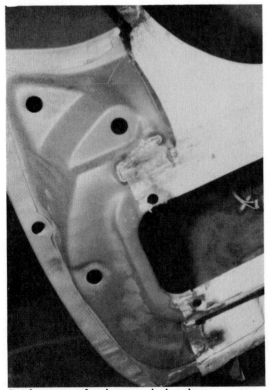

Replacement fenders made by the manufacturer require minimal welding along panel seams.

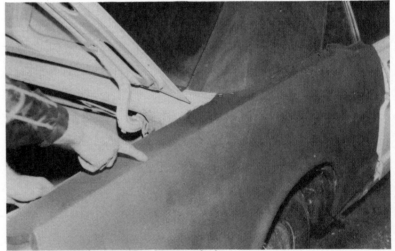

Replacement Mustang fenders made by aftermarket suppliers are welded along the fender crease. Applying heat to this seam is likely to warp the metal.

filled with lead or plastic filler. Both leading and the use of plastic filler are described in the next chapter.

Since seams on all metal patches have to be sealed by welding or brazing, the ideal method for attaching a hand-formed patch is to simply cut out the rusted metal and fit a patch into the hole. This technique works best where there is access on both sides of the hole, as on rusted spots over the headlights that are especially common on fifties-era cars. In areas like this you can use a hacksaw to cut away the rusted metal. Smooth the edges of the hole so that you can cut a patch to fit. Unless the rust damage is located on a flat panel, the patch will have to be shaped to match the contours of the surrounding metal. A flat patch can be cut to the dimensions of the hole, otherwise you should cut a piece of light cardboard to fit the hole and use the cardboard as a pattern. Cut the patch slightly larger than the pattern so that it can be trimmed to fit. The patch can be shaped either by pounding the metal with a body hammer and dolly or by pounding the patch against a sandbag. Test the fit frequently. The shape of the patch must exactly match the contour of the metal it replaces. When you have shaped the patch, trim off any excess metal so that it butts snugly against the edges of the cut-out. To get a precision fit you may want to shape the edges of the patch with a grinder. If gaps between the patch and the surrounding metal are within a sixteenth of an inch, you can weld the seam using little or no filler metal.

To weld a tight-fitting patch so that the repair doesn't have to be covered with filler, tack the patch in place with very small welds placed about an inch apart. Weld the seam between the tacks using a small torch tip to control the heat. Too much heat will spread the seam and distort the metal. Use as little welding rod as possible. Where the edges of the patch and surrounding metal touch, you should be able to weld the seam without filler. As soon as you have connected the tacks, pound the seam smooth using a body hammer and a dolly. You will need a torch stand or an assistant to hold the torch. This technique, called hammer welding, takes practice but results in metal repair that can be filed and painted, often without using lead or plastic filler.

Where rust damage is extensive—the floor pan is rotted or the fenders are spongy not just in one spot, but in several areas—preformed patches or replacement panels make the best repairs. Since the early thirties, car body contours have flowed in graceful compound curves. Forming a panel by hand to match the styling features on rusted or severely dented fenders, doors or quarter panels takes a highly skilled metal man's patience and adroit use of tools. Repair panels are stamped to replace original metal so that only welding and finishing skills are needed to install them.

Manufacturers supply replacement fenders and other body panels for most cars made in the seventies and for some sixties models. Where manufacturer's replacement panels are available, they can be ordered from parts clerks at any dealership. When replacement panels are no longer stocked by manufacturers, they may be available from aftermarket companies that supply repair panels to collision shops. Some auto supply stores carry aftermarket repair panels, but the quickest way to check whether aftermarket panels are available for your car is to ask the owner of a body repair shop if you can look through his collection of repair panel catalogs.

Repair panels purchased from the manufacturer often cost more than similar panels from an aftermarket supplier. This cost difference sometimes reflects a similar difference in quality. For example, Ford Motor Company rear quarter panels for sixties vintage Mustangs (which are still available at this writing), replace the original panels perfectly and can be spot-welded in place along easily hidden seams. Aftermarket Mustang fenders are face stampings—patch panels, in effect. They are designed to be welded to the original fender at the car's belt line, a location that is difficult to weld without distortion.

Restorers of collectable cars such as early series Mustangs, 1955–57 Chevrolets, two-seater Thunderbirds, MG's, Austin Healeys, Model A Fords, VW Beetles and many others, can turn to specialty parts outlets for practically all the replacement sheet metal necessary to rebuild an entire body. But for cars where repair panels are no longer available from dealers, aftermarket or restoration suppliers, you can often locate new-

Installing patch panels is an effective way to replace rusted metal. Here David Irwin, co-owner of Central Ohio Mustang in Columbus, Ohio, positions a patch panel over a rusted rear fender section.

David measures one-inch down from the scored line. The rusted section will be cut off here.

old-stock repair panels at flea markets or through advertisements in hobby magazines. The question here is how do you know you're buying a panel that will fit your car. If you have access to a parts book you can shop for replacement fenders, rocker or quarter panels by number. New-old-stock parts are frequently tagged by flea market vendors or have the manufacturer's parts tag or number stamped on them. Since repair panels tend to be "generic" (that is, a given fender or rocker panel may fit several models and possibly different makes of cars), manufacturer's parts books usually include this interchange information as well.

When my dad was looking for replacement rocker panels for his 1941 Cadillac convertible coupe, he discovered that Cadillac shared the same panel with Buick and Olds. He was able to locate new-old-stock rocker panels for a Buick sedan which were longer than he needed for the Cadillac, but could be cut to fit.

When you are unable to reference repair panels by part numbers, compare the contours of the replacement panel to the same area on the car. You can also measure key areas of the panel, the distance from a wheel well to the front or rear edge of a fender panel for example, and compare the dimensions with your own car. If the dimensions of the replacement panel are longer than required, but the contours appear to match, you may be able to cut the panel and make it fit.

In cases where you are unable to locate replacement or even used panels from any of the sources already mentioned, you may be able to find solid doors and fenders or cut repair

The patch panel has a ridge that fits behind the fender to make a rigid seam.

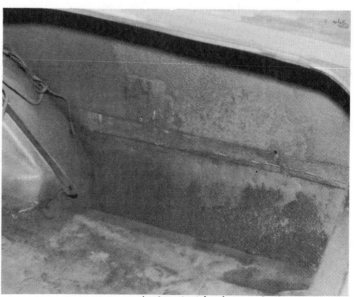

A view inside the trunk shows the repaired fender. This seam has to be caulked so that it doesn't trap moisture.

panels from sound metal on a junked car. For example, on 1965 and 1966 Chevelles the contours of the front and rear wheel arches are almost identical. Since rear wheel arches rust far more frequently than fronts, it is still quite feasible to locate a mid-sixties Chevelle with solid front fenders and cut out a section of the front wheel arch to repair rust on a rear fender. In a situation of this sort, you might either purchase and remove the entire fender or have the junkyard operator cut out a section of the fender for you with a torch. Later you can cut the patch piece and weld it in place.

Repair Panels

Repair panels can be formed from sheet metal to replace flat areas such as floor pans. Where angles or contours are required, pound the metal against a wooden block or use a body hammer and a dolly to create the proper shape.

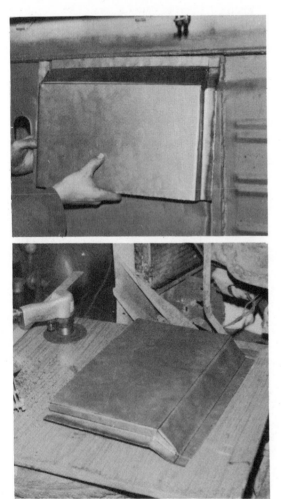

Flat panels can be fabricated from sheet steel, as is seen in this handmade Mustang floor panel.

Rusted metal has to be removed before a new panel can be welded in place.

If you are replacing an entire panel, a fender or door for example, start by removing the damaged panel. Doors remove easily by unbolting the hinges. Front fenders are also usually bolted in place, but rear fenders of most cars built since the early fifties are welded to the body. Remove welded panels by cutting along the seams. Where spot welds are visible, cut or drill out the welds to remove the panel. Don't worry about damaging the section you are replacing, but try not to bend or tear the metal where you will be attaching the new panel.

To install a repair panel, position the panel over the damaged section. Make sure that the outside contours of the patch follow those of the original panel. Now mark a cut-off line along the seam edge of the patch. Commercial repair panels are usually stamped with a flange that slips behind the cut. To allow for a flange draw a cut-off line about an inch below the previously marked line and cut the damaged panel along the lower mark. Hand-formed repair panels or patch sections cut from another panel can be welded to the damaged panel either with a slight overlap or a butt seam, following the same methods used with small rust patches mentioned earlier.

Prepare the seam by sanding the damaged panel to bare metal along a strip six to eight inches wide above the cut, then reposition the patch. Carefully check alignment of the patch for the last time and position it with visegrips or sheet metal screws. Once the patch is firmly clamped, tack weld the seams. The critical welding step comes next.

Working on the floor of a car is much easier from this angle. A later section shows how it's done.

Replacing floor panels is a major undertaking but little finishing work is required.

Unlike welding a small patch, the greater heat required to weld a repair panel greatly increases the chance of warping the metal. The same welding techniques used with small patches apply to repair panels, but heat build-up must be controlled by using a small flame and welding first at one end, then the other end of the seam to distribute the heat across the panel and by using a heat dam of wet rags around the welding area. Brazing (using a brass rod and lower heat), rather than welding, the seam is another way to reduce the risk of warping the panel.

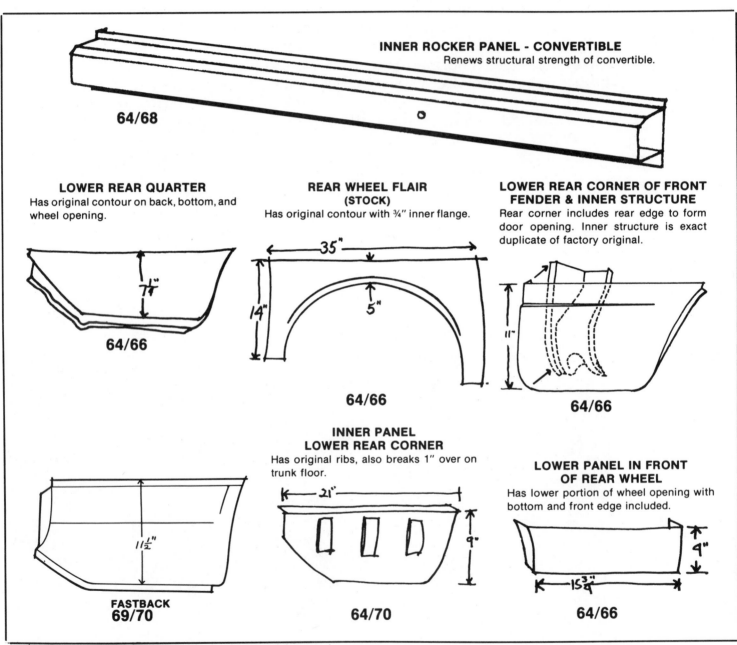

INNER ROCKER PANEL - CONVERTIBLE
Renews structural strength of convertible.

64/68

LOWER REAR QUARTER
Has original contour on back, bottom, and wheel opening.

64/66

REAR WHEEL FLAIR
(STOCK)
Has original contour with ¾" inner flange.

35"

14"

5"

64/66

LOWER REAR CORNER OF FRONT FENDER & INNER STRUCTURE
Rear corner includes rear edge to form door opening. Inner structure is exact duplicate of factory original.

11"

64/66

11½"

FASTBACK
69/70

INNER PANEL
LOWER REAR CORNER
Has original ribs, also breaks 1" over on trunk floor.

21"

9"

64/70

LOWER PANEL IN FRONT OF REAR WHEEL
Has lower portion of wheel opening with bottom and front edge included.

9"

15¾"

64/66

Repair panels are readily available for late model special-interest cars like the popular early Mustangs.

Rust isn't the only form of metal damage hobbyists contend with. Dents are common in cars that have seen active service before being set aside for restoration. Straightening small dents, the kind that occur commonly in parking lots, takes more patience than special skill. Repairing collision damage involves many of the same skills used to rout rust. The techniques of dent repair aren't complicated and the best way to learn is by doing.

You will need a few basic body tools, at least one body hammer (a special hammer with a large flat head) and one or two dollies (hand-held metal blocks used to back the hammer blows). Hammers and dollies come in a variety of sizes and shapes for straightening flat areas, reshaping contours and working in confined areas. Sears and discount stores like K-Mart sell auto body tool sets that include assorted hammers and dollies. Body tools are also available from auto supply stores and restoration suppliers that advertise in hobby magazines. In addition to dollies and body hammers, you may find a dent puller useful to straighten metal damage that can't be reached from behind. Other useful body tools include assorted metal files and pry bars. You can make pry bars yourself, or use shop scrap.

My Mustang convertible hails from Virginia, but a leak in the trunk weather seal had caused rust in the lower section of the rear fender and pin holes in the fender lip. This photo shows bodyman Joe Chambers spot welding a patch over the pin holes.

Before repair, the Mustang showed rear quarter rust that is typical for this make and model.

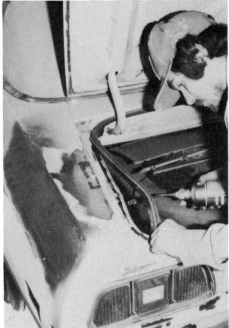

Joe uses a propane torch to heat the glue so that he can pull the weather strip loose from its channel. Since leaking weather seal caused the leak, the rubber molding should be removed and replaced.

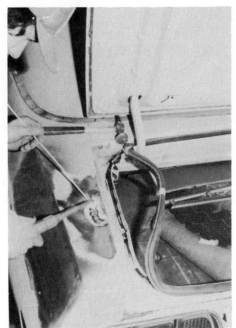

Next Joe seals the seam around the patch with brazing rod.

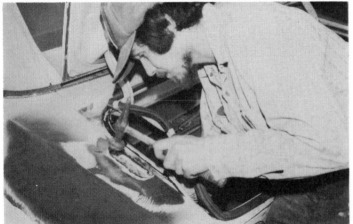

While the metal is still hot he taps the patch lightly with a body hammer. A body dolly should be placed underneath the hot metal to spread the force of the hammer blows.

Grinding smooths the braze and removes traces of flux that could cause the paint to blister.

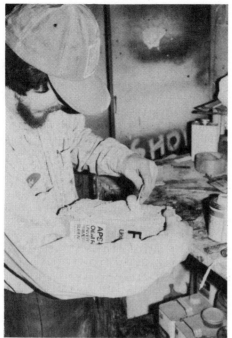

Body filler mixes easily and is used to cover the metal repair.

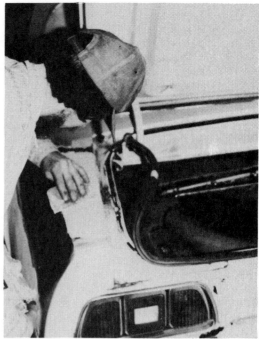

The filler is spread over the patch and surrounding surface with a plastic squeegee.

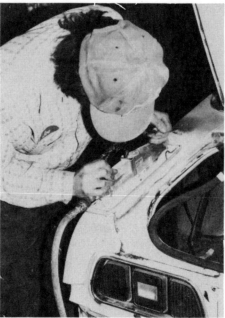

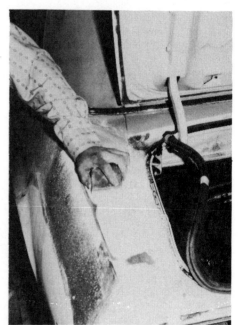

Body filler is grated to remove ridges and high spots, then sanded smooth. Block sanding follows machine sanding to prepare the surface for priming.

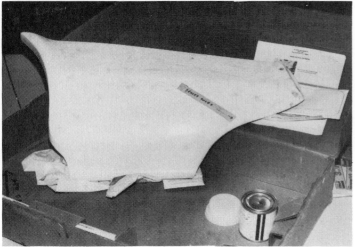

The fiberglass patch from Glassline Panels, Tuckerton, New Jersey, perfectly matches the Mustang's rear quarter contour.

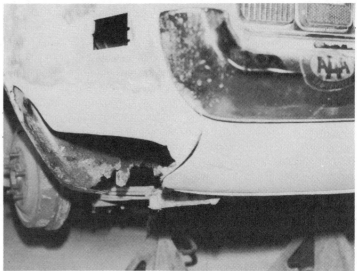

Before installing the panel, rotted metal was cut away.

The fiberglass panel is bonded to sound metal with pop rivets.

Panel seams are covered with body filler. To create a smooth contour, the filler extends several inches beyond the seam.

To get started, you need access to the damaged area. Fender dents can often be reached from inside wheel wells, in which case the wheel may need to be removed in order to give enough room to swing the body hammer. Rear fender dents are often accessible from inside the trunk. Fenders on cars built through the forties can be unbolted and removed for repair. Dents on some door panels can be reached by removing the upholstery. In other cases the reinforcing panel may block access to the dent with a hammer, but it is usually possible to insert a pry bar through a hole in the reinforcing panel to push out the dent. If the car's interior has been removed for sandblasting or chemical stripping, dents on side panels or roof are more easily accessible.

To straighten a dent, begin by hammering the depressed metal against a dolly. Work from the edge of the dent toward the center, gradually smoothing the metal. If you start by banging away at the center of the dent you stand a good chance of stretching the metal. As you work across the dent, first smooth the metal by pounding against the dolly. In doing so you will create slight waves in the metal. To smooth these high spots and depressions hold the dolly against a low spot as you tap down a nearby bulge. Test the metal with your hand as you work around the dent. Pound from one side, then the other until all ripples and hollows feel smooth. Check your progress by running a file across the dent; the file will graze high spots and leave paint in the low areas.

Though convertible weather hadn't arrived, the refinished Mustang looked perky as springtime. The finished rear panel shows no traces of being repaired.

Deep dents should be heated with a welding torch, then pounded smooth. A propane torch does not produce enough heat to make the metal malleable. Use a torch tip that will give a broad flame and spread the heat evenly over the damaged area. When the metal is pliable, work rapidly with a body hammer and dolly to smooth the dented area. Heating not only reduces the force necessary to drive out the dent, but keeps the metal from stretching. Stretched metal is indicated by raised areas that can't be flattened without bowing the metal nearby. To shrink stretched metal, heat the bowed area with a torch then flatten the spot by striking the metal sharply against a dolly.

Dents that are located so that both sides can't be worked with a hammer and dolly, such as those on hoods and trunk lids of late model cars, can usually be straightened with a pry bar. Tire irons work well for this purpose, as do sections of pipe, flattened at one end, or single leaves from a scrap spring. Where a dent is covered by an inner panel, there are usually openings through which a pry bar can be inserted to reach the dent. Tap out the dent using the pry bar and body hammer in much the same way as you would with a hammer and dolly. Work from the edge of the dent toward the center. Special pry bars with curled ends can be made to straighten fender flanges.

To prevent stretching, metal should be heated before it is smoothed with a body hammer and dolly.

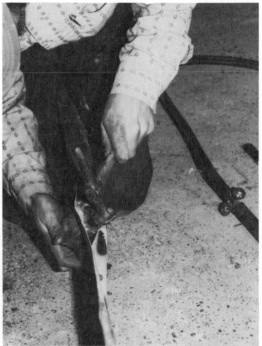

While the dent is smoothed from one side, a body dolly is held against the other to distribute the force of the hammer blows and help form the correct contour.

Dents that can't be reached with a pry bar can be straightened with a dent puller. This tool has a sheet metal screw attached to a metal rod. A hole is drilled in the dent, then the puller is screwed into the hole. With the puller firmly attached to the metal, a weight that slides on the rod is slapped sharply back against the handle. The impact of the weight hitting the handle snaps the puller, forcing out the dent. Usually a series of holes have to be drilled and the puller exerted against each one to smooth the dent. The holes can be filled by brazing later.

Fender, door, hood or trunk panels that are severely dented should be replaced or repaired with patch panels, using the same techniques described for repairing rust damage. After a damaged panel is removed, check for signs of structural damage underneath. This will have to be repaired before outer body panels can be replaced. Repairing major collision damage takes an experienced bodyman's skill, but mangled body panels or frame members can be straightened with a cable winch. One end of the winch will have to be securely anchored to the base of a tree or a metal eye-bolt embedded in a concrete floor, another vehicle, or similar immovable object. The

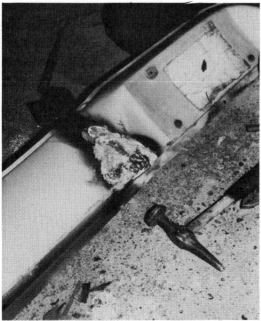

Straightening dents is a slow process, but with patience the metal slowly returns to the correct shape.

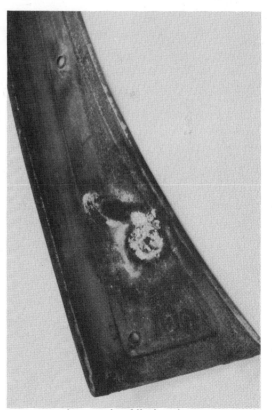

Holes can be filled with a variety of patches. In this case a Model A dash panel has been patched with a plug from an electrical box.

other end of the winch must be secured to the damaged area. One way of doing this is to place heavy-gauge steel plates on both sides of the dent. Drill holes through the damaged body metal and the metal plates. Bolt the plates together and fasten the winch cable to the outside plate. Cautiously straighten the dent with the winch.

Once rust and dent damage are repaired, patch seams and minor surface imperfections have to be filled before the area can be primed and painted. The next chapter deals with the art of leading and the use of plastic fillers. Leading is the craftsman's approach to filling metal repairs; using plastic fillers is a more expedient method.

Mustang convertibles are prime targets for underbody restoration.

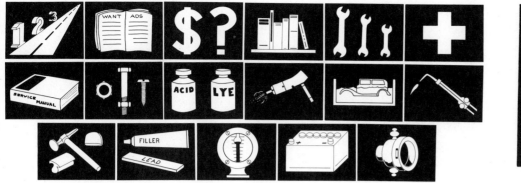

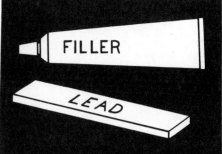

14

Filling Metal Repairs—The Finishing Step

Rust damage should always be repaired with new metal and dents should be hammered as smooth as possible before any filler is applied. In cases where rust damage has been repaired by hammer welding, it may be possible to file the seam smooth enough so that the area can be primed and painted without using filler. Similarly, skilled bodymen are often able to smooth dents without resorting to filler. But for hobbyists who are still learning body repair, some filler is usually needed.

There are two methods and materials that can be used to fill minor surface irregularities resulting from rust and dent repair. The traditional method uses a solder alloy containing lead and tin. Leading, as this method is commonly called, is done by heating the repaired area with a torch then spreading a thin layer of solder over the repair. Properly applied, lead filler will last as long as the car. The supplies needed for leading are expensive. Currently solder alloy costs nearly $10 for a half-pound bar. Besides solder, leading requires special tools including hardwood paddles that are used for this job.

The modern method uses plastic filler. Bondo, as plastic filler is commonly called, is cheap and easy to use. In comparison with the price of lead, $10 will buy a gallon of plastic filler at a discount mart sale. Plastic filler is applied and can be smoothed using common tools and does not require heat. As a result, plastic filler can be used to smooth dent repairs, for example, without melting undercoat protection or burning surrounding paint. The advantages of plastic filler are the cause of its association with sleazy back-alley repair shops. Because it is easy to use, plastic filler is also easy to abuse. Another drawback to using plastic filler is the fact that the material is water-porous. This means that when plastic filler is primed and wet sanded, moisture can penetrate the filler. If this happens, the trapped moisture will eventually bleed to the surface and blister the paint.

For these reasons, purists have continued to prefer leading to plastic fillers. Properly applied, plastic filler has nearly the same permanence as lead, though lead is more flexible and should be applied to areas that are subject to vibration and stress.

Filling Metal Repairs With Lead

I still remember that mid-winter restoration clinic twenty-odd years ago when a fellow car club member demonstrated leading, as he called it. Warren herded us out to the section of his barn where his shop was located, picked up a Model A fender and gave it a sharp rap with a hammer. Then, as abruptly, he proceeded to pound out the dent. It was a bone-chilling January day in western New York and Warren knew he couldn't keep his captive audience long. With the dent roughly straightened, Warren clamped the fender in his bench vise and

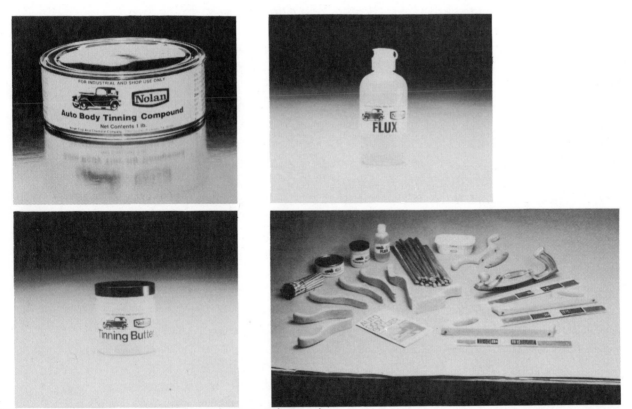

For leading to be successful, the right materials must be used. Metal must be treated with flux and tinning butter or a special tinning compound in order for the lead to stick.

scoured the rippled surface with his grinder. We stomped our feet to drive the frost needles out of our toes and watched as Warren laid bare a circle of gleaming metal. The next few minutes were magic. The yellow flame of his torch flicked back and forth warming the steel. A moment later he was spreading a silvery film of solder with a wooden spoon. He took a few swipes across the solder with a file and the dent vanished. The magic ended and we slogged back through the snow to warmth. Warren's wife beckoned us into her kitchen for hot coffee and cookies baked in the shape of Model A hubcaps and conversation soon drifted to plans for our first spring tour.

Some years later I, too, was repairing a damaged Model A fender and there the similarity with Warren's demonstration ended. I tried to remember what I had witnessed and asked the auto supply clerk what items I would need, besides lead. He assured me that only lead was required and sold me several sticks, enough to fill a number of damaged fenders.

Since I didn't own a torch, wooden paddles or other tools needed for leading, I had enrolled in an evening auto shop course taught at a nearby vocational high school with the intention of using the school's equipment. The instructor said he had worked with an old-time bodyman who used lead on those rare occasions when he couldn't prime and paint his repairs. From our combined experience, he felt confident that we could figure out the leading technique, fill the fender and give the rest of the class a memorable demonstration in the process.

I had a nagging feeling that I would need more than just sticks of lead. Having wired our house, I knew that flux was needed for electrical soldering. Wouldn't I also need flux for body soldering, I wondered? The leading demonstration was scheduled for the last class, so I also felt the pressure of having to get the procedure right the first and only time I would have access to a torch, leading paddles and other special tools.

I had sandblasted the fender and would be using lead to smooth a fist-sized patch covering a hole in the fender's crown. A circle of observers gathered, the instructor lit the welding torch and passed it to me (I hadn't taken the welding class yet). The demonstration began. I licked the metal with the torch until the patch glowed red, then I dabbed on the lead. It ran off the fender in a stream, indicating that the metal was too hot. I let the fender cool and tried again. This time I aimed the torch at the lead stick. The silver stream that ran from the stick froze to the fender. I felt a surge of confidence. Leading really wasn't much harder than Warren's demonstration had made it seem. Next I would spread the mound of lead with a paddle, file the repair smooth and be finished. I cautiously heated the lead and mashed it down with the paddle as soon as the lead softened. The paddle scorched and sizzled as I spread the lead with smooth, swift strokes. Ah, the satisfaction of craftsmanship.

Then a gob of lead stuck to the paddle and as I pulled, the filler broke loose in a chunk and fell to the floor.

Disgusted, I put down the torch. The instructor said he remembered the old-timer using battery acid as a flux and electrical solder to tin the metal. We poured acid from an old battery and raided a coil of solder from the electrical shop. But the jinx had stuck. I was nervous and had lost my confidence. On the second or third application some of the lead bonded, so the demonstration wasn't a total flop. And for me, at least, it was memorable. But I wasn't able to fully understand what went wrong until I read an ad featuring leading supplies and learned that bars of lead are just one of the ingredients for successful leading. Those other items the auto supply clerk told me I didn't need—flux, tinning compound and a lubricant for the paddles—are essential. Without them, lead won't stick.

Leading, or body soldering to use the correct term, looks simple as child's play when you watch a craftsman at work and with the proper supplies the skill isn't difficult to learn. But working with lead requires safety precautions that hobbyists shouldn't overlook. When sanding body solder use a file and a hand sander, rather than a power grinder, to minimize lead dust. Avoid inhaling or ingesting the metal by wearing a respirator designed to filter lead dust and take simple but often overlooked precautions like keeping coffee and snacks out of the work area. Lead dust that collects on food or beverages, even a cigarette will be ingested or inhaled. The amount of lead dust a hobbyist is exposed to in a restoration project is quite minimal. But since lead is a recognized health hazard it is wise to heed cautionary warnings.

Body Solder, What Is It?

Body solder is a mixture of tin and lead. The particular alloy, that is the proportions of tin and lead the solder contains, varies according to the job. Two factors determine which alloy is best suited to bodywork. First, the alloy should contain a high enough percentage of tin to make a strong bond with the base metal. Second, in order to spread the filler in a thin layer, the metal has to stay pliable over a broad heat range. An alloy with high lead content turns from a solid to a liquid state so abruptly that it may run off the metal before it can be paddled. Alloys used most commonly for body soldering contain either twenty-percent tin, eighty-percent lead (20/80) or thirty-percent tin, seventy-percent lead (30/70). Of the two, 30/70 gives better adhesion, greater flex and since it is a softer alloy, it is easier to file. Plumber's solder, as the British call 30/70 alloy, melts at 490°F, as compared to 530°F for 20/80 solder. The lower melting point reduces the risk of metal warpage. However, 30/70 solder does not have as wide a working temperature range as 20/80 alloy and the latter's reduced tin content also makes it cheaper. Either alloy is suitable for bodywork. Solder alloys with lesser or greater amounts of tin should be avoided.

Solder bars are not always marked with the alloy content so it is important to buy from a supplier who is familiar with the requirements of auto body leading. Restoration suppliers that market body solder and accessory products advertise in hobby magazines.

How To Prepare The Surface

Even if body solder would adhere to a corroded surface, you wouldn't want to apply filler over rust. The repair area must be stripped of paint, grease or other coatings and stripped of every hint of rust. Either sandblasting or chemical stripping and derusting provides an excellent base for metal repair. Small areas that are not badly rusted can be cleaned with a grinder and a wire brush clamped in the chuck of an electric drill. It is important to avoid touching bare metal, as fingerprints leave oily deposits.

Body solder won't stick to bare steel. In order for the solder to make a good bond the metal surface to be coated with filler has to be treated first with flux, then tinned with a high tin alloy. Restoration suppliers are the recommended source of flux and tinning preparations. While these products are available from some auto supply stores, they are not widely stocked. Flux is

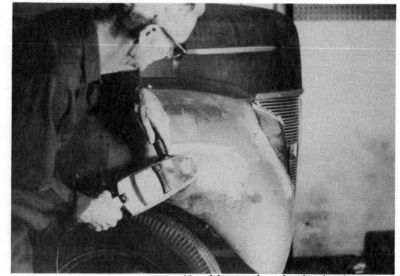

Metal has to be absolutely clean before beginning the leading process. Beginners should practice on horizontal surfaces first.

sold in liquid and powdered form, and as a special paste that contains a mixture of flux, tin and lead. To apply liquid flux, gently heat the metal then brush or spray on the flux. Powdered flux is applied with a wad of steel wool. The trick here is to heat the metal so that the flux will melt and adhere to the surface, otherwise the powder just rolls off in little balls.

After the metal has been treated with flux it should be coated with a very thin layer of high-tin-content solder, usually 50/50-alloy electrical solder. The tinning step forms a bonding base for body solder. While the metal is still hot from applying the flux, tin the repair area by melting a small pool of 50/50 solder and wiping it across the surface with a wad of steel wool. Clamp the steel wool with pliers or wear a welding glove to keep heat, transferred through the steel wool, from burning your fingers.

Heat is a critical factor throughout the leading process. The metal has to be brought up to working temperature for the solder, but care must be taken not to overheat and warp the metal. If a welding torch is used for body soldering, select a wide tip and adjust the flame for low heat. Keep the torch moving to distribute the heat over the repair area. if the metal begins to turn red, you know the temperature is too hot. A propane torch will also melt solder and is less likely to overheat the metal.

Tinning paste, or butter as this product is often called, combines flux coating and tinning in one step. Besides ease of application, this compound offers a major advantage to begin-

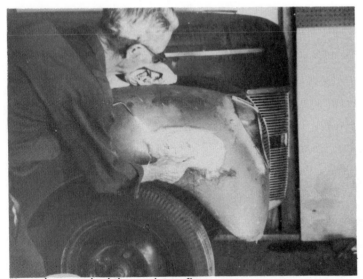

Heat the metal while applying flux. This is especially important if you are using a powdered flux, otherwise the flux will bead up and roll off the metal. The rags shown lying on the fender are used to wipe the surface after the flux has been applied.

After treating the metal with flux, apply tinning paste or tinning compound to assure that the body solder will make a proper bond.

ners. When it is heated to the proper temperature the paste turns from dark gray to bright, glistening silver. Tinning paste is smeared over the repaired area in the same manner as solder.

How Is The Lead Applied?

Experienced bodymen can apply solder to vertical or horizontal panels with equal finesse. Beginners should stick with horizontal work surfaces. If you are filling a repair located on the side of a fender or a door, you should probably take the panel off the car and place it on saw horses so that the work surface is flat. A welding torch is not necessary for body soldering. A propane torch used to sweat solder into plumbing joints will work as well and, depending on your skill, a propane soldering torch may be easier to handle. If you are using a welding torch, use a large tip and adjust the flame so that it spreads out in a soft yellowish cone. Heat the repair area by moving the flame over the metal surface in a circular motion. To apply the solder, heat the tip of the solder bar until it softens, then press the solder onto the repair area so that it sticks and begins to crumble. Aim the torch higher on the bar and twist the bar loose from the mound of solder that has adhered to the work area. Repeat this process until you have built up a sufficient mound of solder to cover the repair area.

Solder is smoothed and spread across the repair area with a hardwood paddle that is handled very much like a cement

In preparation for applying body solder, heat the metal with a low-oxygen flame.

Work the flame back and forth from the solder to the metal. The solder will turn shiny and become pliable before it starts to melt.

trowel. As solder is heated, it turns shiny and begins to soften before it reaches the molten stage. At this point, the near-liquid solder can be spread. The paddle may burn and stick to the solder unless it is dipped frequently in tallow, boiled linseed oil, or machine oil. If more solder is needed to cover the repair area, melt additional lumps of solder and repeat the paddling process.

As long as the solder sticks and is paddled reasonably smooth, the job is a success up to this point. The last step, smoothing the solder, looks like the easiest part of the whole process. Maybe it is, but this is the step where beginners make their biggest mistakes. Because solder is softer than the metal it covers, it is easy to undercut the correct contour while filing the

Hardwood paddles are used to spread a thin layer of solder over the repair.

After spreading the filler, cool the metal with wet rags.

To smooth the filler, begin filing at the edges and work toward the center.

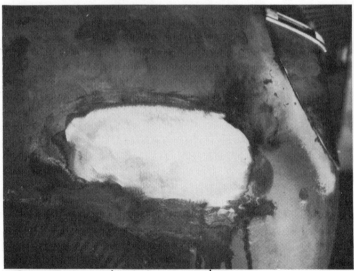
Before priming and painting, treat the finished repair with Metal Prep.

solder smooth. Solder should be shaped using a vixen file. These deep-toothed metal files are available in limited quantities from the restoration supplier listed at the end of the chapter.

Shape the filler by working from the edges of the repair area toward the center. Old-time bodymen wet the file with turpentine to keep from grating the soft metal, and rub wax into the teeth to keep the solder from sticking. Bar solder is expensive so it is a good idea to collect the shavings on a scrap of clean cardboard and save them in a "mush tin" for the next leading job. If a steel container is used to hold the filings, the solder can be melted with a torch, scooped out with a paddle and spread directly onto the repair area.

After the filler has been shaped with a file it should be sanded smooth. Remember to wear a respirator while sanding body solder and avoid wiping your face with your shirtsleeve or glove while working with lead. Before spraying a coat of primer on the finished repair, neutralize any traces of flux by wiping the area with ammonia or a solution of sodium bicarbonate. Treat the repair area with Metal Prep or a similar product containing mild phosphoric acid solution to etch the metal for painting. Properly applied, body solder delivers the two important qualities restorers look for in a filler: invisibility and endurance.

Using Plastic Filler

Plastic filler must be applied over bare metal and should be used only to smooth minor surface irregularities. These preparation steps apply to leading as well. In actual application, plastic filler is extremely easy to use. The secrets to success are purchasing fresh filler and following the mixing instructions on the can. Plastic filler is sold both by auto supply stores and discount stores. Professional bodymen who use plastic filler recommend buying the product from an auto store, however, claiming that auto supply stock tends to be fresher and of higher quality.

Plastic filler must be mixed with hardener before it can be used. Before mixing the two ingredients, stir the filler to a smooth consistency, then scoop a gob of filler out of the can and place it on a scrap of cardboard, plywood or other smooth surface. Hardener is supplied in a tube and is usually colored red or blue. Add hardener to the gob of filler following the mixing proportions listed on the can. Stir the hardener and filler until the two are mixed thoroughly but don't "whip" the mixture, or you will get air into the filler. The filler will change color as the hardener is stirred into it. A consistent color conveniently indicates that the two ingredients are mixed fully. A paint stirring stick works well to scoop and mix plastic filler.

Spread the filler with a plastic squeegee. Work quickly and spread the filler across the repair area in smooth strokes. Once the filler is in place, leave it alone. As the filler hardens it will start to crumble if you are still trying to spread it at that point. The filler will harden in about fifteen minutes. Smooth the filler using a grating file following the same procedure recommended for filing body solder. Work from the edges of the repair area to avoid undercutting the filler. Two or more applications may be necessary before the repair is completely filled and ready for priming.

Because plastic filler is water-porous, it should always be applied over a metal or fiberglass backing and should not be used to plug holes. If plastic filler is wet-sanded after priming, the spot should be warmed with a propane torch to dry out any trapped moisture. Be careful not to burn the filler.

Remember, the less filler used, the better. This advice applies whether the filler is lead or plastic. Both products have their merits and their drawbacks. Which you choose depends on a number of factors including cost, available tools, whether the repair area can be safely heated and your preference for using the traditional or modern body repair method.

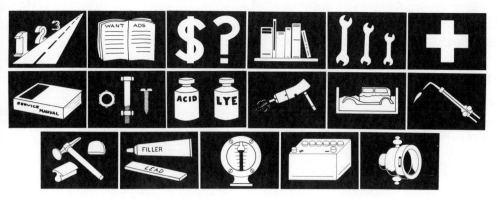

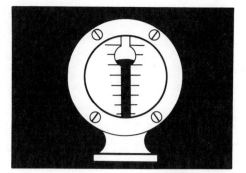

15
Restoring Small Parts

A car is, after all, a vast mechanical puzzle and the sum of its parts. Although old-car parts suppliers are filling their catalogs with reproduction stock, restored original equipment is still preferable to the sometimes poorly constructed replacements. Rebuilding those small parts that are dog-eared and nonfunctional keeps your restoration authentic, and can turn Saturdays or long winter evenings into profitable spare hours. Refinished parts always sell better at flea markets than those gleaned off the top of a scrap pile.

Virtually all parts—mechanical or accessory: lights, instruments or trim—are potential targets for restoration. The examples given here include a motometer, Model A Ford horn rod, Model T ignition switch, water pump and antique tools. The types of parts and repair steps described are representative of the items and methods you can use working on your own hobby vehicle, whether it is modern or antique, sporty roadster or handy pickup truck. This chapter is intended to stir your mechanical imagination. Restoring small parts requires only a basic mechanical aptitude, yet these are the same items most often replaced with reproduction parts.

Each of the parts I've chosen to describe has a history. Perhaps a glimpse at their background will show novice collectors what goes into obtaining rare authentic parts.

The horn rod came from a Model A coupe found curled up against a stone wall in a back-pasture junkyard. The coupe changed hands on the agreement that all other Model A parts on the premises would be removed, too. I scavenged a roadster cowl, two transmissions and a stainless steel headlight among the weeds. All this for $25, a bargainer's steal, but at the time a sacrifice to the family budget.

The Model T switch nearly got left behind when we carted home a pack rat's collection of A's and T's, plus vintage Nash parts on a series of rainy Saturdays. The switch missed a toss into the scrap pile because it looked like an interesting challenge to rebuild.

The motometer was purchased on an October day in 1956, when I skipped school to scout Model A's, at my uncle's once-in-a-lifetime invitation. The search paid off with the motometer and a roadster we stiff-hitched home that afternoon. We spied the motometer perched on a doodlebug and bought the part for twenty-five cents, the price of a pack of cigarettes at the time. The alcohol had dried in the capillary tube, so the gauge sat on a bedroom shelf at the parental homestead for a dozen years or so.

The water pump with its attached two-blade fan kept falling off the storage shelf, so it was lumped into the menagerie of parts slated for restoration. Finally, the Ford script wrenches were lying at the bottom of an old tool box when they caught my eye.

Before restoration, none of the parts worked. I had broken the motometer capillary tube in a premature rebuilding attempt and the chrome had worn off the gauge's diecast head. The horn rod refused to trigger the oo-gah. The Model T switch had not only grown a scaly coat of rust and lost its key, but the switch knob also refused to budge. The water pump shaft had an hourglass figure from running dry on sloppy bearings.

Locating a new capillary tube held up the motometer repair. For a brief period a supplier of motometer parts ran display ads in several hobby magazines, then went out of business. I caught its closing and was able to purchase the parts I needed. Later, a *Cars & Parts* "Tool Bag" column noted another source for motometer parts. The secret to restoring long-out-of-style items like motometers often lies in carefully reading hobby

Small parts often require only common tools and simple repair methods. Here a penknife is used to pry out old packing around the motometer tube.

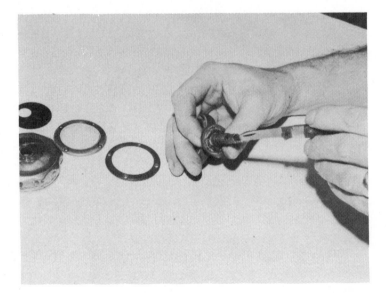

magazines for sources of hard-to-get supplies. Fortunately for restorers, when supplies are available they usually include far more detailed instructions than would be found with new parts.

When repair kits aren't available, restoration may be as simple as soldering a wire. That's all it takes to repair a Model A horn switch. In this case, though, a packet that included the correct length of wire, a replacement contact nub, insulation and instructions made the job practically fool proof. Horn rod repair kits are sold by antique Ford parts dealers.

Rebuilding the Model T switch began with straightening and cleaning the rusted metal, but repair stood at an impasse until one of the vintage Ford suppliers located a stock of Model T ignition parts.

Restoring small parts requires both mechanical and cosmetic overhauling. The top plate on the Model A horn rod is cast-aluminum and simply needed buffing to renew its original luster. The diecast motometer head had to be replated, as did the horn button. If the plater listed in the Yellow Pages isn't interested in replating your old car parts, don't plead with him. Instead, contact a plating shop that accepts odd lots of small parts. Plating shops that advertise in hobby magazines should fit the bill.

Metal parts like the Model T switch and the tools first had to be stripped of old paint and rust, then refinished. A plastic bucket holding a half gallon or so of rust remover, dilute phosphoric acid, sold by auto supply stores under product names

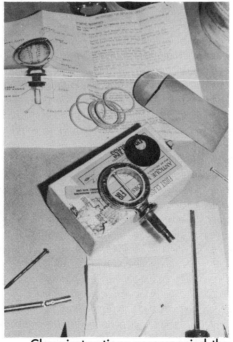

Clear instructions accompanied the motometer repair kit.

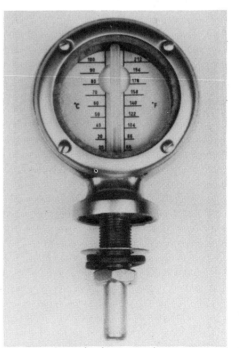

A rebuilt original motometer.

like Metal Prep and Rust Remover, cleans small steel metal pieces in a few hours. Be careful not to dip nonferrous metals in the acid bath. They may be dissolved by the solution.

After cleaning small parts, follow the standard refinishing steps. A yellow-gray residue left on the parts from the acid bath helps prevent rerusting and acts as a wetting agent to ensure a good paint bond. Prime and sand the parts, filling the deep pits with glazing putty. A glossy finish coat will recall the parts' original appearance.

An airbrush makes an ideal tool for spraying small parts such as the Model T light switch, tools and water pump casting. If an airbrush isn't available, these items can be primed with a brush and the final finish applied with an aerosol spray. Painting with lacquer allows the finish coat to be lightly buffed with rubbing compound after it is thoroughly dry. After buffing, only a trained eye would notice any variance between the finish of parts sprayed with an aerosol can as opposed to an airbrush.

The motometer parts arrived carefully packed and wrapped with a detailed instruction sheet that took all the guesswork out of motometer repair, even the first time around. The step-by-step instructions explained how to remove the capillary tube, glass and scale plates. With the old tube out, the new capillary tube slid easily into the replated motometer head and was sealed in place with plaster of Paris. For stumper jobs where instructions aren't available, inquire among fellow hobbyists for someone who has had experience with the repair you are attempting. Technical exchanges like *Cars & Parts* "Tool Bag" or *Skinned Knuckles* can help as well. If you have a spare part, it can be used for experimentation. In this case, carefully note each disassembly step and be prepared to sacrifice the extra part in the learning process.

The Model A horn switch only required buffing to restore its original shiny luster.

Using reproduction parts to overhaul original equipment is not a guaranteed solution. The new packing nut that came with the water pump repair kit was related to the original brass nut by divorce. The new pump shaft and bearings worked fine to replace worn internals; with the old brass nut buffed to a polish and screwed in place, the restored pump looks completely original. It's a good policy to use original parts where they show, and hide the reproduction hardware inside.

The English-language assembly hints on the instruction sheet that came with the water pump kit also appeared in Spanish, French and an Asian character set. In effect, the English text said that rebuilding a Model A water pump is only slightly more complicated than plugging in a toaster. On the back of the sheet, in English only, a red-lettered, boldface warning insisted that the bearings be replaced using a press. (Now you have one more reason for building a hydraulic press from the plans in this book.) The crude option, trying to beat new bearings in place with a hammer, usually ends up confirming Murphy's Law: "If there is a fifty-percent chance for success, that means there is a seventy-five-percent chance of failure." If you lack a press, have a machine shop remove the old bearings and install the new ones. The job just takes a few minutes. Sliding the new shaft through the bearings was as simple as the instructions indicated. Painting the housing, wrapping the packing nut with graphite cord, tightening it and greasing the pump completed the repair.

Car manufacturers follow paint schemes on mechanical as well as body parts. Since color codes for mechanical parts aren't included on the car's data plate, the old part may have to be carefully examined for a patch of original paint that can be used as a refinishing guide. For popular makes like Model A's

The refinished Model T Ford ignition switch and rebuilt carburetor have been restored to a show-quality finish.

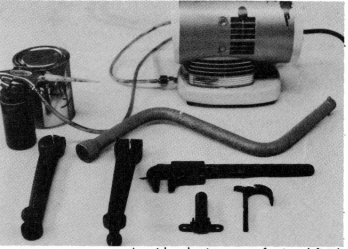
An airbrush gives a professional finish when restoring small parts.

and T's, judging sheets specify the proper color schemes used on chassis parts. Model A water pumps should be painted engine green. Here's a case where restoring the part based on original paint can trick you. It is possible that an original Model A water pump casting will show traces of black paint, not green. That's because rebuilt and replacement water pumps sold by Ford and auto parts stores were painted black. Restorers want to represent their cars as factory original, so green is the proper color.

When repair parts aren't available, the only alternative may be to have a machine shop custom-make a replacement. This work is costly and the shop will need either an original part to copy or a draftsman's blueprint. The story behind a brass water pump packing nut I received once as a Christmas gift may suggest a cost-saving alternative.

A teaching colleague was restoring his Model A phaeton and assigned the water pump packing nut as a design exercise for his drafting students. Later a machine shop student followed the drafting layout to turn several nuts out of brass stock. The project spanned several weeks and called for cooperation between two departments, and students worked a practical exercise that produced several custom-made replacement parts.

Restoring small parts gives the same sense of satisfied craftsmanship that comes from major projects, but can be done with minimal expense and can funnel cash back into the gap left by hobby expenses if some of the items become flea market stock. Refinished tools, for example, make great flea market items. They can be foraged cheaply at garage sales and recycled through a simple cleaning and painting process. Instead of painting tools with a coat of brittle lacquer, they can be refinished with a tough sheen of baked enamel. A description of the baked enamel process can be found in the refinishing chapter. Rebuilding small parts keeps the storage bins from overflowing, but more important, it's the little items that keep a restoration authentic.

Nathan and I enjoy occasional flea marketing, one of the pastimes of the old car hobby.

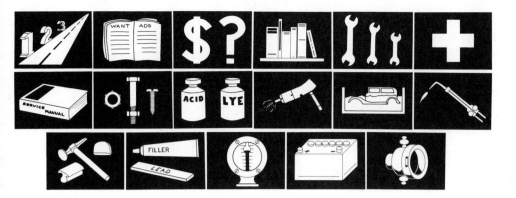

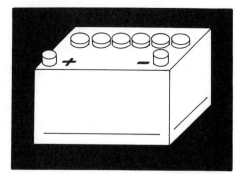

16

The Theory And Practice Of Electrical Troubleshooting

The last several chapters have described procedures for stripping, derusting and repairing the car's sheet metal. However, it would be an unusual hobby car that didn't need some mechanical attention as well. Body and mechanical repairs usually progress separately. Before both are completed and finish painting and upholstery work is begun, it's time to check the car's wiring. If the wiring is badly deteriorated, the car's wiring harness should be replaced. (Instructions for replacing a wiring harness and suppliers of new wiring are included later in this chapter.) Otherwise, electrical repair may be limited to troubleshooting lights that don't work or other inoperable electrical components. Even if the car's wiring appears sound and the electrical system functions properly, unforseen electrical problems can develop. So whether or not the wiring seems to need replacing or repair it's useful to understand the basics of electrical troubleshooting when you operate an older car.

Electrical systems that are trouble-free when cars are put away for winter storage don't always work as well at the end of several months' rest. The windshield wipers on our Mustang that operated perfectly last fall refused to budge when my wife turned them on in the midst of an early April shower. After checking the circuit, I discovered that slight corrosion on the electrical contacts had caused the wiper motor to fail. The repair took less than fifteen minutes. By troubleshooting the problem I spared myself a repair bill that might have included the cost of a new wiper motor.

While the principles of electricity haven't changed, car manufacturers have applied these principles in a number of different ways. Back in the old days, American cars and light trucks ran on 6-volt electrical systems. Old-style 6-volt batteries with three cell-caps are easily spotted in engine compartments that are refreshingly free of air conditioning, power steering, pollution hoses and related clutter. Buick and Packard, among others, squeezed 6-volt batteries into a Coney Island sandwich shape to fit snugly beside straight-eight power plants. Along with radical style changes, the mid-fifties brought engineering advances that swept 6-volt electrical systems into obsolescence. New batteries with six cell-caps instead of three, kicked out a hotter 12-volts to start the new higher-compression V-8 engines and to power accessories that ranged from push-button transmission selectors to photo-electric headlight dimmers; power seats, windows and suspension levelers, even power-operated trunk latches and hideaway hardtops. The American switch-over to 12-volt electrical systems didn't signal an engineering breakthrough. Europeans had used 12-volt systems for years. Increased voltage simply reflected a different application of electrical principles based on an equation named for the German physicist, Ohm.

Electrical Theory

Ohm's law represents the relationship between electrical voltage, current and resistance by the equation $E = I \times R$. The symbols E, I and R stand for voltage measured in volts, current measured in amps and resistance measured in ohms. Voltage is commonly represented as pressure; and resistance as constriction on the flow of current. Just as by increasing pressure more liquid can be pushed through a given-diameter pipe so, too, increasing voltage allows the current flow to remain the same even though the wire size is reduced. When auto engineers substituted 12-volt for 6-volt electrical systems, one advantage was the cost savings that resulted from the use of smaller-diameter wire.

The $E = I \times R$ formula also has a practical application for car restorers. Since 12-volt electrical systems use thinner-diameter 18–20-gauge wire and 6-volt systems require larger-diameter 14–16-gauge wire, electrical repairs on cars equipped with 6-volt systems should always be made with wire the same gauge as original. Automotive wire purchased from an auto supply store or discount mart is intended for use on modern 12-volt electrical systems. Using larger-gauge (thinner-diameter) wire to repair a 6-volt system could mean dimmer lights, underpowered accessory motors and overheated circuits.

Battery cables should also match the car's electrical system. When old 6-volt cable insulation frays, exposing bare wire, or the cable clamps break, hobbyists are tempted to buy a new plastic-clad replacement cable from an auto supply store or discount mart. Before making the purchase, take a close look at the wire diameter where the cable clamps to the terminals. The wire core on the new battery cable is likely to be about the diameter of a pencil, whereas the core of an original 6-volt cable may be as thick as a cigar. Installing a 12-volt battery cable on a 6-volt system increases resistance and constricts the current flow. In warm, dry weather, when the car's engine starts easily, a 12-volt battery cable may seem to work fine on a 6-volt system. In cold-weather starting conditions, the reduced electrical efficiency may seem symptomatic of a dead battery even though the fault most likely lies with the undersized cable.

When battery-cable insulation frays or clamps break, you should either purchase a heavy-gauge replacement cable or salvage the original by wrapping the decayed insulation with friction tape—not plastic electrical tape that dries out and un-ravels, but the cheaper old-style black fabric tape. This sticky-coated wrapping will last through years of driving. To repair a broken clamp, solder or bolt a replacement onto the cleaned cable end. With the repaired 6-volt cable back in place, the battery should snap the starter into action even in cold weather.

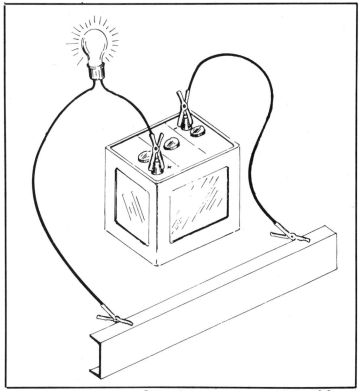

By acting as a common ground for both the battery and light circuit, the car's metal chassis completes the circuit loop.

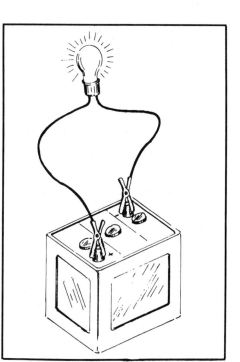

A light bulb connected across the battery terminals illustrates a simple circuit.

Electrical Circuits

Electrical current flows through closed loops, called circuits. Car makers sometimes show a diagram of the car's electrical circuits in the owners manual and always include wiring diagrams in service manuals. General shop texts like Chilton's and Motor repair series also contain wiring diagrams. Instruments, lights, accessory motors, fuses, switches and ignition are represented on these circuit maps by standardized symbols. Individual circuits are traced by color-coded wires.

Tracing short circuits to correct problems such as a fuse that blows every time the electric wipers are switched on, a horn that won't blow, signal lights that don't blink or an electric fuel pump that quits every few minutes requires patience, a few special tools and basic knowledge of how an electrical circuit works.

A battery stores chemical energy. It does not contain a completed circuit. When a wire connects the pole of the battery, the circuit is completed and current flows through the wire. This example calls for a note of warning: Never connect a wire directly across the battery poles. A circuit should always contain a resistance, such as a light bulb, matching the car's voltage to control the current flow. If current is allowed to flow freely, the circuit—including the wire and the battery—will heat up

When a bare wire touches ground, the circuit is cut short at that point. If this break occurs ahead of a light or other source of resistance in the circuit, the short will quickly discharge the battery.

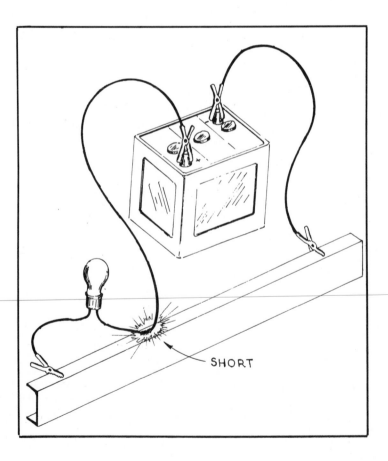

SHORT

very quickly and the battery could explode. Resistance acts like a valve to control the current flow. When a circuit breaks and allows current to flow to the battery without passing through a resistance, a short circuit results. If the short circuit contains no resistance besides that created by the wiring, it will rapidly heat the wiring and drain the battery. For this reason, short circuits are a common cause of electrical fires.

Because car bodies, frames and engines are made from steel and iron in most cases, electrical circuits do not have to run through a wire loop to and from the battery. As long as the battery is connected to the frame or body metal, a circuit starting from the battery will return through the vehicle's ground. Negative-ground electrical systems follow a reverse path.

When wiring insulation rots, unravels or burns off during sheet metal repairs and the exposed wire touches body or chassis metal, current will flow to ground at the point of contact. Electricity always takes the course of least resistance and will bypass lights or motors it is supposed to operate if it can find an easier path back to the battery through ground. Current that follows an alternate path due to defective wiring makes a short circuit.

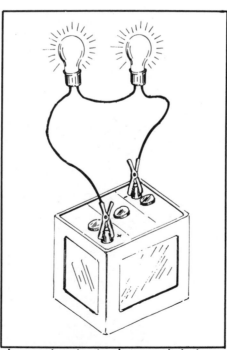

In a series circuit when one light burns out the circuit is broken.

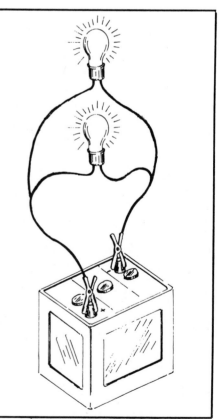

In a parallel circuit, each light is powered by a separate power loop. If one burns out it won't effect the other.

Electrical components can also fail to operate if the circuit is broken. Dirt or corrosion on the ground connection or a loosely attached ground wire can interrupt the current flow. This is a problem that restorers of fiberglass-bodied cars often face. Since fiberglass acts as an insulator, wiring circuits for lights, instruments and power accessories have to be grounded directly to the metal chassis. When the ground straps are missing, electrical problems could result.

An electrical circuit can be intact and fail to work if a burned-out switch or light breaks the circuit loop. Tools and supplies needed to track down and repair defective wiring include: a test light, wire cutters, knife, soldering gun, solder, flux and a roll of electrical tape. You can make a test light from a discarded taillight socket, but commercial units are inexpensive and easier to use. Volt-Ohm meters, abbreviated VOM, are useful for measuring voltage and electrical resistance. Although a VOM is a luxury item for most hobbyists, this instrument gives precise current readings and can be used to check the internal resistance of faulty electrical components.

Electrical Troubleshooting

Begin troubleshooting by locating the problem circuit on a wiring diagram. Follow the circuit's path to find which lights and electrical accessories are linked with the problem component. If a fuse is included in the circuit, check to see whether it is blown. A fuse is blown when the wire inside the glass tube (or lining a groove in the insulation for European-style fuses) is broken. Fuses serve as safety valves to break the circuit when the current exceeds the fuse amperage rating. Sometimes a fuse fails due to age or undetermined reason. If a blown fuse

Tools used to test electrical circuits are shown on the bed of a 1938 Chevrolet pickup. A multimeter gives resistance and continuity readings. The other two items are test lights, one store-bought, the other homemade, used for checking current flow.

has broken the circuit path, then repair may require simply replacing the fuse. If the new fuse blows when lights or electrical accessories are turned on, finding the trouble will require electrical detective work.

Even if the fuse in a problem circuit looks good, replace it temporarily at least. A fuse can look intact and still fail. If the new fuse does not blow, check to see whether current is reaching the fuse block. Checking for current flow, also called a continuity check, is done by grounding one lead of a test light then touching the test light probe to the upstream side of the fuse block or to a wire leading to the power source. The test light will light if current is reaching the fuse. If the circuit is dead at the fuse block, trace the circuit back toward its power source using a wiring diagram. The circuit may include a switch. Switches and fuses are sometimes connected in series. Any circuit that has lights, or any electrical components, connected single file so that the current only has one path to follow is called a series circuit. If you remember those old-fashioned strings of thin, fluted Christmas tree lights that quit when one bulb burned out, you're acquainted with series wiring. An open switch or worn switch contact can have the same effect if it is wired in a direct line with the fuse.

Switches fail when their contacts become corroded or when spring tension holding the contacts together weakens. You can check to see if the switch is defective by bridging its terminals with a length of wire. If the circuit works when the switch is bypassed, replace the switch. When bypassing the switch isn't effective, check the switch terminals with a test light to see if

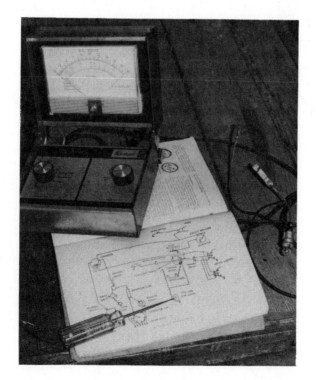

Wiring diagrams on older cars are often simple and easy-to-read, as the diagram for this Chevrolet pickup illustrates. The test light probe points to the problem area, a nonworking taillight.

current has passed that far. A disconnected or broken wire at a main junction block may have cut out the circuit.

In automobile wiring, components beyond the switch and fuse are usually connected in parallel. A parallel circuit gives alternative paths for the current to follow so that lights, a radio and other electrical accessories can operate independently of each other. For example, one blown headlamp doesn't knock out the whole lighting circuit.

Electrical troubleshooting is accomplished by a step-by-step process of elimination. When a taillight fails to operate, the logical first step is to check the bulb. A broken filament (the tiny curled wire inside the bulb) indicates a burned-out bulb. As with a fuse, even if the filament looks intact, it's a good idea to try a new bulb. Sometimes the break in the filament can't be seen. If the new bulb fails to light, remove the bulb and check current flow to the socket by probing the bulb contact (a spring-loaded prong in the bottom of the taillight socket) with a test light. Check the circuit's ground at the same time by clamping the ground lead of the test light to a spot of clean bare metal (the car's bumper is ideal if the lead will reach). If the test light indicates that current is flowing to the bulb contact, clamp the

To test the light for current, remove the lens and bulb, then turn on the lights and hold the test light against the contact in the bulb socket. Note that the clip from the test light is attached to the bumper to assure a proper ground.

Here's why the taillight won't work. The wires have been snipped and routed to a marker light.

test light's ground lead to the side of the taillight socket and check the current flow again. A test light that flickers, lights dimly, or doesn't light at all, indicates a taillight socket with a bad ground. When the circuit is grounded through the taillight assembly, a loose light assembly may break the ground contact. Otherwise, check for a loose or broken ground wire. If the test light failed entirely, then the problem lies nearer the power source.

Windshield wiper, power top or other accessory motors that fail to operate can be checked in much the same way as a defective light. Make sure that the switch operating the accessory is on before checking current flow. Test current flow to the motor by connecting the test light's ground lead to an external ground such as the car's frame. If the test light cannot be attached to an external ground and still reach the motor, connect the test light ground to the motor or to the ground wire terminal at the motor. Check for current flow by touching the test light probe to the terminal that should be delivering power to the motor.

When current is reaching the motor but the unit won't operate, ground the motor with a short length of test wire. If you are sure that current is flowing to the motor and that it has a good ground but it still won't work, then the unit itself is defective. An accessory motor can be tested for an internal short using a VOM meter. If the motor is defective, it should register a higher-than-normal resistance reading on the VOM. The problem, here, is that motors used to power automotive accessories have such low amperage ratings (1 amp commonly) that even the increased resistance caused by a short inside the motor is difficult to detect with the less-expensive VOM meters hobbyists are likely to use. If you are still curious and want to check an ap-

A view underneath the pickup shows the rotted remains of an original wiring conduit. If the metal cable was still intact it could hide a short caused by frayed insulation.

parently defective motor, select the lowest amp scale on the VOM and attach the meter leads to the motor terminals. A normal resistance will barely register on the meter's dial. A high resistance reading, indicated when the needle moves across the dial, is caused by a short circuit inside the motor winding. A motor with an internal short is defective and will either have to be rebuilt or replaced. It is usually easier to find a repairman who can rebuild a vintage electrical component than to locate a replacement. Electrical repair services advertise in hobby magazines such as *Hemmings Motor News.*

When a fuse blows as soon as you turn on the switch, the circuit is probably shorting-out somewhere inside the wiring harness. To locate the hidden short, connect a wire from the battery, fuse block, switch or other power source directly to the inoperable component. If the component works, the short lies ahead of the unit you are testing. To isolate the short, connect the jumper wire to other inoperable components in the circuit. When you reach the section of circuit that breaks the power chain, you will probably find it easier to run a new wire outside the wiring harness rather than trying to replace the defective wire inside the harness. Either cut the defective wire where you solder the jumper wire onto it, or disconnect the old wire at the terminal or fuse block where you connect the new wire.

Installing A New Wiring Harness

Replacing a wiring harness is a job that will vary in complexity, depending on the model and vintage of the car. A

The homemade test light is used to check current flow to the ignition points.

The multimeter is a highly versatile tool in that it measures resistance in the circuit as well as current flow.

wiring harness on a Model A Ford, for example, matches the car's well-engineered simplicity. The first step in replacing a harness is to remove the old wiring. Save clips that hold the harness to the frame or body metal and note the path the harness follows. If you removed the harness in an earlier disassembly stage, hopefully you made a drawing of the harness path. Rubber grommets (which look like miniature rubber doughnuts) are typically placed around the wiring harness where it enters or exits the body at the firewall or through fender wells, for example. If these grommets are dried out or missing, they should be replaced. (A source of replacement rubber parts is included in the list of suppliers at the end of this book.) Slightly oversize replacement grommets can be pinched into a smaller hole by cutting the grommet and removing a thin slice of rubber.

In order to install a new wiring harness correctly, you should follow a wiring diagram. If you can't locate a wiring diagram for your car (a source of wiring diagrams for all American cars built since 1915 is listed at the end of this book), you must tag each terminal and wiring lead as the harness is removed. Information on the tag should note the color of wire that attaches to the lead or terminal. If you have a wiring diagram, you should check it against the color coding found on the car before removing the old harness. Compare the color coding of the new and old harnesses as well to avoid later problems. This double-checking may seem unnecessary, but two wiring dia-

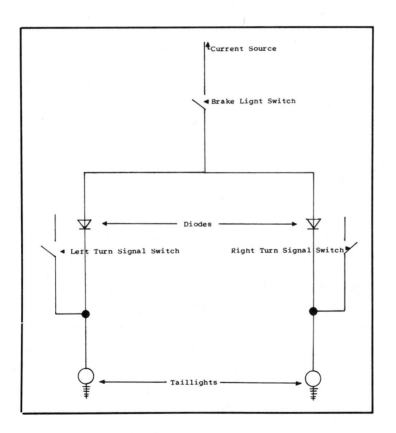

Sample basic circuit for rear signal lights.

grams I consulted as I replaced the wiring harness in my Model A showed contradictory color-coding for the wires connected to the main junction box. I had to trace the current flow through the circuit to determine which diagram was correct.

After the old harness is removed, thread the new harness completely in place before connecting the leads. This way, if the harness has to be rerouted it won't have to be disconnected as well. With the harness in place, check to be sure that all leads reach the appropriate terminals, then begin plugging in the harness. Follow the color coding on the circuit diagram and match each component to its symbolic representation on the print. In cases where the harness contains leads to connect power accessories not included on the car, tape the ends of these leads to avoid shorts. The harness may not include necessary leads for accessories such as electrical tachometers that were dealer options and installed using an auxiliary wiring harness. If the car has an accessory not included in the harness, the original auxiliary harness may serve as a pattern for making a replacement. If the auxiliary harness doesn't exist, either, because you have added the accessory or discarded the original wiring, you should be able to make a replacement following the wiring diagram. If any circuits or electrical components fail to operate after the new harness is installed, troubleshoot the problems using a test light and following the guidelines already mentioned.

Electrical Maintenance

Attention to a car's electrical system shouldn't be limited to repairing and replacing the wiring and electrical components. Electrical maintenance is as important as mechanical maintenance. Scrape oxidation from the battery posts and cable clamps periodically. Clean the battery posts, case and cable clamps with a solution of baking soda and warm water. A tablespoon of baking soda added to a quart of warm water makes an effective solution to wash off accumulated grime and the white powdery residue that collects on battery clamps. Be sure that the battery caps are screwed tightly in place to keep the baking soda solution from spilling into the cell openings. After the clamps and battery posts are scraped and washed, wipe them dry and coat them with Vasoline. The lubricant helps the clamps slide onto the battery posts, but more importantly, it keeps the posts and clamps from corroding. If the battery water is below or near the plates, refill the cells with distilled water.

On older cars that use bulbs rather than sealed-beam headlights, small and sometimes single taillights, you should check the bulb ratings and consider installing brighter bulbs.

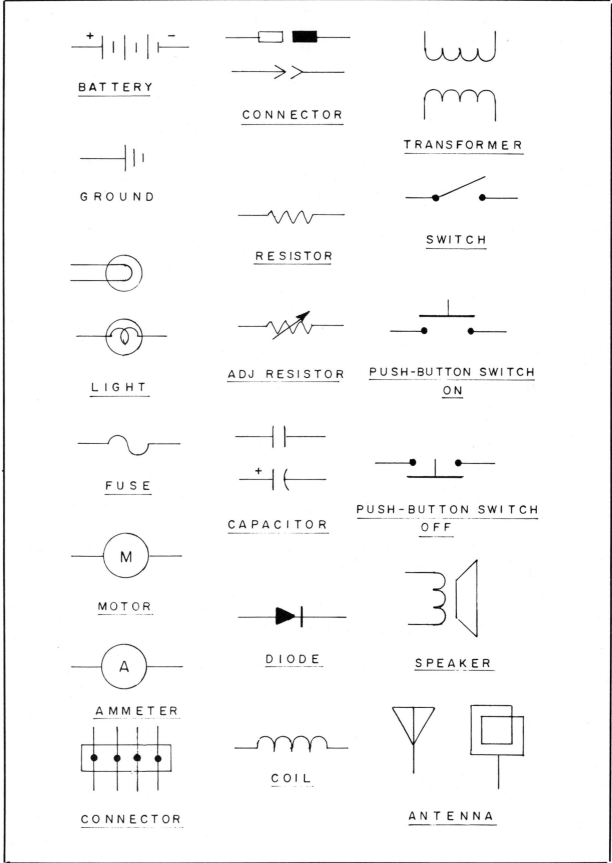

BATTERY

GROUND

LIGHT

FUSE

MOTOR

AMMETER

CONNECTOR

CONNECTOR

RESISTOR

ADJ RESISTOR

CAPACITOR

DIODE

COIL

TRANSFORMER

SWITCH

PUSH-BUTTON SWITCH
ON

PUSH-BUTTON SWITCH
OFF

SPEAKER

ANTENNA

Wiring diagrams use descriptive symbols to represent components in the car's electrical system. This chart is a helpful reference to use when studying wiring diagrams.

145

Dim headlights are not safe for night driving and barely visible taillights are equally hazardous. A bulb's brightness is indicated by amp ratings that are often printed on the face of the bulb or on the shank near the contacts. If the bulbs are rated low (1–2 amps for 6-volt systems), consider replacing them with brighter 3–4-amp-rated bulbs. Remember that increasing the bulb amperage means that the lights will draw more current. This is another reason for repairing or replacing the car's wiring.

Collector cars that are driven with regularity should be equipped with directional lights for safety. Few of today's drivers recognize hand signals, so they can't be expected to react when they see a driver's arm sticking out of the window or pointing toward the sky. The objection most hobbyists have to installing turn signals is their reluctance to add a nonstandard set of lights—two in the front and two in the rear. Turn signals can, however, be installed and integrated into a vintage car's existing parking and taillight circuits using modern diodes. The process is simple.

You will need a vintage-style signal-light switch that mounts on the steering column. These can be made or originals can be purchased at flea markets. Connect the wires from the turn signal switch to the taillight and parking light circuits as shown in the Signal Light Circuit diagram. Add diodes to the circuit just ahead of the signal light junction. Connect each diode so that the color band is on the side toward the signal light junction. Before soldering the wire to the diodes, slip a piece of shrink tubing over the wire. After the diode is soldered in place, pull the tubing over the diode and warm the tubing with the tip of the soldering gun or a hair dryer. The tubing will shrink, insulating the diode.

The diodes should be rated for double the car's voltage (12-volt diodes used in a 6-volt system, for example). Their purpose is to allow the brake or parking light circuits to operate both lights, but the signal light circuit to operate only one light. Diodes are available from the electrical suppliers listed at the end of this book.

Beyond knowledge of fundamental electrical principles, troubleshooting requires only common sense, patience and a few basic tools. The successful troubleshooter's frame of mind is expressed in the reply a Vermont lad is said to have given to the fellow who asked him how he found his lost horse. The lad remarked, "I thought, if I was a horse where would I go, and I went and he had."

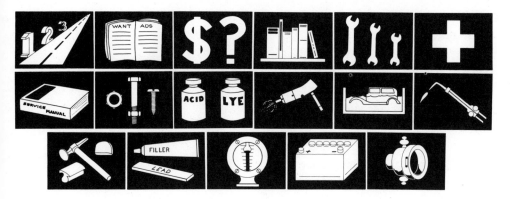

17

A Restorer's Brass Cleaning Recipe

Brass parts won't corrode like steel, but they do tarnish. When a vintage carburetor is dismantled or trim screws are removed, often the only way a sight check indicates that the parts are made of brass is the telltale yellow gleam on a shaft or threads that have been covered. Brass is a decorative metal and thus restored brass parts should exhibit their potential golden glory. The problem is that brass can't be cleaned by acid stripping or sandblasting. Polishes like Brasso rejuvenate well-preserved brass after a session of vigorous rubbing, but hardly touch badly tarnished brass. I used a draftsman's electric eraser to clean badly tarnished brass throttle screws and plugs on Model A Ford carburetors, until John Nelson, an avid clock restorer and friend whose tool illustrations appear in the appendix of this book, showed me a better way.

Visiting John's house is to pass time in a clock shop. More than a dozen time pieces tick and tock in and out of beat in the living room, joined by chimes and cuckoos from other quarters. The heart of nearly all decorative clocks is a wonderfully intricate gear tower made all of brass. As John pulled the mechanism out of a newly restored clock to show me what made it tick, I wondered how he had the patience to clean each tiny shining brass gear, cog and shaft.

"You just soak the whole mechanism in a vat of cleaning solution, help the process along a bit by scouring the brass with a toothbrush, and the entire unit cleans sunshine-bright in a matter of minutes," John explained.

He did add a word of caution. Commercial-strength ammonia is a main ingredient in the brass-cleaning solution. Its fumes quickly fill a room and will gag all but those with the stoutest constitutions. John saves his brass cleaning for warm weather and works outside on his driveway.

The mixing proportions given are for a gallon batch. This quantity should be sufficient for small parts. A plastic tray, available at photography shops, works well for soaking the parts if the job is done in open air. The solution can be stored in a plastic gallon bottle.

The Brass Cleaning Recipe

8 ounces 28% commercial-strength ammonia (sold by blueprint supply stores)

4 ounces oleic acid (from a pharmacy)

4 ounces liquid detergent

2 ounces acetone (available in hardware stores)

To three-quarters gallon water add oleic acid, mix well, then add detergent and acetone. Slowly add ammonia.

Some "clumping" may result as ammonia is added; shake well.

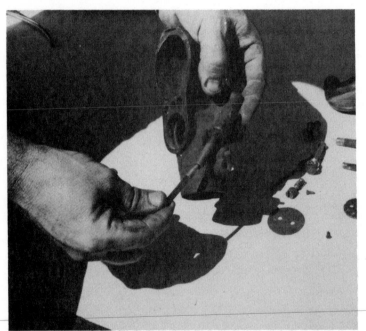

On thirties and earlier vintage cars, mechanical parts such as this Model A Ford cast iron carburetor contain numerous brass components. Some of these, namely the throttle and choke levers, and idle adjustment assembly, are visible on the part and should be restored to a shiny finish.

Model T's and other antiques frequently sport brass horns and headlamps. Cleaning these large brass parts is also a simple process with the cleaning solution.

Allow solution to age three to four days.

Shake before using.

Pep up aging solution with new ammonia.

When using the solution indoors, keep it in a tightly closed container. Store the solution in a brown bottle or away from light.

Helpful Hints

Blow warm air from a portable hair dryer to drive moisture out of tiny crevices in the parts.

John uses four-aught (0000) fine steel wool to burnish the cleaned brass parts, making his restored clock mechanisms gleam. Commercial-strength ammonia fumes are undeniably obnoxious, but the results of using this clockman's cleaning solution are worth enduring the temporary unpleasantness. The telltale smell, of course, evaporates shortly.

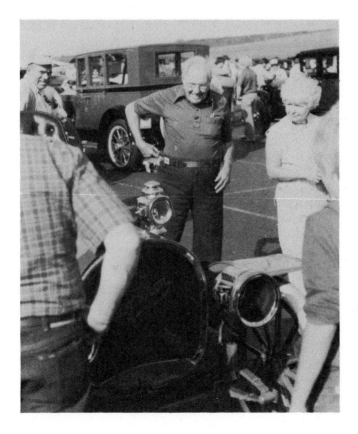

Gleaming brass parts highlight any restoration. Bill Cameron, a contributor to the stripping chapter of this book, beams proudly at the debut of his Cameron roadster.

SECTION II

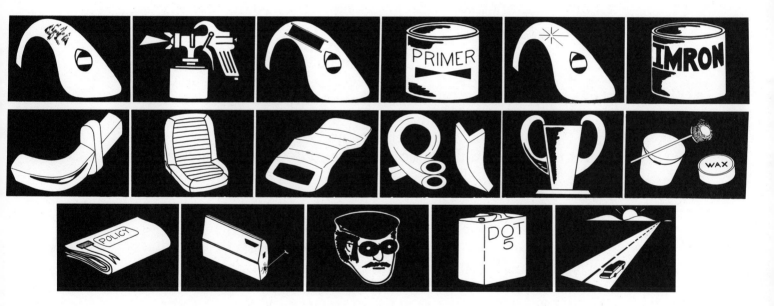

1

Introduction To Refinishing

The car hobby is a wonderful way to develop a sense of accomplishment and build new skills. If you are an admirer of snappy-looking cars, the type of person who turns his head to watch restored relics chug by, then you're not so far from the refinishing processes described here as you might think. If you own a collector car (this handy catch-all category includes just about any car an automobile buff considers worth his time and trouble), no doubt there are areas of your car's appearance that you've earmarked for improvement. Maybe what your car needs is a new coat of paint to cover the stone chips and parking-lot nicks or seat coverings to replace worn and torn front cushions. Or your car's brightwork isn't up to par; the bumpers have lost their sparkle. Somehow the improvements you would like to make get put off. You wonder how to locate a shop that will do the job right and when you consider the cost, you wonder if the improvements will be worth the outlay. That's when you realize that you can do most of it yourself.

Charlie Wilson, President Eisenhower's secretary of defense and earlier head of General Motors, is remembered for his statement that defense dollars should be invested where they would give the most "bang for the buck." Like Wilson's maxim, refinishing makes a greater impression for your hobby dollars than any other stage of restoration or repair. Sure, an engine overhaul will make your car run better, but it won't show off like a new finish. Besides, there are more cars in captivity that could stand cosmetic treatment than there are in need of major engine work.

The real advantage of refinishing work is that unless you are completing the last stages of ground-up restoration, you can still use and enjoy your car while you're dressing it up. Then, too, instead of investing the cost of a modest postwar home to buy a new car, it makes sense to rejuvenate and drive an older model, especially if you like distinctive style. Besides, restoration or renovation is just about the only approach if you enjoy topless motoring. New convertibles are a heartwarming sight, but they're unlikely to hit even the low tide mark on the sales charts.

If you have the inclination to tinker with your car and the patience to learn, you can master painting, upholstery work and other refinishing skills needed to complete a major restoration or rejuvenate your car's appearance. Although an air compressor and spray gun are required for painting, most refinishing jobs require a minimal outlay for special tools—unlike major mechanical work. In fact, if you are restoring your car, you have probably purchased a small compressor, the major item needed for spray painting. If the cost of a compressor exceeds your budget, the tool can usually be rented or sometimes borrowed for the duration required for painting. Remember, too, that the money you save by doing the refinishing work yourself will pay for the tools you need. Portable air compressors cost no more than a portable color TV and can be used to power a small sandblaster and air tools, which makes them versatile additions to any shop.

Kits are a great boon to car hobbyists. For fifties and sixties late model collectables and earlier popular makes, Fords and Chevys especially, upholstery kits are available that can be installed by amateurs and look like the work of professionals. The trend toward kits is increasing and manufacturers are continually expanding the list of makes and models they supply. If an upholstery kit isn't available for your car, you will find that the major kit suppliers are still your best source of original upholstery material. You may not be able to do all your car's upholstery work if you have to start with a bolt of material, but from the instruction in the upholstery chapter you will be able to do at least some of your own work even without the aid of a kit. Once you are aware of what's required for authentic upholstering, you will know how to look for a shop to do the work you can't.

Besides explaining how to do major refinishing work (priming, painting and replacing upholstery), this section also describes the steps you should take to prepare your car's brightwork for replating. Stainless steel and aluminum trim usually need minor straightening and polishing, work you can do yourself. Actual replating, of course, should be done by a professional, but you need to know what happens in the plating process in order to make sure that you receive top quality for your plating investment. The plating chapter takes you into a plating shop for a behind-the-scenes look at the plater's world.

Once refinishing is complete, you'll want to keep your car looking its best. Chapters on how to preserve your car's appearance and protect even its mechanical innards from rust describe procedures to make sure that your refinishing labor isn't wasted. Stepping up from preservation, there is also a guide to preparing your car for show. Why not collect a few ribbons and trophies for your effort? And facing the unthinkable—damage or destruction of your jewel by an accident or fire—there's a chapter on collector car insurance. Theft, the other major risk a hobbyist faces, is the focus of a chapter that offers practical advice for rigging your car with proven devices that will stymie most thieves.

This section is written for beginners and seasoned hobbyists alike. If you are new to repair or restoration you'll find a number of suggestions for building your skills. The refinishing techniques that are described can be applied to individual parts or an entire car. In either case, saving the cost of professional refinishing by doing the work yourself is like having dividends paid to your bank account. With this book as a companion, you can turn your car into an object of pride and feel real satisfaction with what you have accomplished. The challenge is yours.

Refinishing generally means painting and all that process entails; but chapters in the refinishing unit of this book also describe reupholstery and plating, major steps in restoring a car's appearance. Upholstery can be a do-it-yourself project

This cutaway view of a spray gun shows air and paint flow patterns. Note the two adjustment knobs on the spray gun handle. These knobs control flow through the air and paint passages.

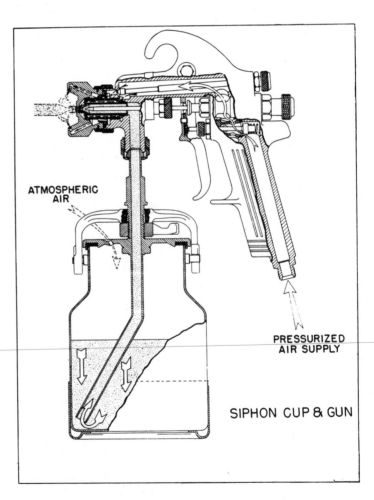

ATMOSPHERIC AIR

PRESSURIZED AIR SUPPLY

SIPHON CUP & GUN

and in communities where trim shops have vanished due to the loss of their convertible top business, reupholstering the car yourself may be your only choice. Hobbyists don't normally attempt to do their own plating, though it is important to know what the professionals have to do to produce a top-quality finish on your car's brightwork.

Of course, painting can be hired out, too. Every community has its share of bodyshops. But that isn't the point. Painting, perhaps more than any other step in the restoration process, requires tight quality control. Unless you are dealing with a painting shop where time isn't important, the painter is bound to take short cuts that are going to stand out on your car's most vulnerable quarter, its appearance. Simply stated, a perfect finish takes perfect preparation. Sure, skill is required but, as in nearly everything else, skill has to be backed by the willingness to repeat all the basic steps again and again until everything is right. This is where having a bodyshop paint your car can compromise refinishing standards. Few hobbyists are wealthy enough to pay someone else for craftsmanship. Most of us can afford a service, be it TV repair or a new roof; few can afford a craftsman's labor of love. That's the ingredient we have to supply ourselves.

Painting is an art, no doubt about it. This statement isn't meant to turn beginners away from tackling their own refinishing work. Restorers by the thousands have mastered the skill of spray painting, as their prize-winning cars testify. To do so they have invested in the proper tools and learned how to use them. They familiarized themselves with painting products in order to pick the right type of primer, paint, solvent and additives for the job. And often they started out by practicing on individual body panels and chassis parts before attempting to paint an entire car.

Spray painting calls for a source of compressed air but it doesn't demand the great volume of air and high pressure required to operate a sandblaster, for example. Portable compressors sold by home improvement centers and major discount department stores, such as Sears, Penneys and Wards, will suit most restorers' needs. A spray gun and its accessories complete the package. The inexpensive guns often included with a portable compressor spray outfit work well for priming car parts or painting lawn furniture, but they aren't designed to apply a quality automotive finish. For the amount of spray painting involved in refinishing a car and the money you will save by doing the work yourself, it makes sense to purchase a professional-quality spray gun from an automotive parts store.

Spray guns used for automotive painting usually operate by siphon feed. This means that air rushing through the spray nozzle siphons the paint from a canister attached to the gun. The canister has a small vent in the top to prevent a vacuum from developing that would stop the flow of paint. The inexpensive spray guns supplied with portable compressors often operate by either siphon or pressure feed. Heavy-bodied house paints, for example, are too thick to spray by the siphon method. For thicker paints, the canister is pressurized and paint is forced out through the spray nozzle. Paint and air can either be mixed externally (that is, outside the gun as in automotive spraying) or internally, before the paint leaves the spray nozzle. Inexpensive spray guns generally offer all four features: siphon and pressure feed, external and internal mix. As a result they can be used for a variety of painting functions, such as spraying your house, but this versatility limits their effectiveness with automotive paints. Professional-quality spray guns are designed for a single purpose—producing mirror-smooth automotive finishes.

Portable compressors and accessories advertised as complete spray painting outfits by Sears and others, come equipped with an air regulator and length of hose. To use them properly, you should add snap-off couplers, a moisture filter and water trap to the system. The standard hose diameter on small compressors is one-quarter inch. For spray painting, a less restrictive five-sixteenths air hose should be used. The pressure drop at the spray gun on a fifteen-foot length of quarter-inch hose averages about three times that of an equal length five-sixteenths-diameter hose. Larger-diameter hose, couplers and filters may be available where you buy the compressor. If not, these items are carried in Sears' mail-order catalog and are sold by most automotive supply stores. Upgrading the air delivery system with these inexpensive improvements plus purchasing a professional-quality spray gun will give you spray painting capacity for top-quality refinishing, plus the capability of powering air-driven tools and a small sandblaster.

As a group, hobbyists have a far too casual attitude toward safety precautions. Professional spray painters wear respirators and spray in areas equipped with high-volume exhaust fans to draw out fumes. To avoid exposure to toxic painting fumes and protect others from painting chemicals, you should observe these three basic safety guidelines: 1—Always wear a charcoal-activated respirator when spray painting. It is also advisable to protect your eyes by wearing safety goggles, glasses or a face shield. 2—Store paint and solvents in a locked cabinet to reduce the chance of fire and keep the painting supplies away from children. 3—Equip your spray area with an exhaust fan. A squirrel cage blower from a hot air furnace adapts ideally for this purpose. You may also want to partition a section of your garage or shop into a spray painting booth by hanging a curtain made from plastic sheeting (sold by agricultural and building supply stores) around the spray area.

Learning to use and care for spray painting equipment is the next step. Regardless of its quality, a spray gun is little better than the care it receives. The cleaning instructions packaged with a new gun give tips that all painters should follow. A spray gun that is cleaned promptly after use, by flushing it with solvent, will seldom give trouble on the job. Although the nozzle can be removed and soaked in solvent, the spray gun itself should never be immersed in thinner. Solvents that loosen caked-on paint will also strip lubricants from packings on the air and fluid valves. If the tiny nozzle orifices become clogged with dried paint, clean them with a broom straw or a toothpick. Spray guns are precision tools; attempting to force dried paint from the nozzle openings with wire or a nail can damage the nozzle. Packings will dry out if they are not lubricated periodically. Signs of dried packings are spitting and irregular spray patterns. These problems can be avoided by regularly applying one or two drops of light machine oil to all moving parts of the gun. While you're cleaning the gun, it's also a good idea to lightly lubricate the canister threads with a petroleum jelly such as Vaseline.

Skill with a spray gun grows with practice, but the following guidelines will get you off to the right start. 1—Always stir paint or primer thoroughly before adding solvent. 2—Add solvent to paint or primer in the proper proportion rather than judging the mixture by watching drips run off the stirring stick, as seasoned pros often do. Mixing equipment need be no more elaborate than a kitchen measuring cup. Be sure to use a glass cup, as painting solvents will "melt" a plastic cup. 3—Always filter the paint as it is poured into the spray canister.

Beginners can profit from spending a few hours watching an experienced spray painter at work. Although he may appear to sweep the gun in an arc toward and away from the surface area, an experienced painter triggers the gun only when the nozzle points directly at the spraying surface. The painter sprays large panels in overlapping strokes with the gun positioned less than a foot from the car's surface. On small touch-up spots, he may fan the area in a sweeping motion.

Before venturing into spray painting, it is important to become familiar with the various primers, paints and solvents, as well as the variety of chemical products that are used to prepare a surface for painting and to enhance the properties of the paints themselves.

There are four basic primer options: primer, primer surfacer, primer sealer and sealer. Primer is a very thin, almost watery coating that bonds strongly to fresh metal. Primer surfacer is the most versatile and widely used preparation product. Since it contains greater solids than ordinary primer, it builds up a base coat that can be sanded smooth to cover underlying blemishes. Recently marketed "high build" primer surfacers with substantially increased solids reduce the tedious sand-and-spray process that is usually required to prepare the surface for finish painting. Primer sealers and sealers are sprayed over an old finish or a primer coat to improve adhesion between the paint layers, create a solvent barrier that will prevent sand scratches from showing through the top coat and keep lacquer thinner from lifting an underlying enamel finish.

Four distinct types of paint have been developed for automotive refinishing. Lacquer and enamel have been the primary refinishing products used since the twenties. In 1972, Du Pont introduced Imron, a tough, high-gloss polyurethane enamel, and Ditzler responded with its competitive product, Durethane. Vinyl paints complete the list. Each has special qualities.

When old timers speak of lacquer, they are referring to nitrocellulose, not the modern acrylic variety. Although nitrocellulose lacquer is no longer distributed by auto supply stores that carry Du Pont, Ditzler or any of the other major paint brands, it *is* sold by paint suppliers that advertise in hobby magazines. Lacquer paints, whether the older nitrocellulose or modern acrylic variety, are distinguished by two qualities that make them well suited for a show car finish. Lacquer is soft, compared to enamel, and this characteristic is both a major strength and shortcoming. The soft surface allows lacquer to be compounded, or "rubbed out." Compounding is a polishing process that results in the characteristic deep gloss finish found on show cars. Since lacquer doesn't dry as hard as enamel, it can be spot painted more easily. The ease with which lacquer can be touched up helps offset the attraction lacquer finishes seem to have for chips and scratches.

Because it is a tougher, more resilient paint, enamel is often applied to chassis parts while lacquer is used more often to cover the car body. Enamel is considered a more difficult paint to spray because it is slower to dry than lacquer. Modern acrylic enamels, however, dry rapidly and can be sprayed as easily as lacquer.

Polyurethane enamels blend many of the best qualities from both lacquer and enamel. The new polyurethane products, notably Imron and Durethane, combine a gloss that resembles the glistening look of wet paint with extreme hardness. Since polyurethane enamel is not an authentic finish, hobbyists are often reluctant to use these paints to refinish the car body. Instead, the durable polyurethane paints are becoming popular for coating chassis parts. Keep in mind that if you are concerned with preserving your car's authenticity, you should use the original type of paint on both body and chassis parts. Methods for determining the original paint are described in the preparation and priming chapter.

Vinyl paints are used to rejuvenate vinyl top coverings. A companion product called "flexible finish" is designed to refinish the plastic facia and bumpers of late model cars.

For spraying, both paint and primer have to be diluted with solvents called "volatiles." Although paint solvents are highly flammable, in this case "volatile" means that paints and primers dry as their solvents evaporate. Because of its soft surface, a lacquer finish remains soluble long after the solvents have dried. As a result, touch-up coats will adhere well even to old lacquer finishes. Not so with enamel. After enamel solvents evaporate, a second drying stage occurs during which the surface layer oxidizes, giving the paint its characteristic toughness. The longer an enamel finish cures, the more mar-resistant it becomes, but this hard surface also makes a cured enamel finish difficult to touch up or repaint without thorough sanding.

Lacquer solvents are called thinners, a name that can easily be remembered when you consider that lacquer paints are diluted 100 to 150 percent by volume for spraying. To assure a smooth, glossy finish, always use a high-quality, brand name thinner. The major paint companies market a range of thinners designed to speed or retard drying and control paint flow for various spraying conditions. Cold weather painting calls for a fast-drying thinner; otherwise the paint may run or penetrate the primer, raising sand scratches and blistering an underlying finish layer. When lacquer is sprayed in hot weather, slower

Pattern	Cause	Correction
	1. Dried paint in one of the side port holes of air nozzle.	1. Dissolve paint in side port hole with thinner; do not probe in any of the holes with a tool harder than brass.
	1. Fluid build up on side of fluid nozzle. 2. Damaged fluid nozzle because spray gun was dropped.	1. Remove air nozzle and wipe off fluid nozzle. 2. Replace damaged fluid nozzle.
	1. Air pressure too high. 2. Spray pattern too wide. 3. Fluid pressure too low.	1. Reduce air pressure. 2. Reduce fan width. 3. Increase fluid supply.
	1. Air pressure too low 2. Excessive fluid velocity or too much fluid.	1. Increase air pressure. 2. Use smaller fluid nozzle orifice, lower fluid pressure.
SPITTING	1. Air entering the fluid supply could be caused by: a. Loose fluid nozzle, or not seating properly due to dirt. b. Loose or missing packing nut or dried fluid packing. c. Fluid connection loose.	a. Tighten fluid nozzle, or clean fluid nozzle seat area. b. Tighten packing nut, or replace missing or dried fluid packing. c. Tighten all fluid supply connections leading to spray gun.

Chart showing typical faulty air nozzle spray patterns.

evaporation is required to prevent "blushing," a color-shift that leaves a dull chalky-looking finish.

Enamel solvents are called reducers. For spraying, enamel paints and primers are diluted between twenty-five and fifty percent by volume. In most conditions, an all-weather enamel reducer can be used that combines a mixture of drying properties to set the paint quickly so that it doesn't run, while keeping the surface fluid so that the paint can flow smoothly.

Polyurethane enamels, notably Imron and Durethane, mix with an activator but are not otherwise diluted. Additives may be used to reduce drying time and extend the pot life of the mixed paint. Enamel reducer is a solvent for polyurethane enamel and is used to flush the spray equipment. Since polyurethane enamel can set up in the spray gun, cleanup should follow immediately after use.

Other painting products include additives to speed or retard drying, add gloss or create a flat finish, and eliminate fisheyes, or tiny circles, that appear when paint is sprayed over a finish containing silicone residue. Wax removers, metal conditioners and rubbing compounds complete the list. Each painting product has a special function. Metal conditioner is used to etch fresh metal and neutralize minute traces of surface rust. It also improves bonding between the primer and metal surface. Thus, treating bare metal with conditioner is an important first step in the refinishing process.

Several major paint companies publish refinishing manuals that explain how to use their products. Addresses for ordering copies of these manuals are listed on page 191. If you are a beginner, you will want to spend some time reading descriptions of the various painting products and visit an auto body repair or restoration shop to see what types of paint are used in different applications before stocking up on your painting needs. That way, when you walk into an auto supply store and the counter clerk asks whether you want lacquer or enamel, primer or primer surfacer, you will know which painting products are best suited for your application.

The chapters describing the priming steps that are the first stage of refinishing are an ideal place to learn the techniques of spray painting. Practicing spray painting while applying primer has the added advantage that mistakes aren't a major setback. If runs develop, a few minutes sanding brings you back to the starting point. Mistakes aren't corrected as easily on the final finish.

Refinishing is one of the most rewarding steps in the entire restoration process. Spraying a glossy finish over dull primer immediately transforms your car's appearance. Refinishing is a process that allows plenty of opportunity to practice and master skills along the way; by the time you reach the last step, spraying your car with a flawless finish, you will be ready for the challenge.

2

A Glossary Of Painting Terms

Painters use a number of specific words and phrases to describe refinishing methods, products and problems. Many of these terms have been used already and will appear, along with others, in the next several chapters of this refinishing unit. The following painting terms are defined here for readers who aren't familiar with their meanings.

ADDITIVES—Chemicals added to paint for a number of reasons: to speed drying for cold weather painting and retard drying in hot weather, to harden the finish and prevent wrinkling, to improve gloss and more.

ATOMIZE—A spray gun atomizes paint by directing compressed air into the paint stream as it leaves the gun nozzle, breaking the paint into tiny droplets.

BLEEDING—The penetration of the underlying finish by solvents in paint or primer. If the solvents are incompatible with the base coat they may bleed through and blister the underlying finish. This condition occurs most commonly when lacquer is sprayed over enamel.

BLISTERING—The result of lacquer thinner bleeding into an underlying enamel finish.

BODY FILLER—Known generically as bondo. Polyester body fillers are both water porous and somewhat brittle. The advantages of body fillers are their ease of application, economy, and the fact that unlike lead, polyester fillers don't require heat.

BODY PUTTY—Or glazing putty, actually a form of concentrated primer. Putty is used to smooth pits or nicks that are too deep to be filled by primer.

CLEAR COAT—Lacquer, enamel or polyurethane paints without pigments are called clear-coat finishes. Clear coats are applied over a color coat to increase gloss and depth or to protect a soft lacquer finish.

CHALKING—A powdery appearance on old and weathered finishes. Sometimes chalky finishes can be rejuvenated by cleaning and waxing.

CHECKING—Line cracks on an older finish caused by aging, often of thick lacquer paint. Checks in the old finish will show through fresh paint unless the blemished base coat is stripped off or the cracks are filled with primer.

COLOR COAT—Also called top coat; it is the finish layer.

DRY SPRAYING—Leaves a lumpy and powdery finish. Dry sprayed paint does not flow smoothly or dry glossy. The causes of dry spraying are varied, but most commonly, the gun is held too far from the work surface (allowing solvent to evaporate before the paint reaches the car) or the air pressure setting is too high.

ENAMEL—A tough automotive finish used by Ford, Chrysler and other makes from the thirties to the sixties. Enamel paints are traditionally thought of as being slower drying than lacquer and consequently more difficult for beginners to master. New acrylic enamels with fast-drying qualities have become popular all-purpose finishes for professionals and amateurs alike. Acrylic enamel is not authentic for cars manufactured before the early sixties, however.

EXTERNAL MIX—Professional-quality spray guns mix air and paint outside the spray gun nozzle. Quick-drying automotive finishes should be sprayed using an external mix nozzle.

FEATHER-EDGE—Spot sanding blemishes such as rust spots on the car's finish with rough-grit sandpaper or a grinder leaves sharp edges that need to be sanded smooth before refinishing. The process of tapering the paint around a repaired area so that the new finish will blend into the old is called feather-edging.

FISH EYES—Small circular blemishes that are caused by a residue of silicone left on the old finish before painting. Properly preparing the surface with a wax remover, using an additive called fish-eye remover and purging the compressor tank before spraying are effective precautions.

FOG COAT—A properly reduced final coat sprayed at slightly increased air pressure and gun distance from the work surface. A fog coat gives a luminescent effect to metallic paints. It is one of the tricks of the trade that is used to give novel shading effects on show car finishes.

INTERNAL MIX—Air and paint are mixed inside the spray gun nozzle. Heavy-bodied, slow-drying paints are sprayed using an internal mix nozzle.

LACQUER—The original quick-drying automotive finish. When nitrocellulose lacquer was first introduced in the early twenties, only dark colors were chalk resistant. Today, lacquer's high-gloss qualities and its ability to be rubbed out make it a restorer's favorite.

METALLICS—Contain small metal flakes embedded in the paint film. The metal reflects light rays, giving the paint a metallic sparkle.

MIST COAT—A highly-thinned final color spray or straight thinner used to blend a touch-up coat into the surrounding finish.

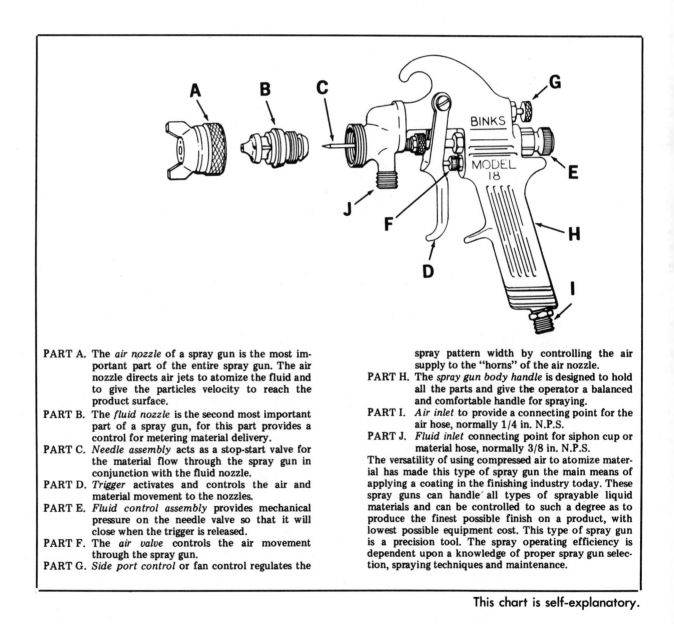

PART A. The *air nozzle* of a spray gun is the most important part of the entire spray gun. The air nozzle directs air jets to atomize the fluid and to give the particles velocity to reach the product surface.

PART B. The *fluid nozzle* is the second most important part of a spray gun, for this part provides a control for metering material delivery.

PART C. *Needle assembly* acts as a stop-start valve for the material flow through the spray gun in conjunction with the fluid nozzle.

PART D. *Trigger* activates and controls the air and material movement to the nozzles.

PART E. *Fluid control assembly* provides mechanical pressure on the needle valve so that it will close when the trigger is released.

PART F. The *air valve* controls the air movement through the spray gun.

PART G. *Side port control* or fan control regulates the spray pattern width by controlling the air supply to the "horns" of the air nozzle.

PART H. The *spray gun body handle* is designed to hold all the parts and give the operator a balanced and comfortable handle for spraying.

PART I. *Air inlet* to provide a connecting point for the air hose, normally 1/4 in. N.P.S.

PART J. *Fluid inlet* connecting point for siphon cup or material hose, normally 3/8 in. N.P.S.

The versatility of using compressed air to atomize material has made this type of spray gun the main means of applying a coating in the finishing industry today. These spray guns can handle all types of sprayable liquid materials and can be controlled to such a degree as to produce the finest possible finish on a product, with lowest possible equipment cost. This type of spray gun is a precision tool. The spray operating efficiency is dependent upon a knowledge of proper spray gun selection, spraying techniques and maintenance.

This chart is self-explanatory.

OEM—Original Equipment Manufacturers produce the paint products used on new cars. These paints will best match an existing finish.

ORANGE PEEL—An uneven finish that looks like the skin of an orange. This condition is a novice painter's trademark since the main causes are improper spray gun adjustment and painting techniques. A slight orange-peel effect can usually be rubbed smooth on lacquer finishes. Enamel is not as forgiving.

OVERSPRAY—Carries paint mist beyond the intended surface onto unmasked areas. Proper masking and an adequate ventilation system are the primary ways to avoid overspraying tires, window glass and surfaces that aren't targeted for painting.

POT LIFE—Once a catalyzed paint is mixed with hardener, an invisible counter begins to tick away the mixture's pot life. Paint thickens as its pot life expires but it usually stays liquid for about eight hours.

PRIMER—Its two main functions are: creating a bond with bare metal and filling minor surface flaws. Contrary to common practice, most primers are water porous and should not be wet sanded.

PRESSURE FEED—Forces paint out of a spray gun canister through the spray nozzle. Pressure feed is used with heavy-bodied house paints, for example, and in automotive spraying when paint is contained in a remote canister.

REDUCER—The solvent used to dilute enamel paints and primers. Reducers are available with fast, slow or medium drying rates. Be sure to select the right reducer for the spraying conditions.

RUB OUT—After a lacquer finish cures, it is usually rubbed out using mild abrasives suspended in a creamy paste. Rubbing creates a mirror-smooth surface, producing a high luster.

RUNS—Drips and sags caused by spraying a cold surface or allowing a heavy coat to build up before the paint has a chance to set. To borrow baseball lingo, a painter's aim is a finish with no runs, no errors.

SAND SCRATCHES—Marks made in bare metal or on an old finish by sanding have to be filled with primer and sanded smooth before painting. Since lacquer solvents can penetrate the primer and swell underlying sand scratches, the prime coat should be sealed before painting.

SEALERS—Have the effect that their name implies. Clear sealers are sprayed between the last primer layer and the initial color coat, particularly when solvents in the color coat might lift old paint or swell sand scratches underneath. Primer sealers combine properties of both products.

SIPHON FEED—Air rushing through the spray nozzle siphons paint out of the spray gun canister. The siphon spray painting technique is best suited to light-bodied automotive primers and paints where a fine finish is desired.

SOLVENTS—Dissolve the solids in paints and primers. Both lacquer thinner and enamel reducer are made of solvents. Active chemicals in the two products are not compatible, however, so thinner cannot be used in place of reducer and vice versa.

TACK COAT—The first layer or coat of enamel should be allowed to dry until it is "tacky." The resulting tack coat holds the next heavier and wetter layer, preventing runs and sags.

TACK RAGS—Specially treated cheese cloth used to wipe dirt, lint and sand particles from a surface in preparation for finish painting.

THINNER—The solvent used to dilute lacquer paints and primers. Thinners are available with fast, slow and medium drying rates. When the weather is hot and dry a slow-drying thinner is used. Fast-drying thinners are used for spraying on cool, damp days. Medium or all-purpose thinner is used to dilute primers and for most spraying conditions.

TOP COAT—The last finish layer. A painter concentrates all his skill on the top coat to obtain a smooth, high-gloss finish.

WET SANDING—Automotive sandpaper is available with waterproof backing. This sandpaper can be dipped in water during sanding to eliminate dust. Wet sanding, as this process is called, extends sandpaper life, but water penetrates most primers and when moisture gets beneath the painted surface it can raise havoc.

ZINC CHROMATE—A fast-drying primer that provides corrosion protection for steel parts that are exposed to the elements, chassis parts in particular. Unlike oil-based, rust-resisting paints, zinc chromate primers use solvents that are compatible with both enamel and lacquer.

3

Preparation Steps And The Priming Process

When I began my first restoration I had a very cold garage, basic Sears tool kit and assorted parts scoured from junkyards that I blithely planned to rebuild into a restored Model A Ford. Eventually summer came, I added to my tool collection and the Model A slowly took shape. But it wasn't until I learned the basic refinishing steps that my rebuilt parts took on a restored look.

Nearly all the parts to my Model A, from the sheet metal to the front axle, had to be stripped of rust and rebuilt before I could even consider refinishing. Not all hobbyists work from the ground up as literally as I did on that Model A. The car's chassis had rested beside a pasture fenceline long enough for a sturdy tree to grow inside the frame rails. The first step toward its restoration was to cut down that tree.

If you are working with newer or better preserved parts that need only light sanding to remove an oxidized surface layer of paint prior to repainting, you can skip most of the preparation steps. More commonly, though, some amount of degreasing and derusting is necessary, followed by dent and rust repair before refinishing can begin.

If you have dismantled your car for restoration and are refinishing body parts and mechanical assemblies individually, you may need to apply the methods for stripping old paint, grease and rust that were described earlier. Once the coatings have been stripped away, you may notice that areas of the frame, undersides of fenders and surface areas where rust has blistered through the paint are covered with tiny pits. Fortunately for restorers, the heavy-gauge steel on vintage cars can be badly rusted, resulting in severe pits, and still leave enough metal to be structurally sound. Metal that is perforated with holes will have to be replaced or repaired.

Before applying the first primer coat, all cracks, tears, pinholes—however tiny—should be repaired. Once the refinishing process begins, the metal can't be worked with heat. Before priming, inspect chassis and body parts for cracked welds or loose rivets on mounting brackets and structural members. Braces for running boards were often riveted to the frame on vintage cars. Frames, too, are often held together by rivets. Loose rivets can be repaired by heating and pounding. Have a professional welder repair cracked or broken welds if you lack welding skills and equipment or weld infrequently and are unsure of your metal-working skill.

When all welding and metal repair is complete, grind or file the welding and brazing beads, then treat the bare metal with metal conditioner (sold by auto supply stores under brand names like Twin Etch, Chem Grip and Metal Prep). Metal conditioner consists of diluted phosphoric acid which etches the metal and removes light surface rust that germinates when steel is left untreated. Apply metal conditioner according to the instructions on the container. Labels on this and other refinishing products are typically marked "for professional use only." This disclaimer against negligent use also reflects a quality standard. The solution will protect metal from rerusting and acts as a "wetting agent" to assure a strong paint bond.

The next step is to fill all deep pits. While lead filler could be used, plastic serves as well and is much easier to work with.

Deep pits can be filled with body filler, commonly called bondo. Unlike glazing putty, which is applied over primer, body filler adheres best to bare metal.

Body filler is smoothed using a grater or body file and 30 grit sandpaper.

It is important to remember that plastic filler bonds to bare metal, but not to a painted surface. Mix the filler according to the instructions on the can. Unless the metal is badly rusted and scarred with deep pits, as is likely to be the case with badly weathered chassis parts, you will need only a small amount of filler. A quart should be sufficient to fill rust pits and minor surface irregularities as well. Spread filler in a very thin layer using a plastic applicator available at the auto supply store where you purchase the filler. Remember, the thicker you apply the filler, the more sanding will be required.

Plastic filler has a short set-up time and should be applied immediately after mixing. At temperatures above 70°F, the filler will harden in twenty minutes or less. As soon as the filler hardens, it can be scraped smooth using a grater (also available at most auto supply stores) and sanded with 36 grit sandpaper. Continue sanding until all trace of filler is removed from the metal surface; only the dots of pink or blue filling the pits should be visible.

The instructions up to this point have assumed that the car has been at least partially disassembled and that you are refinishing individual parts—the fenders, for example, or the frame. This piecemeal approach is common for cars undergoing a show car restoration and is often used to gradually upgrade previously restored or well-preserved original cars. An owner might strip and repaint a car's wheels, for example, while leaving the rest of the car undisturbed. With cars that need cosmetic improvement, but are otherwise well preserved, it is equally common to repaint the whole car. Repainting proceeds from two conditions. Either the old paint layer has been extensively

When the job is finished, the filler covers the pits leaving the rest of the metal surface exposed.

To improve the paint bond, always treat bare metal with a metal prep solution before painting.

stripped by sandblasting or a chemical process, or the original finish is still intact and will be used as a refinishing base.

If you are planning to paint over an existing finish, you should begin the refinishing process by thoroughly washing with detergent and warm water all the areas you intend to repaint. Remember to include the door openings, the underside of the trunk lid, possibly even the firewall, the underside of the hood and other "hidden" areas in addition to plainly visible surfaces. After rinsing and wiping these areas dry, clean the old finish a second time using wax remover, a painting preparation product available at auto supply stores. Any wax residue, but especially traces of silicone wax, can affect paint adhesion and flow, so be sure to clean the old finish thoroughly using wax remover and a plentiful supply of fresh rags. Wipe the finish until the rags no longer pick up a wax residue.

In order to prime and paint an existing finish, the old paint must be sanded thoroughly. To avoid creating scratch marks that may show in the new finish, the old paint should be sanded using 360 or finer grit sandpaper. Coarse 220 grit sandpaper can be used if the old finish is sprayed with primer and the primer layer is sanded and sealed before painting. Scrapes and blisters in the finish should be sanded to bare metal. Treat the metal with metal conditioner to retard rerusting. Small dings caused by stone chips can be filled but dents should be straightened. You can perform minor body work of this nature yourself, following the instructions given earlier. When a spot is sanded to bare metal, the surrounding paint has to be sanded as well so that it tapers smoothly to the raw steel. Feather-edging, the process of sanding the layers of paint and primer so that no abrupt edges can be felt around the bare metal spot, is essential for a perfect finish. If the paint is not sanded to a smooth feather-edge around spots of bare metal, the sanding gouges will show through the new finish.

An artist's airbrush makes an ideal tool for refinishing small parts.

Preparation steps for refinishing fiberglass-bodied cars differ somewhat from those for working with steel bodies. Fiberglass is not subject to parking lot dings or rust but it is prone to cracking. A finish that is marred by criss-crossing check marks indicates aged, road weary fiberglass underneath. Painting over these "crow tracks" won't make the marks go away. The new finish will only highlight the cracks. Most commonly the cracking originates in the fiberglass substrate which means that the old finish must be stripped off using a high-grade water-soluble paint remover. Then the tiny cracks can be filled with thin coats of polyester body filler (the same product used to fill pits on steel parts). Filler will spread more smoothly if it is reduced with lacquer thinner or a product designed to thin polyester putty, such as Marson Corporation's Xtend. After it dries, block sand the filler. Test the surface with your hand and inspect the fiberglass by sighting along flat areas in a good light, preferably sunshine. If cracks remain, apply another thin filler layer. Repeat these steps until all the cracks are filled.

It may seem premature, but before you apply the first coat of primer, you should select the paint for the car's final finish. There are two reasons for this. First, collectors often see refinishing as an opportunity to restore the car to its original color and it is usually easier to determine the original color scheme

Pits and other surface blemishes are filled with a thin layer of glazing putty.

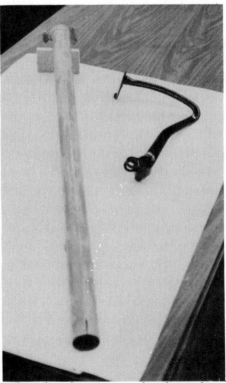

When the glazing putty hardens, the filler is sanded in preparation for another coat of primer.

before coating the car with primer. Second, the type of primer and paint used for the finish coat should match. Although enamel can be applied over a lacquer base, lacquer cannot be applied over enamel. (Lacquer solvents will blister an enamel undercoat.) If you are painting over an existing finish, you will need to determine whether the old paint is lacquer or enamel and select the primer and new paint accordingly. Although professional painters may be able to apply lacquer over a baked enamel finish, amateur painters are advised to work strictly with paints and primers that are known to be compatible.

To determine the type of paint used in an existing finish, rub a small area with lacquer thinner. If the finish is lacquer, the paint will dissolve quickly. Acrylic lacquer will dissolve after vigorous rubbing; enamel will not dissolve at all.

If the car has been repainted and you desire to restore its original color scheme, you can often determine the factory finish by looking inside the trunk, underneath the hood, on the firewall, behind trim moldings and on the dash. Paint shops seldom take the trouble to repaint these areas. For most cars built since the early thirties, you can also determine the factory color scheme from information coded on the data plate, usually located on the firewall. To decode the numbers on the data plate you will need the aid of a coding reference found in the general information section of dealer service manuals. In addition to the color scheme, information on the car's data plate typically identifies the assembly location, engine and drive train configuration and sometimes the month of manufacture.

After finishing the preparation work and selecting the paint, prepare the car for priming by removing the bumpers and trim. Although masking chrome trim is the lesser nuisance, a

The same refinishing steps apply to large or small parts. Housings or castings can be refinished before the parts are reassembled.

more professional finish results if nameplates and other decorative trim are removed. These pieces are usually held in place with clips. The clips holding lettering or nameplates attached to the trunk, hood or fenders may have to be reached from inside these panels. Now blow off dust and any moisture or debris that is trapped in body seams or crevices, under rubber moldings or behind trim with a high-pressure airstream directed through a blow gun. Blow guns are an inexpensive air compressor accessory available at Sears, Wards, Penneys or auto supply stores.

When the surface is ready for priming, mask all areas that won't be painted. These include headlights, window glass and trim that is left on the car. If you are refinishing mechanical parts—a transmission case or front axle, for example—these too may need masking to prevent paint from coating surfaces that should be left bare. Use quality masking tape—the type sold by auto supply stores. It sticks better than the inexpensive discount store variety. Newspaper makes a cheap, effective covering, provided that the sheets overlap and are taped along the edges to prevent paint from blowing underneath. If the grille has been removed, you should tape a sheet of cardboard to the front of the radiator. Several passes of the spray gun across the radiator fins can build up a layer of primer and paint that will reduce the radiator's cooling efficiency. Either remove the tires or cover them with plastic garbage bags. It is often helpful to elevate cars that have a low ground stance by placing jack

For small items, the finish coat can also be applied with an airbrush.

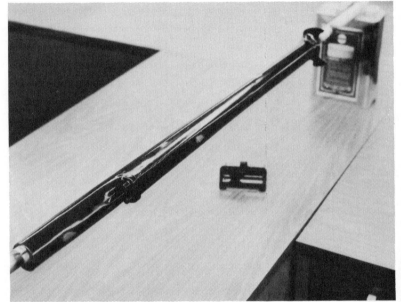

Small blemishes that show up when the color coat is applied can be filled with glazing putty. After the putty dries, it can be sanded and covered with another coat of paint.

stands under the axles so that you can reach the rocker panels, lower fender edges and splash pans with full paint coverage.

If you are refinishing large parts such as fenders, a frame or the entire car, you should spray on the primer layer. But if you are refinishing small parts, hood clamps for example (an overall restoration involves innumerable items of this sort), you can thin the primer slightly and apply it with a brush. For spraying, thin or reduce the primer according to directions on the can. Primer is used to cover bare metal.

Before priming small items, examine the surface you will be spraying under a direct light. Look closely for manufacturer's logos, parts numbers and other details that you don't want to obliterate during the refinishing process. You will have to be careful to apply a light coat of primer over these markings, otherwise they will easily be covered with scratches, pits and other unwanted markings.

Though primer has been used here generically, there are numerous primer products. Lacquer primers are generally used for the filling steps described in this chapter. Enamel primers are harder to sand and do not have the filling capacity of lacquer primer. They are sprayed over smooth surfaces that will be covered with an enamel finish. For quick reference, a chart listing the mixing proportions, spraying pressure, spray gun distance, and number of coats for the major types of primer and sealer is included below.

	LACQUER	**ENAMEL**
Primer (used to cover bare metal)	Red oxide	Nonsanding
Reduction	33% lacquer thinner	12% enamel reducer
Air pressure at spray gun	45–55 psi	45 psi
Gun distance from the work	8–10 inches	8–10 inches
Number of coats	1 to 2 coats	1 double coat
Primer Surfacer (used over previously painted surfaces and for subsequent primer layers)	Lacquer primer surfacer	Enamel primer surfacer
Reduction	80–125% lacquer thinner	50% enamel reducer
Air pressure at spray gun	35–45 psi	45 psi
Gun distance from the work	6–8 inches	8–10 inches
Number of coats	3 or more, repeat as required	2 to 3 coats
Sealers (used to prepare for final finish)	Lacquer sealer	Enamel sealer
Reduction	None required	None required
Air pressure at spray gun	35–45 psi	35–45 psi
Gun distance from the work	6–8 inches	6–8 inches
Number of coats	1 medium coat	1 medium coat

After the first primer coat dries, inspect the surface for pits and other blemishes. Fill these with a thin layer of glazing putty, a form of concentrated primer that comes in a tube and is applied with a rubber squeegee. Both glazing putty and squeegee applicators are available at auto supply stores. Since all blemished areas have to be covered during refinishing, be as thorough as possible in the first application. Spread the putty in thin layers. Glazing putty shrinks slightly as it dries and a thick layer may crack in time.

After the putty dries, usually in less than an hour, sand the putty and primer coat using 220 grit sandpaper. Many bodymen prefer to "wet sand" primer using special water-resistant sandpaper sold by auto supply stores. Wet sanding eliminates dust and stretches the life of the sandpaper, but most primer products are water porous; water that penetrates the primer coat can soak into filler, causing blisters, and possibly rusting the metal underneath the paint. Slower, dry sanding is a safer method. Since dry sanding produces a great deal of dust, you should wear a painter's mask whenever you are sanding as well as spraying. Coarse 220 grit sandpaper cuts easily through glazing putty and primer, making quick work of this first sanding step. To extend sandpaper life, tear a fresh sheet in half, then fold the half-sheet in overlapping thirds like a letter. Wrap this hand-size piece around a small scrap of wood or a rubber sanding block to avoid leaving finger ridges in the primer as you sand.

The first sanding session will quickly cut through the primer coat. Thicker-bodied primer surfacer should be used to build up subsequent primer layers that can be sanded until the finish is mirror smooth. After each primer coat dries, examine the finish for pits and blemishes. Repeat the glazing putty and sanding sequence, using less coarse 360 grit sandpaper.

These accessory starter pedal parts have been painted with baked enamel. It's a useful process, ideal for refinishing small items.

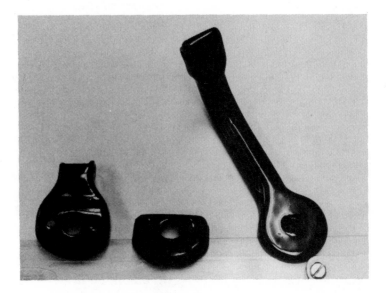

Though the surface will appear smooth after the primer surfacer coat is sanded, it may still have minor imperfections. Wishful thinking won't produce a satin finish, only persistence in the preparation process. One or several more passes through the primer/glazing putty/sanding routine may be necessary, depending on the condition of the parts. To determine whether the finish is perfectly smooth, spray a light coating of red oxide primer over the gray primer surfacer. As you sand, the red coating will highlight low areas, scratches and other blemishes. The final primer coat should be sanded very lightly with 400 or even 600 grit paper. This coat is intended to cover spots of bare metal and fill scratches left from earlier sanding. Very lightly sand edges where bare metal is easily exposed. All bare metal should be covered with primer in preparation for painting.

You may want to spray the sanded primer finish with clear sealer to prevent solvents in the color coat from swelling sand scratch marks or penetrating the primer layer and lifting an original base coat. Sealer also helps prevent new paint from seeping into a porous base coat, dulling the final finish and sometimes causing pigments to bleed from the base layer.

Thorough preparation is the secret of a show car finish. Professionals sometimes reduce the number of repetitive prime and sand preparation steps by using the high build primer surfacer products described in the next chapter. But regardless of the products used, practice and patience are still the essential ingredients of successful refinishing.

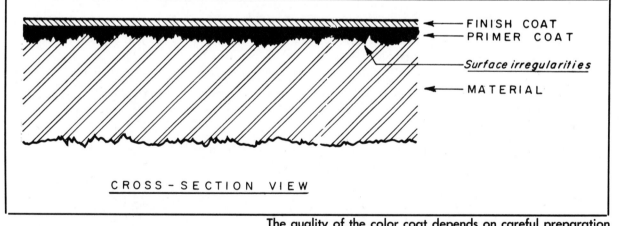

FINISH COAT
PRIMER COAT

Surface irregularities

MATERIAL

CROSS - SECTION VIEW

The quality of the color coat depends on careful preparation during the priming process.

4

Shortcutting Preparation Steps With High Build Primers

The new generation of high build primers are cutting refinishing time for professional restorers and they can do the same for you. Three products, Feather Fill, Eliminator and Du Pont 100S primer surfacer, dominate the one-application primer market. Each of these products has advantages, and each has some limitations in comparison to the others. All provide welcome relief from the repetitious process of spraying and sanding primer coats to fill the pits and blemishes of aged metal.

Before using these, or any primer products, clean the finish thoroughly, to remove all traces of grease, dirt and rust. Treat bare metal with metal conditioner, a mild phosphoric acid solution that removes surface rust and etches the metal to assure a good paint bond.

Two of the high build primers, Feather Fill and Eliminator, are catalyzed polyester products. A liquid catalyst must be added to these primers in order for curing to occur. The colorless hardener is supplied in a small tube and must be mixed in correct proportion with the primer. Too much hardener will cause the primer to set up prematurely. This is a real problem if the primer hardens in the spray gun. If these polyester products are sprayed without hardener, or at a temperature below 70°F, the primer will remain gooey and have to be removed with rags soaked in lacquer thinner. Since catalyzed primers set up rock hard when they cure, the spray gun must be cleaned with lacquer thinner immediately after use.

Apart from adding the catalyst, Feather Fill and Eliminator are sprayed undiluted, just as they pour from the can. Because of their thick consistency and fast-drying quality, these products can be sprayed in heavy coats without causing runs. Novice painters will find that the polyester primers are actually easier to spray than standard lacquer or enamel base primers, providing instructions for adding the catalyst are carefully followed.

Du Pont 100S is a high-solid, acrylic primer surfacer that is reduced eighty percent with lacquer thinner and still sprays twice as thick as standard lacquer primers. Even at 100 percent reduction, it provides fifty percent more surface coating than regular primer surfacers.

Because of their thick consistency, high build primers must be stirred for several minutes before they can be poured into the spray gun. High build primers are applied like any other primer product: Spray an initial wet coat and allow from five to fifteen minutes drying time (depending on temperature and humidity) before applying additional coats. The primer coat must dry thoroughly before sanding. High build primers require thirty-five to forty pounds of air pressure at the spray gun.

The photo sequence shows the high build primer products sprayed on an assortment of weather-beaten Model A Ford chassis and body parts. Each had been stripped to bare metal by sandblasting, but all the parts—a roadster cowl band, front axle and wishbone, running board brackets and rear axle radius rods—were marred with pits and file marks left from smoothing filler rod. The parts were sprayed with several coats of high build primer and allowed to dry thoroughly. Then a light guide coat of red oxide primer was sprayed over the gray

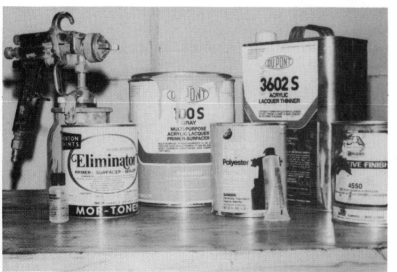

The high build primers described in this chapter include two polyester products: Feather Fill and Eliminator, plus Du Pont 100S and its accessory thinner. Ditzler and other major paint companies also market high build products.

Polyester primers have to be mixed with a catalyst before spraying.

A look inside the can shows the thick consistency that marks high build primers.

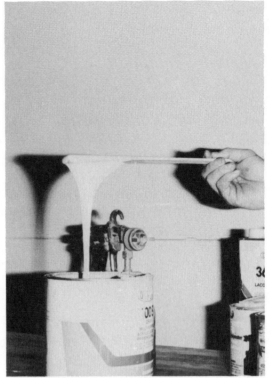

High build primers require thorough stirring before use.

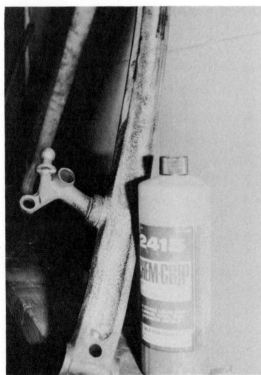

Always coat bare metal with a metal prep solution before priming.

The first primer coat covers most pits and blemishes.

primer base. As the parts were sanded, the guide coat quickly showed low spots and pits.

Dried primer has a dull finish; so, unless a guide coat is used, pits and other blemishes do not show up readily during sanding. The guide coat highlights deep pits, nicks, gouges and other trouble spots that need to be filled with glazing putty before applying another primer layer. To ensure a smooth primer base, use a sanding block and sand only as long as a trace of the red oxide guide coat is visible. Auto supply stores sell plastic sanding blocks that grip the edges of the sandpaper, flex to any contour and fit comfortably in the palm of your hand. Over-

Caution: The lacquer solvents in Du Pont 100S can lift an enamel finish. The trunk of this car has a spot where the high build primer blistered an area of the baked enamel factory finish.

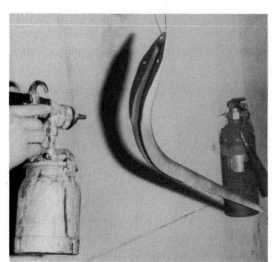

After the high build primer dries, spray a light coat of red-oxide primer to highlight pits and low spots.

This Model A backing plate has been partially sanded to show the contrast between the red oxide dust coat and the gray primer underneath. Pits in the finish are visible as dots of red.

enthusiastic sanding, especially with hand-held paper, will leave ridges and hollows in the soft primer.

As the guide coat was sanded, the Model A parts showed an epidemic of tiny red spots. The thick primer coat easily covered these small pits. Larger blemishes were filled with glazing putty. After the putty dried, it was sanded smooth and another high build primer layer was applied. When this second coat was sanded, all blemishes disappeared. Several coats of standard primer surfacer would have been needed to smooth these badly pitted parts.

High build primers can be sanded with 180 grit sandpaper. This rougher-grade sandpaper quickly smooths the primer buildup, speeding the refinishing process. Those who are experienced with lacquer primers know that using even moderate 220 grit sandpapers can leave scratch marks in the final glossy finish, so the final primer coat should be sanded with finer 360 or 400 grit sandpaper. The high build primers control sand-scratch swelling and provide a suitable base for polyurethane enamel finishes.

Many hobbyists don't realize that nearly all primers are water porous. As a result, they coat carefully prepared parts of a car body with primer, then proceed with other refinishing steps, thinking that they have protected the metal from rusting. When painting time rolls around, they are shocked to find small

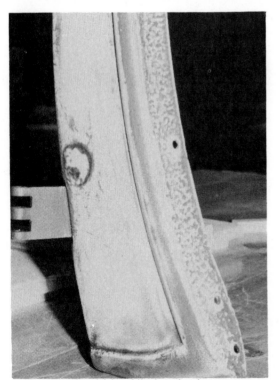

Deep pits should be filled with glazing putty, a form of concentrated primer that is applied from a tube.

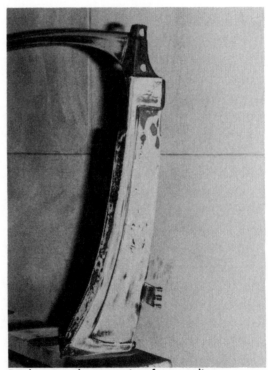

Dark spots that remain after sanding show areas needing another coat of high build primer.

flecks of rust dotting the primer finish. Metal that is covered with primer will rust if it is exposed to moisture either through improper storage or by wet sanding. Yet cars that have been carefully stripped to bare metal are often stored outdoors after priming. Then, too, hobbyists and professionals alike commonly wet sand primer coats. Wet sanding is a process where specially-backed sandpaper used for automotive refinishing is dipped in water during sanding to eliminate dust and extend sandpaper life. Parts that are sprayed with primer should be coated with sealer and stored in a dry area to prevent rerusting. It is wise to avoid wet sanding most primers. Feather Fill is especially porous and should not be wet sanded.

According to the manufacturer, Eliminator is not water porous. As a result, this product is ideal for priming wood spokes or other wooden body parts that must be protected from moisture. It can also be wet sanded. However, because of its sealer properties, Eliminator should never be sprayed over uncured paint or primer. Primer coats that look dry may still hold unevaporated solvents. Once a coating of Eliminator dries, solvents trapped underneath cannot escape and blistering can result. Few painters realize that solvents evaporate over a pe-

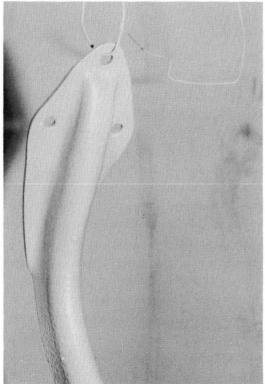

High build primers can be sprayed on thick with little risk of runs and the thick primer coat can be sanded long past the stage where regular primers would be reduced to bare metal.

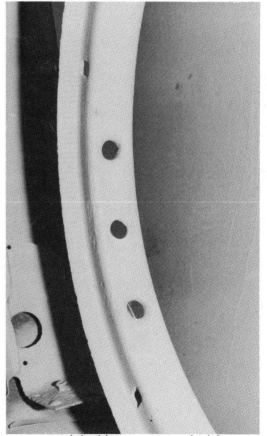

High build primers are ideal for covering curved surfaces like this rim from a Model T wheel.

riod of days, not hours. Although neither Feather Fill nor 100S have sealer properties, this advice also applies to sealer coats that may be sprayed over these primers.

Each of the high build products has advantages and drawbacks. Du Pont 100S is available at auto supply stores carrying the Du Pont product line. Feather Fill and Eliminator are mail-order products advertised in hobby publications. The catalyzed primers are comparably priced; 100S costs about a third less. This cost advantage is offset by the price of thinner that has to be added to 100S. Also, 100S doesn't spray as thick as the polyester products. Eliminator's sealing ability makes it adaptable to wet sanding.

Feather Fill, Eliminator and 100S all have strong odors. You should wear a professional-quality painter's mask and work in a well-ventilated area when spraying any of these products.

High build primers shortcut the repetitious spray and sand refinishing process without sacrificing quality. Properly applied, they quickly transform a rough surface into the smooth foundation necessary for a high-gloss finish.

High build primers make an excellent base for a finish coat of tough Imron polyurethane enamel.

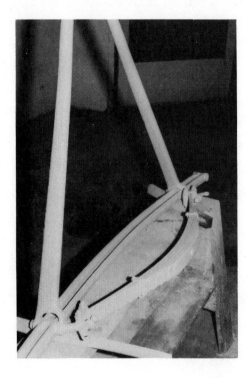

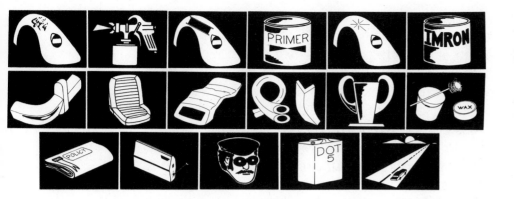

5

Applying A Show Car Finish

Nothing alters a car's appearance more dramatically than a glistening fresh finish. Dull primer may have seemed an improvement over raw metal scarred by repairs, but when you reach the painting stage your car is nearing the end of its restoration or refinishing journey. As a car nears completion, there is a temptation to rush the finishing steps. Yet these are the very steps that shouldn't be hurried. Hold off applying the color coat until you have carefully inspected the primed and sanded finish. Examine the surface closely for any remaining blemishes. Since primer lacks sheen, you will need to inspect the finish under good lighting. Individual parts can usually be carried outside and inspected in sunlight. Rather than looking directly at the finish, sight the surface at an angle. If sanding scratches, grinding marks that have not been smoothed by feather-edge sanding and priming, pits, nicks or blemishes of any kind remain, you should prime and sand these spots again before going on. A final finish can never be smoother than the surface it covers and glossy paint readily exposes a sloppy preparation.

If you don't have access to an air compressor and spray gun you can prime and paint mechanical parts, trim and accessories such as an engine block, valve covers, the air cleaner, horns, hood clamps (on older cars) and similar items using an aerosol spray. Use a special heat-resistant enamel paint on engine castings. On engine accessories such as valve covers and other parts that have a smooth surface you should use a lacquer paint. The plastic spray nozzles on aerosol cans are not designed for automotive spraying, but lacquer can be polished to a glossy sheen with rubbing compound.

Painting small parts with a spray gun gives excellent practice for larger assemblies (the chassis, for example) or for spraying an entire car. Lacquer is easier to spray than enamel, making it a better choice for beginners. Since lacquer sets up fast it is not as likely to run. If orange peel or other signs of amateur spraying develop, they can usually be removed by light sanding with very fine 600 grit sandpaper and polishing with rubbing compound. As a case in point, the national first-prize-winning Model A roadster that my father and I drove to the big Hershey car show in 1958 had been painted by a hobbyist using low-cost spraying equipment. The painter's secret had been to apply a dozen or so coats of lacquer over a very carefully prepared surface. He had sanded the finish between coats and polished the final coat until the paint was mirror smooth.

Spraying enamel requires more finesse. In its nonacrylic versions, enamel is slow drying. As a result, beginning painters are often disappointed by the runs, sags and wrinkly orange-peel surface that develop during their early attempts at spraying enamel. Unlike lacquer, flaws in an enamel finish cannot be sanded and polished away. Unless you are spraying modern acrylic enamel that applies with the ease of lacquer, you should postpone working with enamel until you have developed basic spray painting skills.

Even after all preparation work is completed, several steps remain. First, you should clean up the area where you will be spraying. Spray painting should be done inside a shop or garage, not outdoors, to minimize the chance of dust particles settling in the paint. To avoid cleaning the entire shop each time they paint, some hobbyists partition off a section of their shop for use as a spray booth. As you prepare the painting area, you are strongly advised to install an exhaust fan in a window or doorway to remove overspray and toxic paint fumes.

Don Orr, a New York Boccie instructor and part-time professional restorer, sectioned off his painting area with a sheet of heavy plastic. When he's not spraying, Don rolls the partition up out of his way.

Removing trim before painting gives a more professional-looking finish.

With an exhaust fan, you will also need an air inlet. Furnace filters placed in an open window are effective in preventing dust from being drawn into the painting area. After cleaning you should wet the floor to settle the dust. When all preparations have been made to the painting area, thoroughly wipe the items or surfaces of the car that you will be painting with a tack rag, a specially coated cloth that picks up minute traces of dust. Tack rags are available in auto supply stores.

If you are spraying individual parts such as a steering column, rather than an assembly or the entire car, you will need to support the parts so that you can reach all sides. To minimize the chance of runs, support individual items so that the longest straight or flat surface is horizontal. One way to make sure that all surfaces will be exposed is to suspend the parts by wires.

Fenders, splash aprons and other body panels that may have been removed from the car for straightening and priming prior to refinishing should be painted first on the underside and mating edges, then reattached to the car for final painting. This approach avoids nicks, scratches and gouges that always seem to occur when body parts are bolted together. Where welting is required, attach the fenders loosely so that the welt can be inserted after finish painting.

When you are painting an entire car you will need a systematic approach that will allow you to spray hard-to-reach areas like the center of the hood and top. The accompanying diagram shows two standard painting sequences. Notice that both follow a pattern that leads the painter back to the starting

Two standard painting sequences.

point. When you assemble the spray gun after mixing the paint, be sure to position the air vent on the canister lid so that it is opposite the spray nozzle. Otherwise paint will drip out of the gun onto the hood, top and trunk as you hold the gun at a right angle to the horizontal surface.

As you prepare for painting, you need to know the different mixing and spraying requirements that apply to lacquer and enamel. These specifications are listed below.

	LACQUER	**ENAMEL**
Reduction	125/150% lacquer thinner	33⅓% enamel reducer
Air pressure at the spray gun	35–45 psi	55–60 psi
Gun distance from the work	6–8 inches	8–10 inches
Number of coats	4 to 7 double coats	2 to 3 coats
Flash drying time	5 minutes between coats 1 and 2 10 to 15 minutes between coats 2 and 3	10 to 30 minutes

After mixing, paint should be poured into the spray gun cup through a cone-shaped filter available at auto supply stores. In an emergency, a nylon stocking makes an acceptable substitute. Remember to spray only in a well-ventilated area and wear a painter's mask, available at most auto supply stores, for protection from toxic vapors.

On the show circuit, it is not uncommon to hear glossy finishes described as having so many coats of "hand-rubbed"

Stone chips and repaired areas must be feather-edge sanded and covered with a coat of primer, then sanded again for a smooth finish.

lacquer. Hand-rubbing refers to a process where several coats of paint are applied, allowed to dry and sanded with very fine 600 grit sandpaper. The surface is then wiped clean and several more coats are applied. This sanding and painting process continues until as many as twenty coats have been applied. Following a final light sanding, the last coat is polished with a rubbing compound.

In addition to producing a mirror finish, this elaborate painting and sanding ritual results in a thick layer of paint that is difficult to touch up when chips and mars occur. It is also subject to cracking if the car is stored in cold or fluctuating temperatures. Seven double coats of lacquer sprayed over a well-prepared surface with a blending solvent added to the final coat will produce equal gloss on a thinner paint layer that is easier to touch up and poses less risk of cracking.

Note that instructions for spraying lacquer specify "double" coats. To apply a double coat, the painter sweeps the spray gun across the work surface left to right, then reverses the pattern and sweeps the same area right to left. On the next pass the painter lowers the gun slightly so that the spray pattern recovers fifty percent of the last sweep, in effect applying two coats in one painting cycle.

Adding clear lacquer or a blending solvent to the final lacquer coat increases depth and gives excellent gloss. Following mixing instructions on the can—usually one part blending solvent to one part reduced color—spray one or two medium coats at 35 psi. Allow fifteen minutes drying time if a second coat is to be applied.

A carefully prepared primer base is the secret to a show car finish.

Newspapers can be used to mask window glass and trim. Be sure to tape overlapping sheets so that paint spray doesn't blow underneath the paper.

Enamel dries more slowly than lacquer, so runs are more likely to develop when a heavy layer is applied. Consequently, an enamel finish seldom consists of more than two or three coats. To spray enamel successfully, first apply a light "tack coat." Wait fifteen minutes or so for the tack coat to set, then spray a wet second coat. The tack coat will hold the heavier second layer, allowing for depth and gloss. Allow twenty to thirty minutes for this paint buildup to dry before applying a third coat. In most cases the first two coats will be sufficient. The trick to spraying enamel is to build up a glossy finish without creating runs. Sensing the moment when enamel starts to run is a skill painters learn with practice.

Runs and sags that develop when you spray that little bit extra aren't the end of the world if you are painting individual parts, but they are a colossal nuisance if you are painting an entire car. To remove runs, you simply back up one step. First, though, the paint has to dry. If you try to sand enamel while the paint is still fresh, the finish will roll up in little curds, glaze the sandpaper and leave a lumpy surface. After the enamel dries thoroughly, the runs can be sanded smooth and the spraying process repeated, beginning with the tack coat.

Enamel can't be rubbed out like lacquer, but it can be polished. There is an important distinction in terms here. Rubbing compound abrades like fine sandpaper. With lacquer, rubbing compound produces a glossy finish, but when rubbing compound is used on enamel, the result is a dull, lifeless look. Even polishing compound, a product that is available at most discount store car-care departments, can dull enamel unless the polish is applied in a watery consistency. The right product for polishing enamel is Liquid Ebony, a mail-order item available from Lentinforese Automobile Restoration Supplies, P.O. Box 203, Brooklyn, New York 11228.

If the grille is removed, place a piece of cardboard in front of the radiator to prevent a paint build-up that could reduce the radiator's cooling efficiency.

Few amateur painters realize that painting conditions and spraying techniques can alter the shade of the final finish and cause color variations on parts that are painted separately, or from panel to panel if you are painting the entire car. Shop temperature, the speed at which you sweep the spray gun, air pressure at the gun and amount of thinner or reducer added to the paint all have an effect on the paint color. Increasing temperature, gun distance, pressure and solvent ratio produce lighter colors. Decreasing these variables has the reverse effect. Of course it is possible for the change in one factor to cancel the effect of another. For example, if the sun comes out while you are painting and warms the shop five degrees by the time you have sprayed half the car, but you stop to refill the spray gun at that point and add slightly less thinner, the two conditions should balance each other. Knowledge of the spraying techniques that can cause color change is important to avoid a patchwork painting effect or to touch up slightly faded paint.

Touch-up painting is a job every restorer tries to avoid; yet it seems that newly painted cars have a magnetic attraction for dings and scratches. You can park your family car in a supermarket parking lot every Saturday without having grocery carts run into it or other shoppers pull up so close that they can't open their car doors without scraping yours. Not so with a freshly painted collector car. Grocery carts will appear to be aimed by kamikaze pilots and wherever you park your car, even in a far corner of the lot, will be just six inches from another shopper's favorite spot. Touch-up painting is inevitable and time consuming, but it's nice to know that chips and scratches can be repaired.

Limiting spot repair to a panel, a door or fender, for example, makes the job easier. Otherwise, new paint has to be blended into the existing finish. Lacquer is softer and therefore easier to touch up than enamel. In fact, a seasoned alkaline

Lightly sand the last coat of primer before painting. Note that the taillights and the rear bumper have also been removed.

enamel finish may have hardened to the extent that it can't be satisfactorily spot painted; acrylic enamel usually can. Prepare the surface for touch-up painting as you would for applying an overall finish coat. Clean the area you will be repainting, then scuff the finish by light sanding. Smooth the finish around damaged areas by feather-edge sanding. After sanding, prime the touch-up area and cover any surface imperfections with glazing putty. Smooth the primer with light sanding using very fine 600 grit sandpaper. (Coarser grit sandpaper can leave scratch marks that will show in the finish.) If you are repainting a panel or fender, you will need to mask the surrounding area to protect the finish from overspray. Mask along panel seams or moldings, much as you would if you were applying a two-tone finish. Do not mask off an area within the actual panel you are repainting. These preparation steps, minus priming, also apply to painting contrasting colors on moldings and reveals.

The spraying technique for touch-up work differs from that used to paint the whole car. The first coat is sprayed dry in a small circular pattern extending several inches beyond the touch-up area. If you are painting over primer you may need to apply several dry coats to build up the color to match the surrounding finish. When the paint is dry, wipe the touch-up area with a tack rag, then apply a wet mist coat of thinner, or thinned paint with blending solvent added, to blend the spot repair into the surrounding finish. Once the paint dries, remove the masking paper and tape—but don't rush this last step.

Wet sanding between coats with 600 grit sandpaper helps assure a mirror finish.

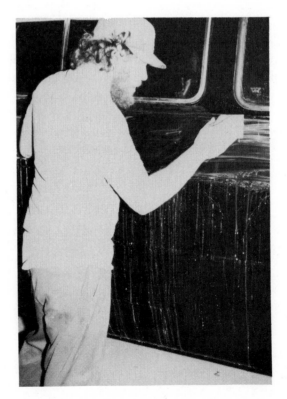

Blending solvent is only one of many additives designed to extend the versatility of modern paints. Adding fish-eye eliminator prevents a walnut burl or fish-eye effect that can be caused by traces of silicone wax that were not removed in the preparation steps. Hardener added to acrylic enamel gives a faster drying time and a more chemical-resistant finish. The latter factor may be important if your car will be parked outside. Flexible additives designed for painting plastic bumper aprons on late model cars have a range of applications on parts that are subject to vibration or flex. Vinyl paints are also available to touch up worn or discolored upholstery panels and vinyl tops.

Hobbyists who don't have access to spray painting equipment can still refinish smaller individual parts by applying a baked enamel finish. Although manufacturers paint entire cars with baked enamel, a hobbyist's baking facility is normally a kitchen oven, which limits the size of the parts. The first step in applying a glossy baked-enamel finish is to prepare the items as you would if they were being spray painted. Be sure to disassemble lights, horns or any other items containing electrical components before baking. Sand the primer and apply a medium coat of enamel with a fine camel-hair brush. Neither the primer nor the finish coat should be applied too thick or the paint may blister. Place the freshly painted parts in the kitchen oven and bake them at 350°F for one half to three quarters of an hour. As the paint bakes it will flow into a hard, glossy, factory-looking finish. If you use this technique, be sure to provide plenty of ventilation while the parts are baking since the paint will give off a strong odor.

Like anything young and tender, a new finish requires special care. Allow the finish to cure before washing, and then always wash your car in the shade using cool water, avoiding either very hot or very cold water. Never wipe off a dry finish or park your car under trees or in areas where soot will collect on the finish. With care and occasional spot repair the finish can be kept looking new for years.

FOUR TOP NOTCH REFINISHING MANUALS OFTEN MISSED BY HOBBYISTS
Instruction and practice are the two keys to improving any skill—and painting is no exception. Major manufacturers of refinishing products publish top-quality manuals intended in part to promote their products and, more importantly, to teach amateurs how to use them and keep professionals up to date.

A Guide To Better Automotive Refinishing
Document #A2325
The Martin-Senour Company
5422 Dansher Road
Countryside, IL 60525

Du Pont Refinish Shop Manual
Document #E-40832
E. I. Du Pont De Nemours and Co.
Refinish Sales
Wilmington, DE 19898

Ditzler Repaint Manual
Document #7699
PPG Industries, Inc.
Ditzler Automotive Finishes
2155 West Big Beaver Road
P.O. Box 3510
Troy, MI 48084

Air Spray Manual
Document #TD10-1
Binks Manufacturing Company
9201 W. Belmont Ave.
Franklin Park, IL 60131

6

Imron, The Toughest Paint On The Block

Imron is a Du Pont product. The folks with the good chemistry call it the paint with the "Wet Look That Lasts." We've all seen the gloss a film of water gives to even chalky, dull paint—Imron always looks just washed. This glossy sheen is just one of the paint's qualities. Toughness is the other. To illustrate Imron's resilience, Du Pont sprayed the paint on a sheet of aluminum foil, crumpled the foil in a ball, then smoothed it out again. The paint coating stayed bonded to the foil. (Try that trick sometime with nitrocellulose lacquer.) Bryan Allen coated the *Gossamer Albatross*, a feather-light pedal plane, with Imron and from its looks the paint may have been all that held the craft's gauze-like structure together.

Because of its limited color selection and the fact that the paint is not an OEM automotive finish, Imron is seldom used as an exterior coating on collector cars. However, Imron has generated enthusiasm among collectors who have sprayed the paint on chassis parts. Lacquer provides a glossy finish, but chips when struck by road debris and is easily stained by dripping gas, grease and oil. Enamel is tougher and more chemical resistant than lacquer, but lacks the gloss. Imron combines the best qualities of both. An Imron finish can be wiped clean of grease, oil and road grime with gasoline without even dulling the paint's "wet look." A glistening coat of black Imron both protects and beautifies a car's partially hidden running gear and other chassis parts.

Imron is most commonly used on trucks and four-wheel-drive rigs. A hometown bodyshop sprays four-wheel-drive vehicles with Imron regularly. Its customers are wild about it. To demonstrate Imron's toughness, the painters set out four-wheel-ing in a gold metalflake Bronco soon after the Imron coating had dried. They spotted a wild raspberry patch on a hillside and charged through it. I was sure the finish would be a maze of scratches, but when they returned the paint still looked flawless. "Imron is tough and flexible," the bodymen explained. "So it's resistant to most of the conditions that mar a car's finish."

The best preparation for Imron is to strip the parts to bare metal, then prime and fill all surface imperfections. The polyurethane paint can be applied over enamel but should not be sprayed over lacquer. Imron bonds well to Du Pont 100S multipurpose primer sealer, a product described in the high build primers chapter. The catalyzed high build primers, Feather Fill and Eliminator, also make a good base for Imron. Du Pont recommends using Corlar, a special epoxy primer, as an undercoat. Remember that the spray gun must be flushed and cleaned with lacquer thinner immediately after using catalyzed primers, Corlar or Imron. If you allow the catalyzed or epoxy products to dry in the gun orifices, you may wind up buying a new spraying outfit.

Safe use of Imron demands that you wear a charcoal-activated professional painter's mask, spray in a well ventilated area and avoid breathing the paint vapors. In toxic doses, Imron's fumes can induce Acute Respiratory Distress Syndrome (ARDS), a potentially critical condition resulting from intense irritation of the lungs and consequent internal secretion that can, in fact, cause death. In order for ARDS to occur, Imron would have to be sprayed in an unventilated area by a painter who did not wear a mask and inhaled the vapors while the paint dried. None of the modern paint products can be safely applied under these conditions.

Imron mixes with its activator in a 3:1 ratio by volume. Using a kitchen mixing glass assures the proper proportions. Imron should be sprayed only in a well-ventilated area and the painter must wear a charcoal-activated respirator.

Imron mixes 3:1 by volume with its activator, Du Pont 192S. The mixture will harden in about eight hours so you should plan ahead and mix just enough paint for the job at hand. A kitchen measuring cup works well to mix paint and hardener in accurate proportions. (Since the polyurethane paint will dissolve a plastic cup, you should use a glass measure.) If the paint is used shortly after mixing with the activator, no further reduction is necessary. As the pot life begins to expire, the paint will thicken. If you are mixing a large quantity of Imron, you should have a can of Du Pont 8485 S reducer on hand to thin the paint as thickening occurs.

Imron is sprayed much like regular enamel. For solid colors, set the pressure regulator for fifty pounds of air pressure at the spray gun. If you are spraying an Imron metallic, you should set the regulator to supply sixty-five pounds of pressure. Spray an initial medium coat and wait ten to twenty minutes for the paint to become tacky. Leave the painting area while the paint dries to minimize your exposure to Imron's vapor. Apply a full second coat over the tack base. If a third coat is needed, wait another ten to twenty minutes before spraying. For greater flow, you can reduce the third coat fifteen percent with Du Pont 8485 S.

Properly applied, Imron sprays smooth, blends evenly and holds firmly. As the paint dries, its luster seems to grow. The parts in the accompanying photos, a Model A front axle and wishbone, brake backing plates and fender brackets, sparkle with Imron's glossy radiance. For added brilliance you can spray a cover coat of Imron clear. You can also apply Imron clear as a protective coating over a regular enamel finish. If the finish has dried more than thirty-six hours, it should be lightly scuff sanded before the Imron clear coat is applied.

Placing the work in a horizontal position minimizes the chances of runs or sags.

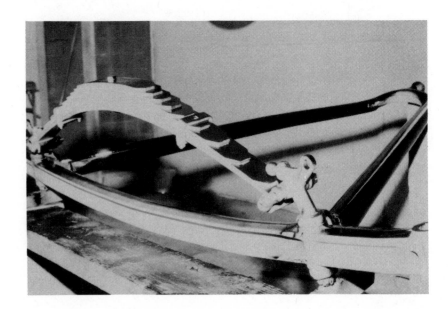

Du Pont's Imron isn't the only polyurethane enamel on the market. Ditzler makes a competitive product called Durethane and Martin-Senour markets Nitram. Imron appeared first and is generally better known, but all three paints have comparable specifications. Preparation and spraying instructions for the Ditzler and Martin-Senour polyurethane products are similar to Imron. Ditzler recommends spraying Durethane enamel over a Durethane primer base. Martin-Senour recommends coating bare surfaces with Vinyl Wash Primer and existing finishes with Primeez Primer-Surfacer prior to applying Nitram.

The parentage of polyurethane enamels can be traced to the aircraft industry, where temperature extremes, high abrasion and the importance of smart-looking finishes demand tough paints. The air-dry polyurethane products developed by Du Pont, Ditzler and Martin-Senour meet demanding aircraft industry standards at prices slightly above the cost of regular automotive paints.

There are some collectors who would coat the chassis of their cars with boot black if that were the original finish; they seem ethically opposed to using high-technology products for restoring old cars. Others who hope to go through a car's restoration only once use the best products available. For this group, which includes me, it makes sense to coat chassis parts with the toughest, best-looking paint available, namely a polyurethane enamel such as Imron.

Imron should be allowed 15 to 20 minutes curing time between coats. When the paint sets, large parts like this front-end assembly can be tipped on end to coat the underside. Note the large ventilation panels in the rear of the spray area.

The freshly painted Model A backing plate sparkles, showing Imron's jewellike "wet look."

7

A Plating Primer

Several years ago a friend who worked as a high school guidance counselor was struggling to fit his old car hobby into the financial demands of raising a family. He managed to rejuvenate the bumpers on his Model A Ford roadster for a $1.98 cash outlay. Sunshine sparkling off the shiny bars added a finished look to the recently repainted car. "Who did the plating?" I nearly blurted out before a wrinkle and a seam in the bumper face gave the trick away. The bright extensions were tightly wrapped in kitchen foil, carefully scotchtaped to the backside.

Kitchen foil "plating" may be one step up from aluminum paint but it is hardly a satisfactory alternative to the lustrous chrome plating that highlights a collector car. The plating process is a mystery to most hobbyists and rumors of careless platers who lose items or buff away distinctive markings and contours on diecast trim, combined with generally high prices, have made most hobbyists somewhat apprehensive about sending their parts out for plating.

Nearly everyone who has doted over a collector car has experienced what they feel to be substandard chrome plating. Yet while this experience seems to be a common bond among car fanciers, the stunning brightwork seen on show cars is equally familiar. One solution to the search for quality chrome plating is to ask the owner of a car with flawless brightwork for the name of the shop that did the plating. Personal referrals can help locate a reliable plater, but you should also know what to look for as you scout a plating shop.

For car hobbyists living in America's industrial heartland, plating shops are often as close as the Yellow Pages. But for many others the nearest plater may be located hundreds of miles away. Whether you deliver your parts directly to a plating shop, or ship them, you should always talk first with the plater. Perhaps that's the reason why word of Glen Schultz's plating shop in tiny East Topsham, Vermont, spread through the north country like a spring grass fire. Glen loves to talk. Despite the fact that his shop was stacked with tubing for modern tables he had no trouble recognizing the parts John and I brought. "Yup, I've plated plenty of Model A spark levers," was his response.

Vermonters have managed to side-step the twentieth century race to nowhere. They've kept time for fishin' and talkin'. In fact, nobody does business in Vermont without talking, about the weather, always plenty of that, and taxes, "Terrible, ain't they?" Glen wanted to talk about our parts and what we were working on—and he wanted us to see his shop. Items from vintage and late model cars alike lined the shelves and stuck out of boxes shoved under chairs in the bookkeeper's office. We walked past the plating tanks on duckboards that led into the buffing room. There we met Gary Garone, Glen's partner, buffing a speedboat muffler the size of a Civil War cannon. Over the noise of the buffing wheel Glen Schultz described the vintage speedboat that a customer was restoring as familiarly as one would talk about a friend's pet project.

To Schultz, the secret of customer satisfaction lay in communication. Sending out parts without talking to the plater is a bad practice, he insisted. Hobbyists should always talk with the plater about their parts; otherwise they may expect finish quality that the plater can't give. The first thing a customer should establish is whether the parts are worth plating. About twenty-five percent of the items hobbyists send to plating shops have deteriorated beyond the point where they can be economically replated. This figure holds true especially for diecast trim.

Diecast is a manmade metal, Schultz explained. Because pot metal, as diecast is often called, is porous, it often absorbs minute traces of liquid when immersed in the initial copper plating solution. If this happens, the chrome finish may look great for a month or more before tiny bubbles begin to develop

In preparation for buffing and replating, the plating layers are stripped off by reverse electrolysis.

under the plating. Asked how hobbyists can be sure of getting quality plating on diecast trim, Schultz recommended starting with items that have as few pits as possible. These pieces can be buffed smooth with minimum cutting and will be less likely to absorb fluids during the plating process. "If diecast were a nonporous metal, the plating never would have pitted to begin with," he added, "because pot metal is not prone to corrosion."

During the conversation with the plater, a customer should explain what he or she wants, then should let the plater explain the results that can be expected. "Plating quality depends to a great extent on the condition of the parts the customer brings in," Schultz stated. "When I hear people complaining about poor plating," he added, "the first question I ask is, 'What shape were the parts in before plating?' Trying to get a smooth chrome finish on pitted parts is like me giving you a screwdriver to pound a nail with. You'd do a lot better job with a hammer. Good plating rests fifty percent with the parts and fifty percent with the plater. A good plater is interested in his work and one measure of this is whether he cares to talk with his customers."

Plating isn't spread on with a putty knife. Trim pieces have to be buffed smooth in order for replating to make them look like new. Quality plating depends on the depth of the pits, the thickness of the base metal, the skill of the craftsmen buffing the parts and the length of time the replated items spend in the plating tanks. Trim parts can be immersed in the copper plating tanks for as long as five or six hours to build up a thick plating layer that can be buffed to fill pits and other surface imperfections. Quality plating results from a triple layer of copper, nickel and chrome; a thick coating of the first two metals is the key to a rich chrome finish.

Careful buffing is the secret of restorative plating.

Many hobbyists think that in order to get quality plating, they've got to buff their own parts. It isn't true. Chrome is a very hard metal that is virtually impossible to remove by buffing. Before parts can be buffed, the chrome layer has to be stripped off by electrolysis. Sandblasting or other abrasive methods should never be used to remove chrome plating. "Let the plater buff your parts," Glen Schultz advised. "He knows how." As I watched Schultz and his partner work their heavy-duty buffing wheels, I wondered where the rumors of platers skipping this key step started. "If a customer insists on buffing his own parts, he will have to accept a plated finish that reflects the work he has done," Schultz remarked. Proper buffing cuts away base metal to remove pits. Applying a chrome finish is like spraying bare metal with clear lacquer. Plating doesn't hide imperfections.

Customers can assist the plater and help assure quality plating by completely disassembling their parts and making necessary repairs. Convertible top latches and plated lights are common examples of items that should be disassembled before taking them to a plater. If you inspect items like these closely, you should soon discover how they come apart. Latches are often held together by small pins that can be driven out with a punch. Be sure to save the pins for later reassembly. Plated

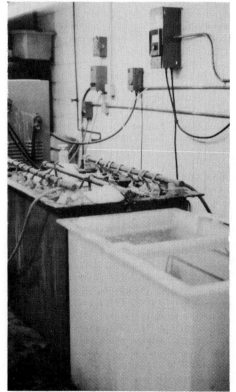

Base layers of copper and nickel give the distinctive bluish luster found in quality chrome plating.

Plating time determines the thickness of each base layer. Badly pitted parts are often recycled through the copper plating/buffing process to obtain a smooth surface for the chrome finish.

199

lights should be completely disassembled, including removing the light bucket from its mounting bracket.

Hubcaps for cars made in the thirties and forties are often covered by chrome plated or stainless steel skins. Stainless steel skins can often be straightened and buffed to look like new. This process is described near the end of this chapter. For re-plating, chromed skins should be removed by carefully straightening the skin where it wraps around the edge of the hubcap. Plated skins can usually be recognized by traces of rust. If you've inspected the hubcap carefully and can't decide whether it is stainless or chrome, polish a portion of the cap with chrome cleaner. Chrome shines with a more brilliant luster than stainless.

Although shops that offer restorative plating may make repairs on rusted or damaged parts, most commercial plating shops won't. So if you are planning to send your parts to a commercial plater, you will either have to repair rusted or cracked metal yourself or find a shop to do the work for you. Thin metal parts like hubcap skins that are peppered with holes usually can't be repaired and should be replaced. On thicker metal such as a chrome plated windshield frame, small holes can usually be filled by brazing. Finish the repair by filing the braze smooth with the surrounding metal. Cracks in thin metal headlight or taillight shells can often be repaired by silver sol-

Thorough washing precedes each step of the plating process.

Fresh chrome plating is honey-colored. The bright chrome luster appears when the parts are rinsed with water.

dering or very careful brazing. Even broken pieces of pot metal trim can be mended using special Lumiweld rods designed for welding zinc diecast and aluminum. (Sources of Lumiweld rods are included in the supplier listing in the appendix.) Although easy-to-follow instructions are included with the rods, you should practice on scrap parts before attempting to repair a piece of original trim.

"Buffing parts in preparation for plating is like planing a board. And you can't plane a board smooth if it's full of nails," Schultz explained. That's the reason it is so important for hobbyists to disassemble items before plating. It is also important to point out logos, part numbers or other markings that the plater should not remove during buffing. It is advisable to circle markings with a magic marker as a reminder for the plater to buff that section lightly.

For the average time-worn, dog-eared old car part, the plating process begins with chemical cleaning to remove paint, grease and other coatings. Next, all existing plating layers are stripped off by reverse electrolysis. Chrome plating is removed in one tank, nickel in another. The item then passes to an acid vat for derusting. These preparation steps are an essential part of the plating process. As with early stages of restoration, the plater has to undo before he can renew.

Once the parts are stripped to bare metal, they can be checked for previously unnoticed flaws. If you are having a

Quality plating is distinguished by prompt service, careful accounting to prevent lost parts, and a deep luster that seems to shine out of the metal itself.

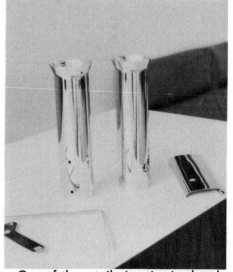

One of these tail pipe tips is plated with show chrome, the other with a standard high-quality chrome finish. The careful examination necessary to tell the two apart may not justify the extra cost of super-quality show plating.

commercial plater replate your parts you may want to inspect and make any necessary repairs at this stage. Otherwise, in a commercial shop, the parts proceed to the buffing room where seventy-five percent of the plating effort takes place. Buffing is a craft. Items are buffed to remove pits; but soft diecast trim parts, particularly, have to be buffed very carefully to avoid cutting away the item's shape and contours.

Cost constraints often determine when the parts are ready for plating. Customers shouldn't leave a plating shop without establishing quality objectives for their parts with the plater and receiving a cost estimate for the work to be done. The actual plating fee should not exceed the estimate by more than ten percent. A plater who grossly overruns his estimate without notifying the customer that he has encountered unexpected problems and receiving authorization to proceed violates the customer's trust and doesn't warrant further business.

At the same time, hobbyists should realize that plating is a labor-intensive operation and as a result, restorative plating can be costly. Glen Schultz used the 1935 Ford radiator grille hanging in his bookkeeper's office to illustrate this point. "To make an item like this look new, I could spend a week polishing each grille slat with a hand-held buffing wheel," Schultz said. "If I spent that amount of time, what would the customer say when I showed him the bill? I estimated $150 for plating this piece, so I'll soak it in acid to take off the rust and buff it so that it will look very good from a straight-on view, but it won't be like new—for $150 it can't."

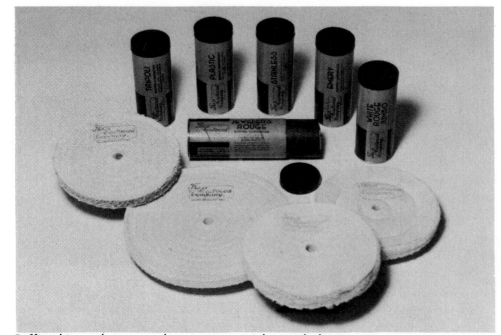

Buffing kits and compounds to restore stainless and aluminum trim are available from Sears or hobby suppliers.

After old plating has been removed, necessary repairs have been made and the parts have been buffed, they are dunked in detergent to remove the buffing residue. Following cleaning, they proceed through a second reverse electrolysis bath to purge any remaining contamination. From the electrolysis bath, the items pass through a water rinse, then are dipped in a mild acid solution for about two minutes. The cleaning procedure is necessary to prepare parts for the first plating step. Any contamination, even fingerprints or dried-on detergent, will show through the chrome finish.

Before passing to the plating tanks, the parts are rinsed again to remove all traces of acid. Acid contamination in the plating solutions could release deadly cyanide gas. Consequently, platers take great care to make sure that parts are thoroughly rinsed after acid cleaning and between each step of the plating process. The amount of time spent in the plating tanks varies with the condition of the parts. Copper plating can last from twenty minutes to four hours. The copper layer has three purposes: It provides a suitable base for the nickel layer; it enhances the luster of nickel plate; and, because copper is soft, the copper layer can be buffed to fill pits in the base metal. Badly pitted trim pieces may require several sessions in the copper tanks and buffing after each pass through the copper plating cycle.

By repeating the copper plating and buffing steps, restorative plating shops are able to turn out a high-quality finish even on severely deteriorated parts. Shops that specialize in restorative plating advertise in car hobby magazines. The process is expensive but for hard-to-replace items it may be the only satisfactory way to renew badly deteriorated brightwork. Wherever possible, you will be money ahead to hunt for better

Attaching a buffing wheel to an electric motor scavanged from a discarded refrigerator, freezer or dryer makes an inexpensive tool for polishing and restoring brightwork.

parts rather than pay the labor cost entailed in restorative plating.

Most commercial platers will not take the effort to buff and plate parts more than once. These shops generally function on a production basis and survive by high-volume work. Replating car bumpers and odd trim pieces for car hobbyists has to fit in around the edges of their production schedules. For this reason many commercial plating shops aren't enthusiastic about replating old car parts, which is the first sign of trouble. Never plead with a plater to take business he doesn't want. When commercial plating shops are cool toward car buffs, it's because doing a customer's small job right means more than just interrupting their production work. They know from experience that hobbyists generally expect high-quality plating on substandard parts. For optimum quality and to take advantage of the cost savings production shops offer, the parts sent to a commercial plater should be in reasonably well-preserved condition.

Quality plating is distinguished by careful buffing and a penetrating bluish luster that seems to lie deep in the chrome finish. This rich coloring results from layering thick coats of copper and nickel under the chrome. Nickel plating takes about twenty minutes. Afterward, the parts are rinsed again, then pass to the chrome tanks for the final step. Chrome plating requires only a few minutes. When parts come out of the chrome tanks they are covered with a glistening butter-colored film. The shiny chrome finish appears after the final rinse.

Commercial platers like Glen Schultz attempt to give hobbyists maximum quality for their plating dollar. Ultra-high-quality show plating, sometimes called ten-point chrome, requires more attention than commercial plating shops can give without disrupting their production schedule. Custom platers that spe-

Aluminum parts, like these Model A light-switch castings, are easily restored by buffing. The plastic horn button, too, can be renewed to a glossy finish with light polishing.

cialize in restorative chrome plating can provide a top-quality ten-point finish, but the extra effort for perfection is reflected in the price. The labor required to improve an item's quality five percent may double the plating cost. If you want top-quality plating for show purposes, you may be money ahead to purchase new-old-stock chrome trim and have the parts replated to a high-luster finish. Whether you are using a commercial or a custom plater, you should sample the shop's service with a small order before making a large commitment.

Replating isn't always necessary to restore a car's brightwork. Where dealer replacement and reproduction bumpers and other chrome trim are still available, as is the case for some of the late model collector cars such as the popular Mustangs, replacing dull and dented trim is generally cheaper than having the old parts replated. To determine whether replacement trim is still available for your car, call a dealer's parts department. If new trim isn't available through the manufacturer, check hobby magazines such as *Hemmings Motor News, Cars & Parts* or *Old Cars Weekly* for ads featuring reproduction trim parts.

Stainless steel and aluminum trim can be rejuvenated without a professional's services. All you need to restore the satin luster of aluminum and stainless trim is a buffing wheel and assorted polishing compounds. The process itself is straightforward and is easily learned with a little practice. Buffing wheels are available from hobby suppliers or can be ordered from a mail-order catalog such as Sears. Several different types of buffing wheels are available. You will need at least two: one for fast cutting, another for finish polishing. To mount the buffing wheels you can either purchase a buffer motor or use a salvaged appliance motor. If you use an appliance motor you will need to purchase an inexpensive threaded shaft extension to mount the buffing wheels. This item is also listed in the Sears

Before buffing metal or plastic parts, the buffing wheel has to be coated with compound. Compounds of varying composition are designated by the color of the bar.

catalog. Besides buffing wheels and motor you will need an assortment of buffing compounds, which can be ordered from hobby suppliers.

To restore tarnished aluminum or dulled stainless trim to its original luster, simply coat the buffing wheel with compound, securely grip the item that needs polishing and hold it against the rotating wheel. It is important to note that different metals require different buffing compounds. In addition, buffing normally progresses from a coarse to a mild abrasive. The accompanying chart lists the recommended compounds for buffing different materials at the various polishing stages. The first polishing stage removes the oxide coating from aluminum and scratch marks from stainless. Successive buffing with milder abrasives is needed to restore the metal's original luster.

Buffing also enables hobbyists to restore dented and scratched stainless steel trim. To straighten damaged stainless steel headlight rims, hubcaps or trim spears, use the same approach you would take to smooth dents in body panels. Remove the dents by gently pounding the raised areas with a body hammer. Since pounding against a body dolly can scratch the metal, you should use a rubber pad placed on your workbench or a small sandbag to absorb the hammer blows as you tap the dented area. Dents in rounded contours or creases can be straightened using a dowel or wooden wedge cut to fit the metal's original shape. When the dents appear to be straightened, file the pounding marks smooth, then sand the metal with 100 grit sandpaper to remove the file marks. Filing and sanding may reveal depressions and raised spots that still need to be straightened. Work the damaged area until it is perfectly smooth.

In buffing an item, such as the light-switch casting shown here, hold the part against the down-sweep side of the wheel. Apply slight pressure while moving the part back and forth across the wheel. The oxidized or tarnished finish is quickly removed, replaced by shining metal.

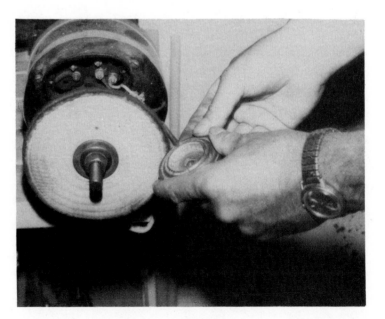

Since trim parts are generally made of thin-gauge metal, be careful not to file too deeply.

Even though the metal will still look rough at this stage, buffing quickly removes the scratch marks and restores the original luster. Before buffing, sand the damaged area with 600 grit sandpaper to remove the deeper sanding marks. Trim that is scratched but not dented, can be prepared for polishing by filing and sanding. Begin the polishing sequence with a coarse emery abrasive. After the scratches and file marks have been removed, polish the item with white rouge to a smooth satin finish. When you're through, no one could tell that damage ever existed.

To preserve a car's brightwork, avoid using abrasive cleaners. Instead, polish the plating with Glasswax, a cleaning product commonly available in grocery stores. To keep shiny metal from tarnishing, coat the car's trim with paste wax at least twice a year. Wax also helps protect a car's plating during storage. When a car is placed in prolonged storage, you should coat the plated trim with a light oil film or a thin layer of Vaseline.

Glistening brightwork is one of a car's most attractive features. For satisfying plating, remember to start with the best possible parts, make sure the plater knows the quality you desire, find out ahead of time what problems the plater foresees, and be sure to get a price estimate before giving the go-ahead. Polishing aluminum and stainless trim is a job you can do yourself.

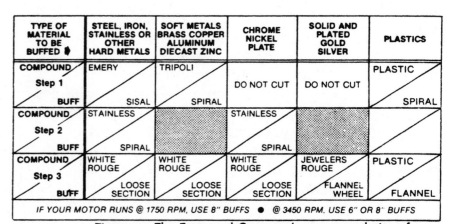

TYPE OF MATERIAL TO BE BUFFED	STEEL, IRON, STAINLESS OR OTHER HARD METALS	SOFT METALS BRASS COPPER ALUMINUM DIECAST ZINC	CHROME NICKEL PLATE	SOLID AND PLATED GOLD SILVER	PLASTICS
COMPOUND Step 1 — BUFF	EMERY / SISAL	TRIPOLI / SPIRAL	DO NOT CUT	DO NOT CUT	PLASTIC / SPIRAL
COMPOUND Step 2 — BUFF	STAINLESS / SPIRAL		STAINLESS / SPIRAL		
COMPOUND Step 3 — BUFF	WHITE ROUGE / LOOSE SECTION	WHITE ROUGE / LOOSE SECTION	WHITE ROUGE / LOOSE SECTION	JEWELERS ROUGE / FLANNEL WHEEL	PLASTIC / FLANNEL

IF YOUR MOTOR RUNS @ 1750 RPM, USE 8" BUFFS ● @ 3450 RPM. USE 6" OR 8" BUFFS

These are The Eastwood Company's recommendations for selecting the correct type of buffing wheel and compound.

8
Installing Seat Upholstery Kits

In recent years vinyl upholstery has become a popular alternative to leather and cloth interiors. Modern embossing techniques have given vinyl panels and seat upholstery a luxury image earlier leather imitations lacked. Good looks, combined with favorable price and the fact that vinyl cleans easily, have made it the standard interior material for most late model sports and sporty-looking cars. Of course, vinyl does have shortcomings. The plastic-coated fabric stretches in hot weather and shrinks in cold. As a result, vinyl-covered seats develop a "baggy" look with use and often tear, either in the seat cushion or along the seams.

It comes as no surprise that car interiors wear principally in the driver's seat—cars really are personal transportation. The difficulty in repairing vinyl seats comes with matching embossed designs. Trim shops can usually repair torn seams and can often replace worn panels with matching fabric, but unless you are refitting the seats on a pickup truck or an older car with naugahyde-style leatherette, trim shops are not often successful in duplicating original vinyl seat coverings. For Mustangs, Corvairs, Corvettes, Triumphs, MG's and other sports and sporty cars that were fitted with vinyl-clad bucket seats, upholstery kits are widely available to restore worn seats with original-style coverings.

If you own a late model collector car with bucket seats that need recovering, you can locate sources of seat upholstery kits for your make and model of car by checking ads in hobby magazines such as *Hemmings Motor News* or *Cars & Parts*. A partial list of upholstery kit suppliers is also included in the appendix. In addition to seat upholstery, these suppliers carry carpets, refurbished or reproduction door panels and, in some cases, headliners, dash pads, even optional leather seat coverings.

The popularity of upholstery kits shows the interest hobbyists have in tackling refinishing jobs that formerly had to be turned over to professionals. Kits have been successful primarily because they make it possible for novices to install professional-looking original seat and other interior coverings and save money in the process. Although installing seat upholstery takes more skill than slipping on a set of seat covers, the job isn't complex. The instructions detailed here describe the process for recovering early Mustang seats, but the steps apply in general to all types of vinyl or leather-covered bucket seats. If you are installing an upholstery kit for the first time, you'll need to pay close attention during disassembly. It often helps to write out a description of each step. Later you can use these notes as instructions for reassembly.

Tools needed to install seat upholstery kits include common workshop items: Phillips and slotted screwdrivers, pliers, a socket set or assorted box wrenches, side-cutters (also called cutter-nose pliers) and a utility or other sharp knife. The rings that hold the upholstery covering in place are easier to install if you use special hog-ring upholstery pliers, but you can get the job done using regular pliers if you don't have the hog-ring variety. Hog-ring pliers are inexpensive and worth the price. They are often sold by auto supply stores and are available from H. C. Fastener Company, RT 2, #27, Alvarado, Texas. Besides these

After removing the bucket seats, detach the seatbacks and frames.

Side trim unscrews from the seatback. Keep an empty coffee can nearby to save screws and other small items.

tools and the upholstery kit, you should also have the following supplies on hand:

A. A sheet of foam rubber approximately one-inch thick, generally available from an Army-Navy store

B. A can of 3M brand 8080 General Trim Adhesive; trim shops will usually sell a can of this special adhesive if you can't find it anywhere else

C. Coat hangers or several lengths of one-eighth-inch welding rod

D. A coffee can to hold miscellaneous nuts and bolts

As you work through the upholstery process for the first time, you should exercise patience. You may have to repeat steps such as fitting the seat covering several times before you're satisfied with your work. That's ok. Hobby work should be pleasurable, not frustrating.

Before you can replace the seat covering, you'll have to remove the seats from the car. On foreign cars, bucket seats will usually slide off their tracks if they can be moved far enough forward. On American cars, the seats are attached to the slides so the entire seat assembly has to be removed by loosening

Seat slides are attached to the bottom cushion. Squirting the threads with penetrating oil will help loosen rusted bolts.

Twist off the hog rings that hold the old covering in place. Slit the corners of the seat cover with a razor blade to keep from tearing the foam cushion as the cover is removed.

the bolts that attach the seats to the floor pan. Removing these bolts isn't difficult if you have a helper hold the bolts inside the car while you loosen the nuts from underneath.

After removing the seats, set up a work area to disassemble the seats and install the new upholstery. A workbench provides the best arrangement because it places the seat at a comfortable height, but you can use a corner of the garage or basement floor as well. To keep the upholstery kit clean while it is being installed, cover the work surface with cardboard, old sheets or towels.

To replace the upholstery, you will have to take the seat apart and remove the cushions. It's a good idea to work on one seat at a time. That way, if you forget any of the reassembly steps, you can use the other seat as a guide.

To take the seat apart, start by removing the folding side supports that attach the seatback to the bottom cushion. Side supports are generally held in place with Phillips-head screws. The screws should be plainly visible. With the side supports removed, the seatbottom and -back can be separated and upholstered individually. Now turn the bottom cushion over and

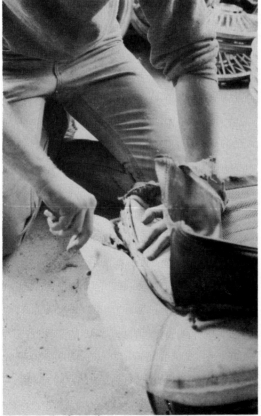

To free the cover, turn the seat over, reach into the slip surrounding the pleated area and snip the hog rings that fasten the cover to the foam cushion.

The bare foam cushion shows pleat imprints and the "listing wire" groove. Before installing the new cover, repair tears or other damage to the foam padding. On worn seats a thin layer of foam glued over the cushion's center section will restore full padding.

remove the seat supports and slide rails. You may have to slide the seat supports out of the slide rails in order to gain access to the bolts holding the slide rails to the cushion. Place screws, springs, assorted bolts, nuts and washers in a coffee can as you remove them so that you will be able to find these small parts when you are ready to put the seat back together.

The back side of the upper cushions may be covered with a stiff panel held in place with clips or screws. If a panel is used in place of fabric to cover the seatback, it should be removed next. By looking at the seat you should be able to tell how the panel is attached. If no screws are visible, pry up gently on the panel to determine the location of clips. After prying the clips loose to remove the stiff panel backing, you are ready to strip off the old seat covering. Begin by cutting the hog rings that attach the cover to the seat springs. The easiest way to cut the hog rings is to grip them with cutter pliers and snap them loose in a twisting motion. Next, slit the old cover at the corners with a utility knife. Cutting the covering not only saves time, but also

To install the cover, fit hog rings over the listing wire and press the wire down into its groove in the foam cushion until you feel the lower wire embedded in the cushion. Interlock the two wires with the hog rings and squeeze the rings shut.

Turn the new cover inside out to feed the listing wire into the slot surrounding the pleats. David Irwin, of Central Ohio Mustang Restorations in Columbus, Ohio, demonstrates this process.

eliminates the risk of tearing the foam cushion as you peel off the old upholstery.

Even after all the visible hog rings are removed and the vinyl cover is cut free, the center pleated section (shown in the photos), which appears on Mustangs and many other cars, will still be attached to the seat frame by hog rings that are fastened through a retaining wire buried in a groove in the seat cushion. These rings have to be removed next, then the cover will pull free.

Before discarding the old fabric, pull the retaining wire (technically called a "listing wire") out of its flap. The function of this wire is to draw the pleats snugly into a depression in the foam cushion. If the listing wire is rusted, as is sometimes the case, a new wire can be fabricated using coat hangers or welding rod. Before installing a replacement wire into a new cover, curl the ends to keep the wire from puncturing the upholstery.

While the seat is disassembled, check for badly rusted or broken springs. If the springs need replacing and you can't locate another set of cushions, a trim shop may be able to rebuild or repair the seat cushions. Otherwise you may be forced to rebuild the springs yourself using cushions salvaged from a junkyard. If the seat frame and support brackets are rusted, you should clean and refinish these parts before installing the new upholstery.

Tears in the foam cushions can be mended with 3M 8080 General Trim Adhesive, a product marketed primarily for trim shops. Seat cushions compress with wear, particularly the driver's seat. To restore full cushion depth, cut a piece of one-inch foam to fit inside the area outlined by the listing wire groove and glue the foam pad to the seat cushion.

When the necessary repairs have been made to the frame and cushions, the next step is to install the new vinyl cover. In preparation, spread out a supply of hog rings where they can be reached easily. If you are using hog-ring pliers, insert a ring in the jaws of the pliers. (With the pliers preloaded, you will have one hand free to position the cover while clamping the ring in place.) Now fold the new cover inside out. If the cover has a flap sewn for the listing wire, as is the case with Mustang seats, slide the wire into the seam. Feed the wire slowly to keep it from puncturing the fabric and guide the wire as it passes through bends in the seam.

Next, position the cover by laying it over the cushion. If a listing wire is used, fit the wire into the groove in the cushion. To fasten the listing wire, slip a hog ring over the wire at about the midpoint, press the ring down into the groove with the pliers until you feel another wire and connect the two wires by squeezing the hog ring closed. Repeat this process until you have secured the listing wire with hog rings spaced at two- to three-inch intervals. Use a liberal number of rings on this critical operation.

If the seat covering has a pleated center section, as is found in Mustang seats, or a waffle imprint, like early Corvettes, check to see whether the insert is aligned squarely on the cushion before proceeding.

Pulling the cover over the cushion should be the easiest step in the upholstery sequence but it usually turns out to be the hardest because while the cover is being stretched over the foam cushion, it also has to be turned right-side out. To stretch and reverse the cover without tearing seams, work from corner to corner and grip both sides of the corners as you work the cover over the cushion. Keep your progress consistent by pulling the cover only part way over a corner, then proceeding to the next.

When the cover is fitted in place it will probably look lumpy and wrinkled. More important at the moment, however, is to check whether the seam secured by the listing wire lies evenly. If it does, the hog rings have been properly fastened. In the event that the seam is loose, indicating that the listing wire is not attached tightly to the seat cushion, the cover will have to be removed and the hog rings fastened correctly.

If each step has been carefully executed, the reupholstery steps should be progressing on cue. The seam connecting the seatbottom or -back (depending on the cushion) to the side

Be careful not to tear the seams as you stretch the cover over the foam cushion.

Lumps and wrinkles are normal at this stage. They smooth out as you fit the cover in place.

flaps contains piping which should be aligned so that it makes a smooth border around the cushion's outside edge. To reposition the cover, slide one hand under the cover so that you can maneuver the foam cushion while you shift the vinyl cover in place with your other hand. When the piping makes an even border around the cushion, turn the seat over and insert short lengths of wire cut from a coat hanger or welding rod into seams on the edge of each cover flap. Pull the flaps taut over the sides of the cushion and attach the flaps to the seat frame with hog rings. To keep the vinyl from tearing, the hog rings should enclose the wire inserted in the cover flap.

After attaching one side of the cover to the seat frame, turn the cushion over and check for wrinkles. Usually small but irksome wrinkles will be found, particularly around the corners. If you try to smooth the wrinkles by shifting the cover on the cushion until it lies flat, you may wear out your patience before you succeed. Professional upholsterers use an easier method: They simply heat the vinyl slightly with steam and when the fabric cools, the wrinkles disappear.

To steam out wrinkles, professional upholsterers slide a small metal tube under the vinyl cover until it reaches the lumpy area. The tube is flattened somewhat at the open end to spread the steam and connects at the other end to a miniature Steam Jenny. Moist, hot air from the tube heats the vinyl until it becomes pliable. Then the hose is withdrawn. This steaming technique smooths wrinkles by softening the vinyl cover and shrinking the cotton backing.

Reattach seat hardware as the last step. Note the hog rings holding cover flaps to the seat springs.

The finished cushion is nearly ready for a test ride.

Amateur restorers can make a similar steam device by connecting a length of tubing to a boiling tea kettle. A short length of bendable copper tubing works well as a heating tube to slide under the vinyl cover. The end of the tubing should be flattened slightly and inserted carefully so that it does not tear either the vinyl or the foam cushion. After steaming the wrinkles smooth, finish attaching the remaining upholstery flaps to the seat frame.

The entire sequence is repeated four times to reupholster a set of bucket seats. When the new upholstery has been fitted to all the cushions, reattach the seat slides to the bottom cushions and the panel inserts to the seatbacks, then reassemble the seats. If the bolt holes for the slides and folding side supports are covered by new upholstery, use a screwdriver or punch to make holes in the fabric for the bolts.

Installing kit upholstery is not difficult if you take your time, are careful to perform each step and make sure the cover fits snugly and squarely on the cushion. New upholstery makes a striking improvement in a car's appearance. Kits duplicate original upholstery, are moderately priced and require only one special tool, hog-ring pliers. The only drawback to reupholstering vinyl bucket seats is that when your friends see your work, they may decide to reupholster their cars—and when they do, they'll want assistance from "the expert."

Upholstering Vintage Cars

Although a visit to a local trim shop might suggest otherwise, wool broadcloth, mohair and genuine leather—the upholstery materials that were widely used in vintage cars—are still available. Car collectors are largely do-it-yourself types, so it isn't surprising that hobby suppliers have responded by producing upholstery kits amateurs can install with professional-looking results. Ford and Chevrolet owners are most fortunate, in that custom-fit interior kits are marketed for nearly all models of both popular makes. Headliner, door panel and seat upholstery kits are also available for a variety of other makes. A list of upholstery kit suppliers is included in the appendix. You can also locate upholstery suppliers by their ads in *Hemmings Motor News, Cars & Parts, Old Cars Weekly* and other hobby magazines.

Although upholstery kits are essential if you plan to replace a car's interior yourself, they can also be used if you are having a trim shop handle the upholstery work. With a quality upholstery kit, you can be assured of an authentic interior, both in construction and material. Then, too, an upholstery shop can install a kit in much less time than would be required to redo an interior from scratch. In most cases adding an installation charge to the price of an upholstery kit still works out to a cost savings over having an upholstery shop construct and replace a car's interior. If you install the kit yourself, you will save the installation charge.

In cases where an upholstery kit isn't available, it is unlikely that you will be able to replace the car's interior yourself. To do so you would need a heavy-duty sewing machine and extensive upholstery skills. Instead, you will need to concentrate your efforts on locating a trim shop that is capable of replacing an older car's interior and willing to do the work. One of the best ways to locate a qualified trim shop is to ask other hobbyists, particularly fellow club members, for recommendations. You should also look at examples of work the shop has produced. Depending on the upholstery shop's experience with collector cars, you may be able to assist in the search for authentic materials. From the upholstery suppliers listed in the appendix and those whose ads appear in hobby magazines you should be able to locate a source that can duplicate your car's interior. Some, like Le Baron Bonney Company in Amesbury, Massachusetts, stock original as well as reproduction upholstery fabrics. To determine whether the supplier can match the fabric in your car, send a small sample of unfaded material from the underside of a seat or similar hidden area. If you send the sample with your letter of inquiry, most upholstery suppliers will send a swatch of their closest matching material for no charge.

Mark Libbey, talented pattern maker and draftsman at Hampton Coach, measures the rear curtain dimensions on a rare 1929 Chevrolet landaulet sedan.

Hampton Coach uses original upholstery pieces for its patterns. Each pattern set represents a $1,500 investment. The patterns assure that each kit will fit exactly like the original.

It's best to begin reupholstering with the old interior intact. Of course, the interior must be removed from a car that needs extensive metal work, sandblasting or chemical derusting. In that case, take photos before removing the upholstery. If an upholstery kit is not available for the car, keep the seats intact, save the door linings, headliner and other interior pieces, take photos and draw diagrams of the position the various pieces occupied before they were removed. If a kit is available and you decide to replace the upholstery yourself, this same advice applies. The hardest cars to upholster are those that have been stripped so that there is nothing left to show how the original interior was installed.

Typically, the upholstery in a vintage car consists of up to 100 separate panels—lining the doors, sides, rear quarters, cowl, even the center door pillars on fordor models—including the headliner and seat coverings. Even so, installing a new interior is more straightforward than it looks. Then, too, the entire interior may not need to be replaced. Kits are sold in sets to recover the seats, replace the headliner and/or the interior panels. In most cases, however, individual upholstery panels, a single door panel for example, are not available for the simple reason that upholstery material fades and when a single panel is replaced the contrast between new and original material is likely to be quite noticeable.

When a car's entire interior needs to be replaced, your first concern may well be where to begin. In most cases when a car's interior is deteriorated to the point that it requires replacing, other refinishing work is needed too. The dash and interior trim may need to be painted or the wood-graining effect restored. The exterior may require refinishing as well.

Arthur Brown shows the back side of a door panel. Note that the fiberboard is reinforced where a pouch is stitched to the panel.

The door panel fits precisely, without trimming.

If you plan to replace the car's upholstery as part of a general refinishing effort that includes repainting, you should decide ahead of time whether to install the upholstery before or after painting. If you attempt to replace the interior after having your car repainted, chances are you'll wind up scratching the new paint in the process. No matter how careful you are, it is almost impossible to climb in and out of a car removing and installing the seats, replacing the carpet, tacking door panels in place, hanging the headliner and completing all the other details of upholstery work without marring the finish. It's also just about impossible to mask upholstery effectively enough to protect the fabric from sanding dust and painting overspray. Whether you decide to paint the car and then install the upholstery, or vice versa is up to you. The choice really depends on which way you feel you can be more careful. Whichever approach you take, make sure you prepare a clean work area for fitting the new upholstery.

Upholstery is installed using common tools and supplies. You'll need a tack hammer, screwdriver, pliers, a staple gun and supply of quarter-inch staples, a utility knife or single-edged razor blades and, for some jobs, a tube of upholstery cement. Special hog-nosed upholstery pliers work better than regular shop pliers for installing upholstery rings, but aren't essential.

Before new upholstery material can be installed, the old covering has to be removed. To recover the seats, both the cushions and the front seat frame will have to be removed from

Stan Brown, owner of Hampton Coach, holds a wooden seatback. His company sells complete ready-to-install seats, as well as upholstery kits.

Lee Atherton founded Le Baron Bonney in response to hobbyists' requests for duplicates of the interior he installed in his Model A roadster. Today Le Baron Bonney upholstery kits are the standard against which replacement Ford interiors are measured.

the car. The seat frame is usually bolted through the floor. Door and other interior panels are often tacked to wooden strips and can be pried loose with a screwdriver. As you remove the upholstery from a vintage car, you may be surprised at what you'll find. Cotton stuffing and burlap were commonly used to cover seat springs. Door panels were usually constructed of fabric covering—wool, mohair, sometimes leatherette—stitched or glued to heavy cardboard backing. Door openings were fitted with a thick, round molding called windlace. Upholstery kits include these original materials along with instructions explaining how to install them.

Once the old interior is removed, you may find that the wooden tack strips and seat springs need repair. Rotted wood will have to be replaced, but tack strips that have split or cracked can usually be glued back together. If the seat springs are badly deteriorated, replacements may be available from the upholstery suppliers listed in the appendix. If not, it is often possible to rebuild rusted or sagging cushions by replacing damaged springs in the old seat frame.

If you're attempting upholstery work for the first time, remember that patience is the key to quality. It's important to install upholstery in the proper sequence. The directions should give you this information. If not, use the sequence in which the upholstery was removed as your guide. As you install the new upholstery, make sure that you position each piece of fabric correctly before tacking it in place. Don't trim off what appears

Although Le Baron Bonney and Hampton Coach upholstery kits are designed to be installed by hobbyists, both companies maintain trim shops for customers who would rather have a professional replace the upholstery in their cars.

to be excess material until you have fitted the surrounding fabric and know that each piece is positioned exactly where it belongs. When you are installing door panels, it's a good idea to place a few tacks around the edges of a panel, then pull the fabric tight and check for fit before tacking it permanently. Whether you are installing a headliner, seat covers or door panels, always center the fabric first, then work toward the edges, checking the fit as you go along.

On a vintage car, upholstery panels are held in place primarily by tacks and various methods are used to camouflage the tack heads. When they don't show directly, tacks are either left as is or color-matched to the fabric. Where the tack heads are apt to show, they are either covered with windlace or trim binding. On doors and interior panels where trim binding could look garish, the heads are usually concealed by a technique called "blind nailing." With this method, upholstery nails are driven almost flush with the fabric, then a large needle is inserted under the fabric and the material is lifted gently over the nail head. The needle should pull *across* the weave pattern, otherwise it may snag the fabric.

Since door panels are constructed of fabric or leatherette stitched or glued to heavy cardboard, it's a good idea to cover

New seat springs are still available for many vintage cars.

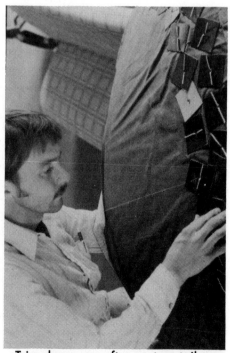

Trim shops can often custom-tailor a new interior for a vintage car, provided they can locate authentic material. Suppliers of vintage upholstery fabrics and quality leather hides advertise in hobby magazines.

the backs of these panels with plastic to protect the cardboard from moisture. Plastic trash bags make an effective covering. Just slit the bag open and spread it out in a sheet, then cut the plastic to fit the door panel and tape it securely to the cardboard. The plastic backing will prevent water that drips past window seals from soaking the cardboard and leaving unsightly water spots on fabric covering. There are a number of tricks like this that should be used when you're upholstering a vintage car.

If you have difficulty smoothing the wrinkles in a headliner, remember that wet wool shrinks as it dries. To prevent being driven to the brink of madness while trying to smooth out wrinkles in a headliner, only to have them appear someplace else, lightly moisten the wrinkled area with a vaporizer or steam iron. Then pull the material taut and retack it if necessary. The wrinkles will disappear as the fabric dries.

Now that you have an idea of the basic steps to follow in order to install an upholstery kit and have learned a few tricks of the trade, it's time to experience an upholstery sequence. Stan Brown, founder of Hampton Coach, the vintage Chevrolet

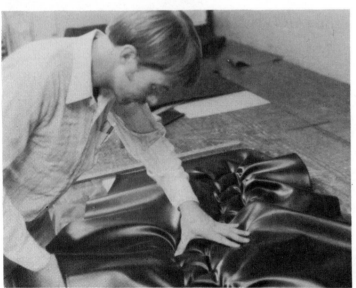

As David Workman at Zane Auto Top in Zanesville, Ohio, shows, the know-how for forming diamond pleats found on very early cars isn't lost to the younger generation of trimmers.

To install an upholstery kit on a vintage car, as in this front seat from a 1938 Chevrolet tudor sedan, the seat frame is re-covered first. Each piece in an upholstery kit supplied by Hampton Coach fits precisely as it should to replace the original covering.

The finished seatback attaches to the lower seat frame at two hinge points. The seat frame usually takes more time to recover than the cushions. Notice how completely the upholstery kit covers the seat frame. Holes for robe-rail sockets are cut after the fabric is tacked in place.

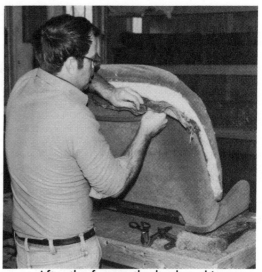

After the frame, the back cushions are covered and installed. The cushion tacks directly onto the seatback. Seat cushions are not removable from thirties-vintage Chevrolet front seats.

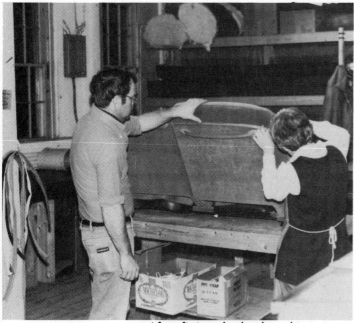

After fitting the back cushions in place, trim welt is tacked along the edge of the seatback to hide the seam.

After tacking the bottom cushion to the front of the seat frame the seat is ready to be installed in the car.

upholstery supplier, provided the series of photos showing the steps involved in recovering a vintage car front seat. The seat in the photos is from a 1938 Chevrolet tudor sedan and is representative of upholstery construction from the twenties up until vinyl replaced cloth fabrics in the late forties and early fifties.

In order to reupholster a front seat you must remove the seat assembly from the car. It's important to note that the photo sequence and instructions given here show how to replace the upholstery, not install seat covers. When you shop for an upholstery kit, be sure to buy upholstery, not seat covers. There is a big difference between the two. Seat covers slip over both the cushions and seat frame. Upholstery kits contain material to re-cover the cushions and the seat frame separately so that each part of the seat retains its distinct appearance. As the photos show, there are a number of steps involved just in upholstering the seat frame. You may be surprised to discover that most hobbyists who install a kit for the first time take longer to cover the seat frame than they do to upholster the seat cushions.

Unless you're a sumo wrestler, you will need help removing the front seat. The seat frame will either slide off its tracks, or have to be unbolted, either from the seat frame or through the floor. When you have the seat out of the car and placed in a clean, comfortable work area, don't just tear off the old upholstery. Remove each piece in the reverse sequence from the way it appears to have been installed. That way you will learn how the seat was put together originally.

When you have the cushions and frame stripped bare, you may find that the springs and the seat frame need to be re-

The upholstery kit for this Chevrolet cabriolet front seat is cut from genuine leather.

paired. You should replace broken or rotted wood in the seat frame and repair or replace broken springs before installing the new upholstery. Hampton Coach and Le Baron Bonney both sell replacement seat springs. You may also want to paint the seat frame before it is re-covered.

Hampton Coach kits come with all pieces properly cut and sewn, and ready to install. But even though the kits include instructions for proper installation, you may also need to recall how you took the seat apart to make sure you position each piece where it belongs.

Cover the lower frame first, then the seatback. Hold off cutting holes for the robe rail trim and ashtray until after you have completely fitted the frame cover. Now assemble the frame parts. On the tudor seat shown, the two frame backs mount on hinges. Seats from a fordor sedan have rigid backs.

As you re-cover the seat cushions, it's not necessary to remove the old burlap from the spring pockets if the material is still intact, but you should replace the burlap and cotton padding covering the springs. If the cushions appear to have settled some with age, you may want to add a thin layer of foam rubber. This extra padding isn't included in the Hampton Coach kit, but foam rubber should be easily obtainable from a local trim shop.

Next, cover the seat springs and the foam, if you added the extra padding, with burlap. Pull the burlap down so that it encloses the springs on three sides and fasten the cloth to the spring frame with hog rings. Heavy cotton stuffing is supplied to pad the springs. You will find that stitching the cotton to the burlap with light thread will help hold the padding in place as you fit the mohair cover. Now fold the cover down over the

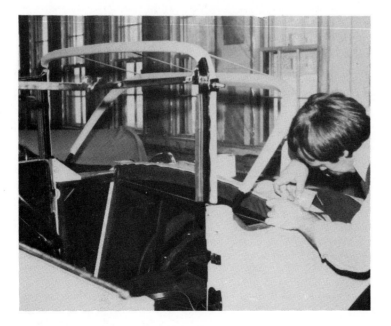

The trimmer here is beginning to install a Hampton Coach interior kit in a 1932 Chevrolet cabriolet. Since vintage cars are framed extensively in wood, most upholstery panels are tacked in place. Before interior upholstery is installed, the top bows are covered and fitted in place.

padded springs. On the seatback cushions, the cover fastens to the springs only at the end that rests against the bottom of the seat frame. On the bottom cushion, the covering attaches to the springs on two sides and the rear.

The fabric that covers the front of the bottom seat cushions on thirties vintage Chevrolets tacks to the lower edge of the seat frame and holds the bottom cushion securely in place. The two flaps that cover the gap between the lower end of the seatbacks and the seat frame are also attached to the bottom cushion, anchoring the cushion to the seat frame at the rear. The cushions for the seatback tack directly to the frame on three sides. You have to stuff these cushions in place, pulling the fabric tight and tacking or stapling it to the wooden seatbacks. After you have finished tacking the covering, you can trim the excess fabric and cover the seam with a strip of Hide-em binding supplied with the kit.

Upholstery work isn't complex, just tedious. Replacing the interior of a vintage car makes a modern collector appreciate those who installed the snugly fitted trim fabrics and upholstery panels on these cars when they rolled down the assembly line. Admittedly, practice helps but, even so, those original upholsterers must have had mighty nimble fingers.

Upholstery kits enable amateurs to install an interior that looks like the work of a professional trim shop.

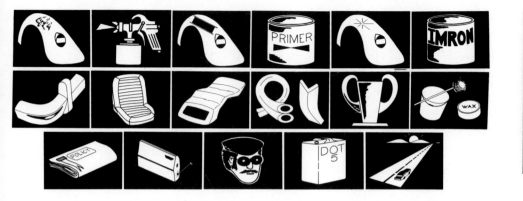

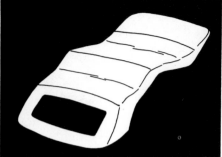

9
Renewing A Ragtop

A few years ago two friends tackled the simple-looking job of replacing the bikini-size top on an MG roadster. One of the pair had seen a top installed and thought he knew the tricks, the other owned the car. The two worked an entire Saturday; yet when they finished, the top looked as though it had blown against the car in a stiff wind and been snagged by the bows.

Replacing a convertible top may look easy, but it requires knowledge of the way the car's top mechanism is constructed and how a top should be installed, careful measuring and equally careful attention to detail during installation. During the heyday of convertibles, convertible top shops did a brisk business; but since the early seventies ragtops have been fading from production, causing convertible top shops to join the endangered species list. That's the reason my friends attempted to install the MG top themselves. As residents of northeastern Vermont, where convertibles never sold briskly, there wasn't a top shop available to do the work for them.

The absence of convertible top shops, combined with a do-it-yourself attitude and the availability of convertible top kits, is prompting hobbyists to learn how to install new ragtops themselves. I was about to purchase a replacement for the original top on my 1971 Mustang convertible and install it myself when the sign "Zane Auto Top" on a freshly painted, well-kept building in downtown Zanesville, Ohio, caught my eye. Since I hadn't fully convinced myself that I could replace the top, I decided to stop, find out whether the shop still installed convertible tops and, if so, check on the cost.

As I walked in I could see a garage door and the workshop area where convertibles were formerly fitted with new tops, but there wasn't a car in sight. Two men were at work re-covering a pickup seat. The senior partner stopped his work. "Can I help you?" he asked.

"Do you install convertible tops?" I responded.

With a twinkle in his eye, Ben Workman, the shop owner, introduced himself and answered that he did install convertible tops as often as the occasion arose. Workman said that even after thirty-three years experience he enjoyed the challenge of replacing convertible tops, the one job in his line of work that could still spring surprises. Although the convertible top business isn't brisk, enough convertibles have survived in Zane Auto Top's southern Ohio location that Ben Workman gets a chance to tune his skills every now and then.

Ben Workman's price to install a new top was so reasonable that I decided I would be foolish to try to replace the top myself. As a bonus, Workman agreed to apprentice his customer in the art of installing a convertible top. He began by explaining that there is a vast difference in the quality of tops. Up until the mid-fifties when nylon tops replaced the earlier canvas variety, shops like Zane Auto Top custom-made each new canvas top. In contrast, nylon tops with their special heat-welded seams are purchased ready to install. Today, both canvas and nylon tops are available precut and presewn for most vintage and late model convertibles. Workman stated that he uses only top-of-the-line tops manufactured in nearby Columbus, Ohio. He advised hobbyists who plan to install a top themselves to make sure they purchase a premium top from a reputable supplier. Workman explained that correct stitching and fit, plus heavier fabric and tighter weave, mark the difference between shoddy and well-made products. He advised against buying the discount tops sold by some of the mail-order auto parts vendors.

In addition to the two types of top material, canvas and nylon, convertible tops also vary in back window design and

Ben Workman, owner of Zane Auto Top in Zanesville, Ohio, removes the rear trim welt as the first step in peeling off the old top.

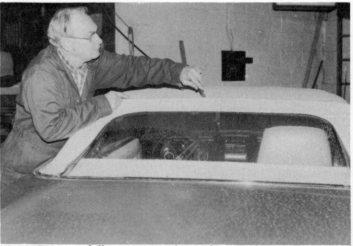

Next, Ben carefully pries out the tacks to avoid damaging the fiber tack strip underneath.

actual top construction. Until the late forties and early fifties, convertible rear windows were made of glass set in small, usually rectangular-shaped metal frames. The later plastic windows nearly filled the zip-down rear curtain, giving much better visibility. In a few flashy designs of the late fifties, the plastic windows even wrapped around the rear quarters of the top, a case of convertibles mimicking hardtops. Plastic windows scratched easily and turned brown, especially when washed with harsh detergents at a drive-through car wash, so for the last stage of rear window evolution manufacturers substituted thin tempered glass for plastic. Glass rear windows were standard equipment on many convertibles made in the mid- to late sixties and early seventies, and options on others. Hobbyists concerned with maintaining authenticity should make sure that when the convertible top is replaced, the new rear window matches the original design.

Convertible rear windows are mounted in a separate piece of fabric that attaches to the top with a zipper. Rear curtains that contain glass windows do not always need to be replaced. If the rear curtain on a nylon top is faded, but in otherwise good condition, its appearance can often be restored by spraying the fabric with special paint made for coating vinyl. When a rear curtain containing an older-type glass window mounted in a metal frame is replaced, the window should be removed and installed in the new top. The metal frames are made of an inner and outer section, generally held together by small bolts.

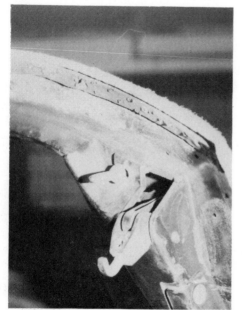

The fiber tack strips on late model convertibles are reusable so long as they aren't badly deteriorated.

Usually the pads have sagged and should be refitted before installing the new top.

By the time a top needs replacing, vinyl rear windows are usually scratched and should also be replaced.

Though Ben Workman was willing to show me how to install a convertible top, he wasn't enthusiastic about the prospect of hobbyists fitting late model convertible tops. He explained that recent full-size General Motors convertibles built from 1971 to 1976, ending with the bicentennial Eldorado model, used an unorthodox scissors-like top mechanism, rather than the traditional cantilever style. Workman described the GM design as "the beginning of the end; an engineering nightmare" that was prone to rapid wear. British convertibles, like the sixties Hillman Minx, also used a scissors design on the front bows to allow the popular continental three-position top stance.

For years convertible tops exhibited an annoying ballooning effect when the cars were driven at cruising speed. To correct this, engineers designed tiny cables that passed through channels sewn in the fabric along the sides of the top and attached the top fabric to the front bow (first bow behind the windshield header) with a retaining clamp. If you are planning to install a convertible top on a late model car, you should study the instructions in the manufacturer's body service manual to learn how to remove and install the side cables and to familiarize yourself with the car's top construction. These manuals are written for mechanics and professional upholsterers, but they are well illustrated and contain views of the cable attaching points, adjustments for the top mechanism and other details that a beginner might overlook. (Body service manuals

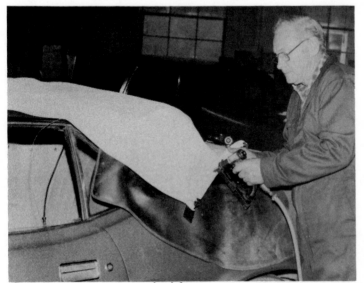

The rear quarters are tacked first. Note the coverings draped across the rear fender to protect the finish. Ben Workman prefers to install a new top before the car is repainted.

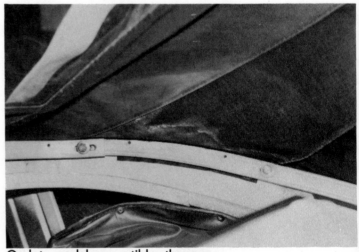

On late model convertibles the rear tack strips are accessed from inside the car.

for most late model convertibles are available from literature vendors at flea markets or can be ordered through literature-for-sale ads in hobby magazines. In lieu of buying a manual, you may be able to borrow a copy from a local dealer and photocopy the relevant pages.) As you read the instructions for installing a top on a late model convertible, you should locate the cables and other details shown in the manual on your car. If you are replacing an older-style canvas top, the job will be more straightforward since you won't be concerned with cables or other restraining devices.

Logically enough, replacing a convertible top begins by removing the old fabric. First, though, you should cover the car's trunk, hood and rear fenders with old blankets or similar protection to avoid marring the paint. To remove the top, loosen it from the windshield header and detach the rear quarter flaps. On older convertibles, the canvas is tacked directly to a wood tack strip. Most late model convertibles cover what appears to be the rear quarter tack strip with chrome trim, leaving you wondering how to undo the fabric. As the Mustang photos show, on newer cars the top fabric is attached to tack strips that unbolt from inside the car. After detaching the rear quarter, lower the top to a "stacked position" and strip the top fabric from the bows by gently prying out the tacks with a screwdriver. On newer cars the top fabric is frequently attached with staples, rather than tacks. These, too, can be removed with a screwdriver. Don't throw the old top away just yet. It will be used to align the new top.

Before installing the new top, Ben Workman always inspects and repairs the tack strips. Since the early fifties, American convertibles have used metal bows with a fiber insert to hold the

Wrinkles in the rear quarter area will be worked out later.

Antiballooning features on late model convertibles include metal strips that clamp the top fabric to the forward bows.

tacks. Earlier convertibles and Volkswagens, up to the demise of the Beetle, used wooden bows. Wooden bows are susceptible to rot and may need repair or replacement. Cracked or broken wood can often be repaired by gluing, but rotted wood will have to be replaced. Since wooden top bows generally have sharp curves that are made by steam bending, replacing them is beyond the skill of most hobbyists. Fortunately, replacement bows are available for many vintage cars from suppliers listed in the appendix and others who advertise in hobby magazines. Deteriorated fiber tack strips should be repaired or replaced. New inserts are available in some cases from auto dealers.

To attach the top to the header bow, the fabric is pulled forward and marked, then tacked in place.

The wrinkles are removed from the rear quarters after the top is fastened to the bows.

With the new top installed, the Mustang is off to the body shop for repainting.

Once the top fabric is removed, the next step is to prepare the top frame. Begin by checking the top pads to see whether they need to be replaced or refitted. The top pads cushion the fabric and fill out the side contours to give the top a well-fitted look. If the pads are worn, they should be replaced. If the pads have stretched so that they fit loosely when the top is clamped to the header, unfasten them, then pull them tight and reattach them to the bows. Along with fitting the pads, you should make sure that the top is correctly aligned. Installing convertible tops was a complex assembly-line operation, so even on new cars the tops weren't always aligned properly.

My 1971 Mustang that appears in the accompanying photos had a strip of foam rubber glued to the windshield header

Canvas tops on older convertibles are installed using the same basic steps as with vinyl tops. The pads are fitted first, then the fabric is tacked in place. Note the extensive wrapping used to protect the finish.

After the top is fastened to the rear tack strip, the fabric is pulled forward until it is snug and tacked to the header bow.

to seal a gap between the header and the top. Since the car appeared to carry its original top and the body showed no sign of collision damage, the top was probably improperly aligned at the factory. Late model Ford convertibles have a cam on the rear side rail that adjusts the fit between the top and the windshield header. By turning this cam, Ben Workman was able to slant the header bow forward, eliminating the need for the extra weatherseal. The top adjustment procedure is fully explained in the Ford body service manual.

Before installing the new top, be sure that the drain holes generally located in the rear quarter panels aren't plugged with debris. If they are, water running off the top will flood the trunk.

If you plan to replace the back curtain, tack it in place first. Be sure that the curtain is centered, then attach it to the tack strips with tacks or staples. Either method works well. After the rear curtain is installed, center the top on the car, zip the rear curtain in place and make any adjustments necessary so that the zipper works smoothly. (During this and later operations, the top frame should be raised so that it is positioned loosely over the windshield header.) Next, fasten the top to the rear tack strips. On late model convertibles these tack strips can be adjusted for fit after the top is positioned.

Now move forward and connect the side cables on tops equipped with this antiballooning feature. Next, pull the top forward so that the fabric is snug against the header bow and mark a line along the edge of the header bow with a pencil or colored chalk to show where the fabric will be tucked under and tacked. Lower the top frame enough so that the fabric can be tacked easily to the header bow. Following the line you just made, tack the top loosely in place, then raise the top so that it closes on the windshield header and check the fit. This process may have to be repeated until the fabric is snug, but not too

After removing wrinkles from the rear quarter sections, trim welt is installed to cover the tack heads on the rear bow.

tight. "Snug" is the word Ben Workman uses to describe a proper fit. Remember that the top fabric will shrink slightly and adjust the fit accordingly.

When the fit is satisfactory, tack the top securely to the header bow. Fold the corners in a similar fashion to tucking in sheets when making a bed. Illustrations in the service manual may also show how to fold the fabric, or you may wish to examine the way the fabric was folded on the original top. After the fabric is securely tacked, trim off any excess with a sharp utility or X-acto knife, then move to the back of the car and tack the top to the rear bow. Note that on 1971 to 1975 full-size GM convertibles, the top fabric is not attached at the rear bow.

Ben Workman checks alignment of the new top on the rear bow by cutting out the section of the old top that was tacked to the rear bow and laying it as a template over the new top. New vinyl tops generally have guide holes to help position the top on the rear bow, but since the holes are punched at the factory they may not be located correctly for every car, the template is used to assure that the new top fits properly. When the new top is positioned, tack the fabric to the bow. The tacks should be centered, evenly spaced and in a straight line. To preserve the wood bow or fiber tack strip, you should coat the tack heads with neoprene weatherstrip adhesive before installing the trim welting.

The front weatherseal and rear trim welts are installed next. Workman explained that top kits usually include a narrow strip of fabric to wrap over the original front weatherseal. He prefers to form new weatherstripping by wrapping a length of ⅜- or ½-inch-diameter soft rubber, as required, with fabric and sewing the ends. The front weatherseal should be tucked far enough under the header bow to compress slightly when the top is locked in place. The rear trim welt must be positioned so that it makes a straight line across the rear bow. On canvas tops,

Care should be taken to make sure the trim welt is straight. Two people can do this job easier than one.

trim welt is often installed to cover the tack heads on the front bow and rear tack rails as well. Here, too, it is wise to seal the tack heads with neoprene before covering them with welt.

The top can be locked to the windshield header at this point, while any wrinkles in the rear quarter are removed by adjusting the rear tack strips or retacking the rear section if necessary. The trick here is not so much removing all traces of wrinkles, as it is getting the wrinkles running the right way. As the top shrinks, small vertical wrinkles will disappear, but horizontal slack will increase. This was the problem with the top my friends installed on the MG—they got the wrinkles going the wrong way. Workman had to fit the rear tack strips three times before he worked out all the wrinkles on the Mustang top. That's three tries by a man with thirty-three years of experience. Removing wrinkles demands patience!

After installation, a new top deserves proper treatment. To keep a convertible top looking new, follow these guidelines: Always unhook the top from the windshield header before zipping or unzipping the rear window. This takes tension off the zipper and helps prevent straining the zipper and pulling the teeth. Wash vinyl tops with a hose and use a quality foam-type upholstery cleaner or a mild detergent. To clean stubborn grime, work the cleaner into the vinyl with a vegetable brush. Sweep or vacuum canvas tops. Never fold a wet top.

Convertibles of all ages were eye-catchers when they were new and are even more of a crowd-gatherer today. After all, the beauty of a convertible with its top up is surpassed only when the top is down.

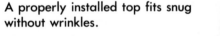
A properly installed top fits snug without wrinkles.

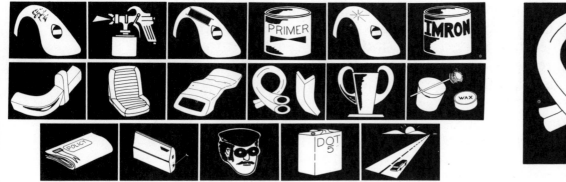
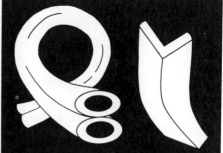

10

Renewing Rubber Parts And Weatherseal

Like the weak link in a chain, any area of a car that has deteriorated will detract from its overall appearance. I learned this lesson on the Model A roadster I drove to high school. The car had been upgraded mechanically, reupholstered and painted. It wasn't a show car, but it ran well and attracted a respectable share of admiring glances. But despite its well-preserved appearance, the car had an ugly spot that could easily have been avoided. The trim welting that lined the seam between the gas tank and cowl was frayed and rotted. Even painting didn't hide the deteriorated welting.

Rubber molding around windows, door and trunk weatherseal, trim welting and other rubber parts harden and crack with time. Although the appearance and condition of rubber moldings are easy to overlook before refinishing, dried out rubber not only blights a car's finished look, but can also cause water leakage. In most cases, replacing rubber parts requires patience more than skill, yet these are the very items that hobbyists often overlook.

Hobbyists bypass replacing rubber parts for two reasons. First, they don't know where to find replacements for worn weatherstripping, window moldings and other rubber parts. Second, hobbyists generally don't realize how easy most rubber parts are to replace. This chapter addresses both concerns.

The first step in renewing rubber moldings, running board mats, weatherseal—rubber parts in general—is to take stock of their condition. Although rubber that has begun to harden can sometimes be rejuvenated, if water is leaking into the trunk or around the windows, weatherseal and window moldings should definitely be replaced. Check pedal pads and running board matting and gravel shields on rear fenders of forties and fifties vintage cars for wear. Look for missing rubber bumpers used as door and hood stops and check to make sure that the rubber grommets usually surrounding wiring and cables passing through the firewall and other body panels are in place. List missing items along with those that are worn, dried and cracked.

Since weatherstripping, running board matting and rubber parts that are glued in place can rarely be removed intact, it is important to locate replacements before stripping off the existing rubber. When a car undergoes a major restoration that requires sandblasting or chemical derusting and extensive body work, the weatherseal around the doors and trunk, trim welting, even window weatherstripping grommets and so on may have to be removed. In this case, it's important to carefully remove the old rubber. Some items may be reused and others will serve as a guide when ordering replacements. To loosen weatherseal without tearing it, heat the metal on the side opposite the one where the rubber is glued. A propane torch will supply adequate heat. When heated, the glue will soften and the rubber can easily be pulled loose. Be careful not to overheat the metal and burn the rubber.

Rubber moldings around the windshield and rear window should be removed and replaced by professionals. If you at-

Water leaking into the trunk after a heavy rain or washing is a sure sign that the weatherseal needs replacing. Along with replacement weatherseal, you'll also need trim adhesive and cleaning solvent. In most cases, the only tool required is a screwdriver.

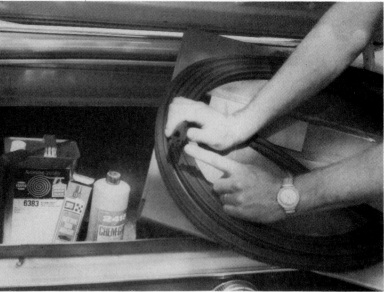

Whenever possible you'll want to use reproduction or factory replacement weatherseal. As seen in a cross-section view, authentic rubber parts will fit the contours of the weatherseal cavity better than a "universal" product. Note the container of metal prep, used to dissolve light surface rust.

tempt to remove the windshield and rear window yourself you risk cracking the glass. Rubber moldings around doors, vent and rear quarter windows can be removed with much less risk to the glass if you follow instructions in auto body repair manuals such as Chilton's body and frame manual or manufacturers' body service manuals. As with other automotive literature, these manuals are available at flea markets and through literature-for-sale ads in hobby magazines. The Chilton manual describes how to remove and replace glass on all major makes of American cars and illustrates important steps with clear photos.

To remove vent window glass, for example, crank the window open and insert a quarter-inch screwdriver between the glass and the top corner of the metal frame. Pry up gently on the frame to loosen the glass. When the glass is loosened at the top, pry the bottom portion of the glass loose from the metal frame. Wiggle the glass to free it from the channel while pulling it out of the frame. Glass that has yellowed or is not made of safety plate should be replaced.

After taking inventory of needed rubber parts, it's time to start scouting for replacements. Weatherseal and other rubber parts are available from numerous sources. Flea market vendors sell new-old-stock rubber items that have been purchased from dealer inventories, as well as reproduction parts. When buying new-old-stock weatherseal and window moldings, squeeze the rubber to test its resiliency. Even rubber that looks new may have hardened, in which case it should not be used.

Suppliers of reproduction and new-old-stock rubber parts also advertise in hobby magazines. Many specialize in rubber parts for particular makes and models. Others, including Metro Moulded Parts in Minneapolis, Minnesota, stock a large variety of rubber parts for a wide range of collector cars. In addition

Remove the old weatherseal by carefully peeling it loose. In stubborn cases you may have to work the rubber loose with a screwdriver or heat the metal behind the rubber with a propane torch to loosen the adhesive.

to specific replacement parts Metro Moulded also carries universal weatherstripping, window moldings, rubber bumpers, grommets and other items that dramatically extend the range of cars the company's parts will fit. Metro Moulded Parts' catalog shows these universal rubber items in cross-section views with dimensions. When ordering universal rubber parts, carefully compare the catalog cross-section with the piece from your car. It is easier to measure the actual profile of old rubber parts from a freshly cut cross-section. Where weatherstripping and window rubber is sold by the foot, stretch out the car's old weatherseal, measure the total length and add about five percent for error and waste. Metro Moulded Parts' address appears in the suppliers listing at the end of this book. The company's catalog sells for $2. It contains illustrations of Metro Moulded Parts' complete inventory and is well worth the price as an aid to identifying the rubber parts that may need replacing.

In cases where new-old-stock and reproduction rubber parts aren't available, it may be possible to repair the old rubber or hand-make your own replacements. Metro Moulded Parts sells rubber sheets, slabs and cylinders from which you can fabricate body-mounting pads and other items. Rick's Auto Parts in Kansas City, Kansas, sells a liquid rubber product that can be used to mold small parts, particularly those that have special markings, or to repair hard-to-find items. To mold small rubber parts,

With the major portion of the old weatherseal removed, a residue of rubber may still be stuck to the metal.

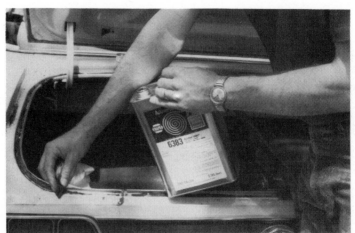

To remove the residue, soften the rubber with cleaning solvent and scrape the channel clean using a knife or screwdriver.

start by making an image of the original part in a plaster cast or by constructing a mold out of cardboard, papier-mâché or wood. Pour the liquid rubber compound into the mold and let it harden. The product cures overnight at room temperature.

Repairs can be made with liquid rubber in much the same way. Examples of rubber parts that could be candidates for repair include running board matting, gas filler or steering column grommets, trunk mats and the like. To repair worn areas on running boards, chips from grommets and other damage to rubber parts, first clean the area being repaired with soap and water. Let the rubber dry thoroughly before applying the liquid rubber. It may be necessary to make a mold to hold the liquid rubber in place. Since liquid rubber has a vinyl appearance, the repair may have a glossier look than the original rubber. If the difference is very noticeable, you may be able to camouflage the repair by coating the part with blackwall paint.

In cases where replacement parts are not available and would be difficult to make, it is often possible to substitute similar parts. For example, a hobbyist was able to install new windshield glass in his Mitchell touring car using rubber molding purchased from a truck dealer. The truck molding wasn't an exact duplicate, but it fit and looked like it belonged on the car.

Many times rubber that has begun to harden can be rejuvenated by applying a coating of ArmorAll. This rubber-renewing product is widely available in discount and auto supply stores and should be applied periodically to all rubber parts, including the tires. ArmorAll softens and restores the wet look of fresh rubber. It also coats the rubber to prevent further oxidation, the main cause of rubber deterioration. ArmorAll is easy

After cleaning the channel, apply a liberal bead of trim adhesive to hold the new rubber in place.

to use. Just spray it on and wipe it into the rubber with a cloth. Since ArmorAll is clear and does not spot paint, it can be sprayed on window moldings and other rubber trim. Any excess that lands on the paint is easily wiped off.

If you are repainting the car, you should wait to replace rubber parts until the painting process is finished. There are two advantages to removing rubber parts and replacing them after the car is painted. First, the surface under the rubber can be coated as well. This is important around the windows where water is often trapped when rubber moldings harden, causing rust. Second, this approach allows you to avoid the painstaking job of masking rubber parts to keep them from being painted.

After bodywork and painting steps are finished, the new rubber moldings can be installed. In most cases you will find that weatherseal, rubber trim and window moldings are easy to replace (Windshield rubber, as previously mentioned, should be fitted by a professional to avoid the risk of cracking the glass). Weatherstripping is glued in place around the edges of the doors and trunk using 3M brand Fast Tack Trim Adhesive, number 08031. This product is often available from auto supply stores or can be mail ordered from Metro Moulded Parts. The trim adhesive comes in a tube and is applied by squeezing a bead of glue onto the rubber. It is not necessary to apply a thick bead, since the glue will spread across the surface when the rubber is pressed in place. Wait until the glue becomes tacky before fitting the weatherstripping. You will find a friend's assistance helpful when installing and fitting the weatherseal. Even though trim adhesive dries quickly, the rubber has to be held tightly in place for a few minutes until the glue sets. During this time the rubber can be repositioned if necessary.

Now fit the new weatherseal into the channel. Note the proper placement, using the old weatherseal as a guide if necessary.

Running board matting and gravel shields found on older cars are glued in place using rubber contact cement. This product is also available from Metro Moulded Parts. Unlike trim adhesive, contact cement is applied both to the rubber and metal surfaces. Contrary to what seems logical, contact cement is allowed to dry on both surfaces before pressing the rubber in place. When using contact cement it's important to remember that the glue bonds instantly as the surfaces touch, so the rubber parts cannot be removed or repositioned. As a result, the parts must be aligned correctly, then pressed to the metal surface. With long strips, such as running board matting, you'll need a friend's help.

When installing rubber window moldings and glass channels you should follow the instructions in a body service manual. To replace door glass moldings, window channels and glass sweepers (the brush-like moldings that clean the glass as it is raised or lowered into the door panel), the trim molding—if one is used—and upholstery panel will have to be removed. With trim and upholstery out of the way and the glass cranked down into the door, the window channels, moldings and glass sweepers can be removed and replaced. Instructions in the body service manual describe the location of retaining clips and give other useful information. If a body service manual is not available, work on one door at a time so that you can use the others as guides to reassembly.

Fender welting is usually installed when fenders (or other body parts where it is used to prevent squeaks in the metal-to-metal seam) are mounted on the car after bodywork is completed. Welting is sold by the foot and is available from Metro Moulded Parts as well as numerous other mail-order suppliers. To fit new welting, measure along the seam and cut a strip to the length required. Next, bolt the fender loosely in place and slide the welting into the seam. The bolts holding the panels

The new weatherseal makes a tight seal against the trunk lid, ending water leaks and possible corrosion.

together will prevent the welting from fitting properly. To make the welting fit, mark the bolt locations then remove the welting and cut V-shaped notches at the marks, using scissors or a utility knife. Now when the welting is installed it will seat properly in the seam. If the car is to be repainted, wait to position the welting and tighten the fenders until after painting. In cases where the welting is deteriorated but there is no other reason to remove the fenders (or other body panels, such as the cowl-mounted gas tank on Model A Fords, where the seams are separated by welting), it is usually possible to slip new welting into the seam by loosening the bolts, removing the old welting, then cutting and fitting a new piece into place.

Station wagons, convertibles and other special body styles have additional weatherseal along the tailgate and top bows, for example, that may also need to be replaced and should be treated periodically with ArmorAll. Inspecting and replacing worn or missing weatherseal and other rubber parts are steps that are easy to overlook. Yet installing new rubber parts isn't difficult, and in most cases the supplies you will need are as easily obtainable as most collector car parts. Attention to such details as a car's rubber parts is a mark of well-executed refinishing.

11

Preparing A Trophy Winner

If you have been watching show car competition from the sidelines and wondered about driving into the fray, you will be encouraged to know that the expense and time it takes to restore a consistent trophy winner in regional shows, commemorations, county fairs and the like isn't beyond a dedicated collector's grasp. Moving from that level to national competition, though, is like stepping out of a penny-ante poker game into the Chicago futures market. Winning in the national league is expensive and takes a perfectionist's fetish for detail. Restoration costs amount to only part of the bill. Stiff competitive standards mean that serious contenders start with solid original cars or older restorations that could be driven and enjoyed without being touched. In preparation for the national show circuit, these cars receive such meticulous refinishing, often done by professionals at great cost, that they rarely set tread on a highway. They are trailered or trucked to shows, often in enclosed vans, stowed under wraps, seldom sat in and never loaded with kids for a Sunday drive.

Prepping a car to national show standards isn't cheap. In calculating the price, start with the cost of a premium automobile, add the expense of a total restoration, where no detail is too insignificant for attention, and expect to meet hidden costs besides. On the show circuit, tales of restoration cost-overruns are even more common than out-of-control budgets for military hardware. Not long ago I met a collector who said he trucked his just-restored Buick convertible to a nationally noted authority on the marque with instructions to nit-pick the car for flaws. The expert studied every detail. He confirmed the quality restoration except for one detail: the top. According to the Buick authority, the top's canvas lining strayed a shade from the authentic hue. So back went the convertible to the upholsterer for a second new top, this time made with canvas specially dyed to match the presumed original shade.

The manager of a plating company specializing in ten-point show chrome reported that a customer had shipped the headlights from a Packard, saying that the rest of the car's brightwork didn't need replating. But the rechromed lights with their rich triple plate made the car's radiator and bumpers look so shoddy in comparison that the owner felt compelled to upgrade all the car's plating to show chrome. The additional expense, well over a thousand dollars, improved the car's appearance, certainly, but mostly by overcoming the imbalance that had resulted from the owner's insistence on show-quality plating for the headlights.

A hobbyist who had worked for years preparing his 1914 Model T touring for national competition said that three days before the Hershey AACA (Antique Automobile Club of America) meet where his car was awarded a national first prize, he had spilled a drop of paint on one of the splash aprons while touching up nicks. The problem quickly spread when the rag soaked in lacquer thinner that he used to wipe up the spot lifted the finish. Fortunately, he was able to deftly touch up the area with an artist's brush, sand the spot with 600 grit paper and compound the finish to a gloss in time for the show. (Lacquer finishes are far more forgiving in this respect than enamel.) This concern for preserving a delicately prepared finish keeps collectors nervously shooing kids and enthusiastic adults back from their cars. At shows, flawless finishes have been marred by fans who have rubbed the rivets of their jeans or belt buckles against the paint.

Immaculate is the word that best describes a show car. New car dealers lay paper mats over the carpet on cars displayed in the show room, but hobbyists who attempt to preserve

Paint chips are inevitable, but the blemishes can be covered with a dab of touch-up paint applied with an artist's brush. You will also need a small can of matching-color paint and thinner or enamel reducer, depending on the car's finish. Clean the chipped area with wax remover or enamel reducer, if your car has an enamel finish.

their cars' just-restored look while moving and displaying them in a series of shows not only cover the carpets with mats but lay soft rags over the door strikers to keep from marring paint on the latches when the doors are closed. It is not uncommon to hear the charge of over-restoration leveled against show cars, particularly those competing for top national honors. Even the undersides of fenders and wheel wells may be waxed.

In national competition flawless attention to detail means far more than an unblemished finish and clean floor mats. In fact the word "detailing" is used to describe a series of procedures that starts with careful research to determine as accurately as possible every facet of the car's original appearance, equipment and construction. This information is used to guide each step of restoration. If chassis bolts left the factory cadmium plated, as they did on Model A Fords, then they must be similarly plated to meet the standards of national competition. The option of buying zinc-coated nuts and bolts at a local hardware store to substitute for originals won't work. Heads on modern bolts lack the thickness of original stock; and, besides, zinc plating has a yellowish cast, whereas cadmium is dull gray. Serious restorers will pay premium prices for NOS parts (new-old-stock in hobby lingo) rather than reproduction items because, even though the quality of replacement stock has improved greatly, the parts may vary enough from original to cost those few critical judging points. Improvements like hydraulic brakes and sealed-beam lights that weren't factory equipment aren't allowed. Signal lights, where they are required by law and installed with a degree of subtlety, don't bring a penalty.

During restoration, detailing means fitting engine and drive train parts to such close tolerances that the car's mechanics will

Lacquer finishes should be cleaned only with wax remover. Wiping the spot with thinner could soften or remove paint. Now carefully apply a dab of paint to the chipped area with an artist's brush.

run with the precision of a clock. Oil leaks are seen as signs of shoddy workmanship, so every gasket and seal has to fit as tightly as a well-soaked rain barrel. Grease fittings are given one or two shots, just enough to lubricate moving parts, then wiped dry. However well preserved an original car might be, even one that had been tucked away in a factory attic (were there such a place), it wouldn't stand a chance against a show-quality restoration.

No detail is too insignificant to pass over. Restorers aiming for national competition make sure the tire valves are covered with old-style metal caps. The modern plastic caps that most of us accept without thinking can dock an otherwise perfect car one judging point each. It's even possible that a show car may never be washed. Unless water is naturally pure, it can spot the paint, soak into wood and penetrate body seams. The dust a prize winner collects while parked on the show grounds will often be whisked off with a feather puff before the car is tucked away under wraps until the next show.

Competition and attendant preparation is much less intense at local shows. The comparison isn't meant to detract from the dedication that goes into building a national winner. Capturing first place amid the best cars in the nation is an exclusive pedigree, a distinction fitting an immaculate restoration. Those of us who lack a perfectionist's stamina can surely appreciate the masterpieces others create, but the more relaxed standards of local meets allow hobbyists who enjoy driving their cars the chance to bring home a trophy. Frame up restorations are common, but not the rule at the local level and original cars that have been upgraded cosmetically, or are exceptionally well preserved, also stand a fair chance of winning first place honors.

Despite the more relaxed standards of local and regional meets, competition at all levels involves much of the same prep-

Allow a few minutes for the dab of paint to set, then build up successive layers until the paint is flush with the surrounding finish. When the paint dries, you can rub the spot lightly with polishing compound to remove all traces of the blemish.

aration when it comes time to get ready for a show. Thorough cleaning always seems to reveal a few paint chips, nicks or scratches in the finish, even on a car that is treated with china doll care. Show car owners put together touch-up kits to fill in the scars and their procedure is a model all hobbyists can benefit from copying. The kits are usually made up of a small amount of paint poured into baby food jars, along with a jar of thinner or enamel reducer, an assortment of artist's brushes, several sheets of 400 and 600 grit sandpaper, a can of polishing compound, assorted soft rags and a can of car wax. The day before a show, or even after the car is set up for display, if competition is keen and judging standards are strict, a dedicated show car owner will inspect the finish for chips and fill the damaged spots with a small dab of paint from the tip of an

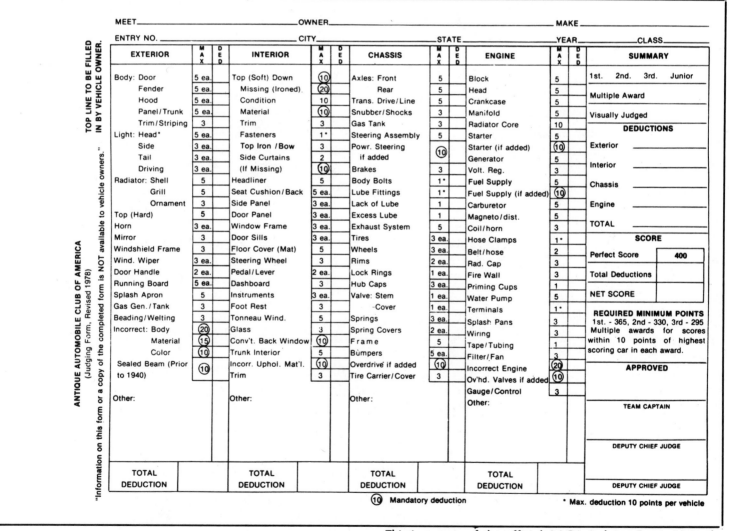

TOP LINE TO BE FILLED IN BY VEHICLE OWNER.

MEET_____ OWNER_____ MAKE_____

ENTRY NO._____ CITY_____ STATE_____ YEAR_____ CLASS_____

EXTERIOR	MAX	DED	INTERIOR	MAX	DED	CHASSIS	MAX	DED	ENGINE	MAX	DED	SUMMARY
Body: Door	5 ea.		Top (Soft) Down	(10)		Axles: Front	5		Block	5		1st. 2nd. 3rd. Junior
Fender	5 ea.		Missing (Ironed)	(20)		Rear	5		Head	5		Multiple Award
Hood	5 ea.		Condition	10		Trans. Drive/Line	5		Crankcase	5		
Panel/Trunk	5 ea.		Material	(10)		Snubber/Shocks	3		Manifold	5		Visually Judged
Trim/Striping	3		Trim	3		Gas Tank	3		Radiator Core	10		DEDUCTIONS
Light: Head*	5 ea.		Fasteners	1*		Steering Assembly	5		Starter	5		Exterior _____
Side	3 ea.		Top Iron/Bow	3		Powr. Steering			Starter (if added)	(10)		
Tail	3 ea.		Side Curtains	2		if added	(10)		Generator	5		Interior _____
Driving	3 ea.		(If Missing)	(10)		Brakes	3		Volt. Reg.	3		
Radiator: Shell	5		Headliner	5		Body Bolts	1*		Fuel Supply	5		Chassis _____
Grill	5		Seat Cushion/Back	5 ea.		Lube Fittings	1*		Fuel Supply (if added)	(10)		
Ornament	3		Side Panel	3 ea.		Lack of Lube	1		Carburetor	5		Engine _____
Top (Hard)	3		Door Panel	3 ea.		Excess Lube	1		Magneto/dist.	5		
Horn	3 ea.		Window Frame	3 ea.		Exhaust System	5		Coil/horn	3		TOTAL _____
Mirror	3		Door Sills	3 ea.		Tires	3 ea.		Hose Clamps	1*		SCORE
Windshield Frame	3		Floor Cover (Mat)	5		Wheels	3 ea.		Belt/hose	2		Perfect Score 400
Wind. Wiper	3 ea.		Steering Wheel	3		Rims	2 ea.		Rad. Cap	3		
Door Handle	2 ea.		Pedal/Lever	2 ea.		Lock Rings	1 ea.		Fire Wall	3		Total Deductions
Running Board	5 ea.		Dashboard	3		Hub Caps	3 ea.		Priming Cups	1		
Splash Apron	5		Instruments	3 ea.		Valve: Stem	1 ea.		Water Pump	5		NET SCORE
Gas Gen./Tank	3		Foot Rest	3		-Cover	1 ea.		Terminals	1*		REQUIRED MINIMUM POINTS
Beading/Welting	3		Tonneau Wind.	5		Springs	3 ea.		Splash Pans	3		1st. - 365, 2nd. - 330, 3rd - 295
Incorrect: Body	(20)		Glass	3		Spring Covers	2 ea.		Wiring	3		Multiple awards for scores within 10 points of highest scoring car in each award.
Material	(15)		Conv't. Back Window	(10)		Frame	5		Tape/Tubing	1		
Color	(10)		Trunk Interior	5		Bumpers	5 ea.		Filter/Fan	3		APPROVED
Sealed Beam (Prior to 1940)	(10)		Incorr. Uphol. Mat'l.	(10)		Overdrive if added	(10)		Incorrect Engine	(20)		
			Trim	3		Tire Carrier/Cover	3		Ov'hd. Valves if added	(10)		
									Gauge/Control	3		TEAM CAPTAIN
Other:			Other:			Other:			Other:			
												DEPUTY CHIEF JUDGE
TOTAL DEDUCTION			TOTAL DEDUCTION			TOTAL DEDUCTION			TOTAL DEDUCTION			DEPUTY CHIEF JUDGE

(10) Mandatory deduction   * Max. deduction 10 points per vehicle

This is a copy of the official AACA Judging Form. Note the point breakdown within each major category, especially for those items that carry large mandatory deductions.

artist's brush. If time allows, chips can be completely hidden by building up several layers of paint, allowing ample drying time for each. When the chip is filled slightly above the surrounding finish, wet sanding with 600 grit paper followed by polishing compound to rub out the fine sand scratches leaves the retouched area ready to wax.

After waxing, a few stray white streaks always remain on trim and welting. For a show, even this faint residue has to be cleaned off. The usual tools for this job are a discarded toothbrush or a toothpick wrapped with a soft rag. White sidewalls must be scoured snowy white. Blackwalls and all rubber moldings are often treated with ArmorAll to preserve the gloss look of fresh rubber. Spoke wheels quickly collect dust and road grime and usually need cleaning before a show. Brass car owners win the tennis-elbow prize for their hours of preshow polishing. There really is no totally effective coating that will protect brass trim without causing more problems than it solves. Cloth covers for brass lights, acetylene generators, radiators and hubcaps retard oxidation that dulls the surface but the only way to prepare a brass-era car for judging is to gather the family and polish every square centimeter of the copper-colored metal.

Local and regional meets vary as widely from national events in judging standards as in the caliber of the cars. Judges at local events may pick the winning cars by their looks, but established national organizations like the Antique Automobile Club of America (AACA) have labored for years to eliminate subjective judging. To accomplish its goal, the AACA has trained its judges and developed a comprehensive judging form used for all its shows. Careful examination of the AACA and other clubs' judging sheets is a must before starting on the competition trail. The AACA's judging form, shown here in its 1978 revision, is broken into four categories: interior, exterior, chassis and engine. Note that individual components are itemized in a point system that totals 400 for a perfect score. According to AACA stipulation, a minimum of 365 points is necessary for a first prize trophy. The purpose for this ruling is to keep nationwide standards uniform.

The AACA form works on the principle of deductions. No bonus points are added for accessories; extra items mounted on a car are judged along with everything else. Major penalties fall to items carrying mandatory deductions such as sealed-beam headlights installed on cars built before 1940, incorrect body color and overhead-valve performance kits. As judges inspect the exterior they are instructed to deduct points for paint overspray on beading or welt, wavy metal, dents, paint chips or a poor finish. The total penalty is compounded by the number of infractions. Inside the car, judges check for nonauthentic upholstery material, stains or wear and tear. Again, multiple deductions are possible.

Tire sizes must be compatible with original equipment, 7.60 × 15 rather than G78 × 15, for example. The engine compartment is scrutinized for grease, new-style hose clamps and nonauthentic accessories, including starters on cars that weren't so equipped originally. Running an incorrect engine carries a whopping twenty-point penalty. According to AACA standards, the only permissible accessories, whether mechanical or dress-

---

NATIONAL MEET JUDGING FORM

Entry No._____

Division_____

Class_____

Meet_____

Location_____

Classic Car Club of America

Final Score_____

Position_____

Date:_____

Year_____ Make_____ Cyl_____Model_____ Owner_____

Body Style_____ Body Builder_____ (if custom) Address_____

Mfg. Serial No._____and if Senior, No._____ City_____ State_____ Zip_____

☐ Check box at left if senior badge was displayed. All Senior cars must display Senior badge to be judged.

Legend of Scores

Unsatisfactory - 0	Good -3
Poor -1	Very Good - 4
Fair - 2	Excellent - 5

Instructions: Judges use numerals in scoring — EXAMPLE: If the item is "GOOD" write "3" in box marked "SCORE". All boxes under "SCORE" are to be filled in.

If top is metal, mark "METAL" under "SCORE". Judges are NOT to total their scores.

Automatic Disqualifications

No fire extinguisher
No safety glass
Non-authentic air conditioning
Non-authentic power steering
Non-authentic braking system
Non-authentic automatic transmission
Non-authentic engine
Non-authentic body

Automatic 1-Point Deductions

Sealed beam headlights, if not factory
Truck tires
Enamel paint unless original factory
Vinyl or plastic open car tops, boots or
    side curtains (exclusive of clear plastic
    used in side curtains)
Synthetic upholstery material
Direction signals —
    if modern or commercial in design
Flexible exhaust pipe where not factory

*ALL DEDUCTIONS FOR AUTHENTICITY **MUST** BE DOCUMENTED BELOW

Mechanical Condition and Maintenance

	Score
A. Engine, Start and Idle	
B. Windshield Wipers	
C. Exhaust System	
D. Brakes (pedal and hand)	
E. Lights	
F. Horn	
G. Tires	
H. Glass and/or Side Curtains	
I. Wiring (neat and safe)	
J. Cooling System (top tank, core, hoses)	
K. Authenticity*	

Section Total_____

Physical Appearance

A. Engine Room	
B. Undercarriage	
C. Body (condition of)	
D. Roof or Top (If all metal, DO NOT score, see averaging sheet)	
E. Plating	
F. Paint	
G. Upholstery (headliners, floor coverings)	
H. Instruments, Dash and Interior Trim	
I. Degree of Authenticity of Restoration*	

Section Total_____

Judge's Name (please print)_____

Judge's Signature_____

Page Total_____

This is a copy of the official CCCA Judging Form. The maximum possible score is 100 points, 5 points for each category. Note the list of exceptions that cause automatic disqualification and the items that cause automatic point deductions.

up, had to be available from the factory. In a dispute, burden of proof that an accessory was a factory option falls on the owner with judges holding final authority in those instances owners are unable to document. Presumably a first place winner in AACA competition represents factory-new condition. Seldom, though, would a car in pristine, as manufactured, condition be good enough. The pressures of competition make winning cars even better than new.

The Classic Car Club of America's famous 100-point judging system was devised nearly thirty years ago by former CCCA president Robert E. Turnquist. The form is divided into two parts: "Mechanical Condition and Maintenance" and "Physical Appearance," with fifty-five points available in the former category and forty-five points in the latter. Although the system is not perfect (for example, it does not include any "in motion" test of the vehicle being judged), it is recognized as an excellent system and has been widely copied. As is true in the AACA and many other clubs' judging events, a fire extinguisher must be with the car on the CCCA judging field on pain of disqualification.

While the AACA and CCCA formats have been widely copied, judging standards vary from club to club. Mustang owners will want to study judging guides for their cars, while mid-fifties Chevy owners should examine Chevy club judging standards. As an example, the national woody club, dedicated to wooden-bodied cars of all makes and models, awards its trophies on strictly noncompetitive terms. The categories include longest distance traveled, ladies' choice, oldest and newest cars at the meet. The woody club is one of several collector car organizations that encourages owners to drive their vintage cars.

The satisfaction that comes from building a show car depends on an honest evaluation of one's purpose for owning a collector car. National competition requires total commitment to perfection but brings rewards on a high order. Cars entered in local and regional competition can be enjoyed for touring and family outings as well.

If competition at any level isn't your idea of enjoying the old car hobby, just dress ma in her best gingham, the girls in bloomers and the boys in knickers, put on your straw hat and wide suspenders, tie a crate of chickens to one running board, a gas can to the other and rumble in as folks just down from the hills. If the disguise is good enough, nobody will ever guess you're part of the show.

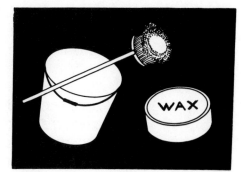

12

Car Care And Storage

Collector cars invariably spend a good deal more time in storage than on the highway. As a result of this pampering, it should follow that very little in the way of special care and maintenance is required to keep a collector car in prime condition. Actually, unless proper precautions are taken, storage is more likely to cause mechanical deterioration than regular use.

As a case in point, in the fall of 1957, my uncle spotted a perky Model A sport coupe while on a Sunday drive. He bought the car on the spot and drove it home. Model A Fords had passed from commonplace by then and for the next several weekends he enjoyed driving the little Ford, a better running rig, he said, than his late model car. When snow came he parked the car in one of his barns for the winter, where it sits today—tires rotted, covered with layers of dust. The next summer he attempted to run it, but the battery was dead and one of the tires kept going flat. A process of gradual deterioration had begun that made driving the little car more work than fun.

Spring and fall car care rituals, along with inspection and maintenance before trips and tours, are necessary to keep collector cars in their prime, minimize upkeep costs and help insure against an embarrassing and troublesome highway breakdown. Tour preparations will vary somewhat with the age and type of car, but should include an oil change, even when maintenance intervals total less than 3,000 miles. Short drives add more contaminants to oil than long runs, especially in brisk weather when running with an open choke can cause raw gas to wash down the cylinder walls into the oil. After changing the oil and filter on cars that are so equipped, jack the car up and grease all the lubrication fittings (several dozen on many vintage cars). Next, add a drop of oil to the generator bearings, if an oil hole is provided, and service any other areas that require routine attention. On older cars this can be a rather long list. The water pump packing nut may need to be tightened and the clutch throw-out bearing greased, for example.

Tour preparations should include a thorough inspection of the lights, tires and brakes. It's a good idea to carry spare light bulbs, including an extra headlight. Check tires for signs of wear and cracked sidewalls that can result from the tires going flat during storage. Badly worn or cracked tires should be replaced. Check brakes for adjustment and, on cars equipped with hydraulic brakes, check the fluid level in the master cylinder. If the fluid level is low, inspect the system for leaks in the brake lines or wheel cylinders. If the car's hydraulic braking system is filled with petroleum-based fluid, a pretour maintenance session may be an appropriate time to have a brake shop flush the lines of old fluid and refill them with a DOT 5 silicone brake fluid. Few hobbyists realize that petroleum-based brake fluid absorbs moisture which accumulates in the system. As a result, hydraulic brake systems containing petroleum-based fluid should be flushed and refilled every few years. Since silicone brake fluid is not water absorbent it helps preserve hydraulic brake systems and does not have to be changed.

Before a long tour, it's also a good idea to give the car a tune-up. Clean and set the spark plugs and points, and check the engine timing. While you are working under the hood, inspect and clean the air and fuel filters. Check the fan belt and water hoses, and replace these items if the rubber shows signs of cracking. Fill the battery with distilled water and top up the radiator.

Even after an extended maintenance routine you should pack a tool kit and assorted spare parts such as an extra con-

Bringing home a collector car raises the question of storage. Old barns offer shelter but little more.

Don Orr's restoration shop in Williamson, New York, is a good example of a spacious, well-planned combination workshop and storage building.

denser, fan belt, the light bulbs previously mentioned, along with any other items you feel would be handy. My father habitually carried a spare generator when he toured in his Plymouth convertible. Hobbyists touring in groups frequently carry adequate spare parts to make emergency road repairs should a mechanical mishap occur to one of the cars in the caravan. As a final precaution, it is also wise to pack a flashlight with fresh batteries and a nylon tow rope.

Along with periodic mechanical maintenance, collector cars should receive thorough cleaning and other preparations preceding any period of extended storage. To assure dependable motoring, another set of procedures should be followed when a car emerges from storage. These car care rituals are usually performed semiannually in the spring and fall. Preparations for storage will take a Saturday, maybe a weekend, and possibly require a stop at a discount mart's auto counter for car wax and cleaning supplies, and a review of time-tested preservation techniques.

The prestorage clean-up routine begins with thorough washing, not only topside, but underneath where caked-on dirt and road grime trap moisture that breeds decay. Since it is important to float dirt off with a gentle wash, rather than forcing it into tiny crevices, cold water from a hose gets the job done better than using a high-pressure spray at a car wash. Besides, the harsh detergent and hot water from a car wash may cut through the wax and abrade the car's finish. Washing is best

An inside view of Mike Worcester's restoration shop near Dublin, New Hampshire, shows parts neatly stacked and waiting for refinishing. Planned storage maximizes interior space.

Of course, if your storage area looms cavernously like this hobbyist's paradise, you can collect cars and parts to your heart's content.

done at home where the kids can help. Vinyl tops on late model convertibles should be washed with mild detergent or vinyl upholstery cleaner, rinsed and wiped dry. Be sure to wash off any detergent that runs down on the finish. Detergents and the minerals that are found in most water supplies leave water spots if they are allowed to dry on a painted finish, so always park your car in the shade for washing and wipe the finish dry, either with a chamois or turkish towels.

Even though a sanitary engine doesn't run any better than one that is covered with grease and oil, a collector car's mechanical heart deserves care, too. To preserve that showroom-fresh look under the hood, spray the engine and other areas where grease and oil have collected with Gunk, a water soluble degreaser. To remove heavy deposits, work the Gunk into the grease and oil with a discarded paint brush. After allowing ten to fifteen minutes for the Gunk to work, wash the area clean. Be careful to avoid spraying water into the distributor, generator and other electrical parts.

After washing, vacuum the interior, trunk and canvas top on older convertibles. Leather and vinyl upholstery can be maintained by wiping the surface periodically with a damp cloth; fabric interiors require occasional sweeping with a whisk broom or vacuuming. During the semiannual cleaning sessions, leather should be treated with conditioner or saddle soap. Vinyl upholstery can be renewed with upholstery cleaner worked into the pores of the fabric with a soft-bristled vegetable brush. To finish the job, wipe the vinyl clean with a sponge or damp cloth.

Were a family car ever treated to a cleaning as thorough as this, the job would be nearly done. Not so with a collector car. Painted metal on the dash and door pillars should be re-waxed, and varnished interior wood treated with silicone spray.

Cleaning a collector car begins with a bath of mild soap hosed off with cold water. These photos feature Steve Olesky of Columbus, Ohio, and his prize-winning Jaguar XK120 roadster.

To preserve the weatherseal around the windows, trunk and doors, spray the rubber with a coating of silicone or ArmorAll.

Cleaning the window glass comes next. Rather than using household glass cleaners or an ammonia solution and paper towels, you might try the following method to make the glass sparkle like crystal. Add a dash of kerosene to a bucket of water. Wash the glass, then wipe the windows dry with a wad of newspaper. The newsprint acts as a mild polish and buffs the glass to a mirror sheen.

Though most hobbyists favor particular brands of wax, traditional Simonize applied over liquid cleaner gives a longer-lasting, tougher coating than most one-step waxes. Whatever your choice, waxing is part of the cleaning regimen. Before waxing, inspect the finish for chips and scratches. To prevent rust spots from developing, touch up these minor blemishes with a dab of paint applied with an artist's brush.

Glass Wax is an effective nonabrasive cleaner and polish for chrome trim. Tires should be coated with ArmorAll to maintain a glossy black coloring and to prevent the rubber from cracking. By the time you have oiled the door and hood hinges and rubbed the door locks with Latch Ease, you'll probably be ready to call an end to the day's work, but mechanical preparations remain.

Car care sessions are intended to ensure that your collector car can be driven and enjoyed year after year. Storage, on the other hand, means idleness, and to a machine, rest doesn't bring rejuvenation, but debilitation. Machinery doesn't count

After washing, Steve wipes the finish dry. Some collectors prefer to dry the finish with a chamois, others use a turkish towel.

Regular cleaning preserves a finely detailed engine compartment.

the days until Friday. An engine has to enter storage thinking it's still running. This means that the spark plugs should be unscrewed and an oil mist sprayed into the cylinders as they're cranked over for the last time. It would be ideal if a supplier marketed petcocks that could be tapped into the bottoms of mufflers for drainage but, lacking this innovation, plastic bags or an old sock tied over the tail pipe outlet and carburetor air inlet will prevent additional moisture from entering the engine and exhaust system during storage.

While permanent antifreeze with rust-inhibiting additives protects a car's cooling system from corrosion it is still advisable to flush and refill the cooling system each year. Water pump life can be extended by adding a can of water pump lubricant to the new coolant.

A debate has stewed for years as to whether gas tanks should be drained before storage. Gasoline does break down in time but usually no serious deterioration occurs during a few months storage. If a car will be stored for a prolonged period of time, the gas tank should be drained. The other alternative is to fuel the car with 87 octane aviation gas before storage. Unlike automotive gasoline, the aviation variety is less likely to deposit a gummy residue on the bottom of the gas tank.

Options for a storage site are usually limited to the space available, but ideal storage conditions include: low humidity, moderate air circulation, fairly constant temperature and no direct sunlight. Avoid barns and outbuildings with dirt or gravel floors because an earth base draws moisture that can keep the underside of the car perpetually damp. As a friend discovered,

A shop vac is ideal for cleaning carpets.

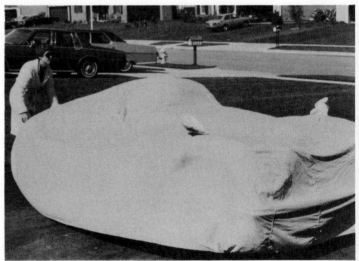

Commercial storage buntings are sewn to fit the car's contours. Whether a car is covered with a custom fit bunting or old blankets, the material should "breathe" to prevent condensation.

improper storage conditions can do more harm than parking a car outside in the elements.

Several years ago a maple sugaring shack on our property in Vermont served as winter storage for a friend's Packard Custom. We jacked up the car and propped chunks of firewood under the axles, then put the Packard's fate out of mind. Occasionally as my wife and I skied past the shed that winter we peeked in at the Packard. Seeing that no appreciable amount of snow had settled on it, I assumed the car was doing fine.

The next spring, when we pushed the Packard out and jump started it, a stuck valve and a car-shaped outline of rust flakes left inside the shed told the true story. The gravel floor had soaked the Packard's floor pan with moisture through six months of storage. Temperature fluctuations during the January thaw had spanned fifty degrees in a twenty-four hour period and resulted in condensation that had bred mildew spots on the car's mohair interior. The brightwork had a glazed-over look and a thick layer of grime had settled on the lacquer finish. As it turned out, in offering my shed for storage, I hadn't done my friend any favors. If the Packard had been stored outside, the engine could have been started periodically and the sun would have dried out the interior. Along with providing shelter from the elements, indoor storage should afford protection from moisture.

Temperature fluctuations and humidity can be controlled by insulating the storage area. If your garage doubles as car

My Porsche Super 90, purchased in Munich, got a morning rub-down in the French farm lane where I'd spent the night.

Car care supplies include cleaning compound, wax, silicone, engine degreaser and tire cleaner.

259

storage and workshop, it makes sense to insulate the walls and ceiling. Fiberglass insulation is relatively inexpensive and can be easily stapled to the studding. Cement, too, draws moisture. This is especially true in an older construction where the concrete was seldom poured over a vapor barrier. A collector I visited recently made the floor of his garage dry, warm and comfortable to walk on by covering the concrete in the area where he stores his cars with indoor-outdoor carpeting.

During storage be sure to keep the car covered. This is particularly important when the car is stored in the family garage, where the finish can be easily scraped or marred. Tailored car covers are available from suppliers advertising in hobby magazines. An equally effective, less expensive covering can be made by sewing old blankets together. Never cover a car with plastic. As the temperature fluctuates, moisture will condense under the plastic sheeting and settle on the car. To protect cloth interiors distribute a handful of mothballs inside the car. Since mothballs could discolor the fabric, they should be placed on the floor mats rather than on the seats.

When a car is stored for long periods, disconnect the battery or, better yet, remove the battery and place it in a warm area where it can be recharged periodically. Coat the terminals with Vaseline to prevent corrosion and place the battery on a workbench or a wooden block, rather than a cement floor. To preserve the tires, jack up the car and place blocks under the axles. Covering the chrome with pastewax or a thin layer of oil or Vaseline will protect the plating from oxidation. Always insure cars during storage. The risk of fire, vandalism or other mishaps makes this precaution a must.

When a car is removed from storage many of the preservation measures just described may have to be reversed to return the car to running condition. In addition, electrical connections have a tendency to corrode during storage; so it is not uncommon for sporadic failures to occur in the electrical system after prolonged storage. To troubleshoot electrical failures, first check the fuse. If the fuse is good, check the current at the light socket or plug connection to the failed electrical component. If the current is flowing to the socket or connection and the component does not operate, lightly sand the socket and metal conductor. In most cases, this simple remedy will repair the failure.

Seals and gaskets may dry and shrink during storage, causing oil or water leaks for a time. The first drives after storage should be local. Check fluid levels frequently until the leaking stops.

Periodic maintenance and proper storage are essential to the preservation and enjoyment of a collector car. For the trouble it saves, car care is time well spent.

13

Protecting Your Collector Car Investment

Disasters always afflict the other guy, right? That's what I thought, too. So when my friend John said, "You're welcome to keep the Model A in my barn as long as you like; the car will be well-protected there unless somebody sets the place on fire," I laughed off his warning. The vandals who smashed out the barn's windows a year earlier had made me wonder if the barn was a poor storage risk, but since signs of vandalism promptly ceased when a neighbor moved in across the street I assumed that the trouble had passed.

I had insured my Model A with J. C. Taylor, the original collector car insurer, primarily for liability protection. It was hard to consider the monetary value of the car that had been given to me by my uncles when I was fourteen years old. You don't sell a family pet or the Father's Day presents your children proudly make in school, and you don't sell your first car, especially when you've managed to keep tabs on it for half its life and two-thirds of yours. Then, too, how could I set a price on a learn-as-you-go restoration begun in sub-zero January temperatures in Vermont? On work days, the blazing fire in the woodstove had only softened the frost on the garage windows by noon. Add the frustration of advertised-as-original reproduction parts that had to be remanufactured to fit and the car's sentimental value far exceeded any price I could set.

Vermont doesn't require drivers with accident-free records to carry liability insurance but even though I intended to use the Model A only for parades and an occasional family outing, I believe that everyone operating a vehicle on the highways has the obligation to protect themselves, their passengers and other motorists by carrying the full liability coverage. As to comprehensive insurance, fire and theft, I probably would have passed that coverage by, thinking the tough Model A that had survived a fit of my uncle's temper would be around long after its present owner had departed. Fortunately, J. C. Taylor, and the other collector car insurers, lump liability and comprehensive in a package. You can't buy one without the other. I had kept a running ledger of restoration expenses and used the final tally to calculate the car's value. At policy renewal periods I increased this figure slightly to compensate for inflation and progressive improvements to the car.

The barn burned to the ground the day after John's prophetically timed warning. The fire cremated the Model A. It had been stored in an insulated, humidity controlled room on the barn's main floor; when the blazing structure collapsed, the cherry-hot Model A fell one story onto the cement floor below. The heat-softened metal contorted on impact. The car's wooden body lay in fire ash, the brass headlight rims, copper radiator and aluminum pistons vaporized. Nothing usable remained.

Although antique car insurance agencies, J. C. Taylor included, deal with their customers through the mail when they write the policies, I was given prompt, personal service less than a day after the fire. The company representative passed his report along to a nationally recognized appraiser who promptly certified the loss. J. C. Taylor's check for the full amount of the policy arrived in less than a month.

I had purchased my coverage from J. C. Taylor principally because my father had insured his collector cars with the company and to my knowledge, its reputation is unblemished. This isn't to say that one collector car insurer is necessarily better than another. In a circle as tight as the car hobby, word of mouth is often the best recommendation and following other collectors' advice may be as good a way as any to shop. A list

Covered with roofing tin and contorted by the heat of the barn fire that vaporized its brass headlight rims, the remains of my first car were a sad sight.

of collector car insurers appears at the end of this chapter. Application forms can be obtained by writing the companies. Several companies include an application form in their ads that appear in old car hobby magazines.

For the past decade old car values have risen so rapidly that replacement costs soon outpace insurance coverage unless policies are revalued regularly. Old car price guides such

A sample insurance form, specifically made up for collector cars.

as *The Gold Book,* covering models 1955 to 1977, *C.A.R. Values,* covering models 1893 to 1981, or the *Old Car Value Guide,* covering models 1897 to 1970, are good references to use in determining your car's current value. Cars in the process of restoration and spare parts also warrant insuring. American Collectors Insurance allows a fixed amount of additional insurance at no extra cost to cover spare parts. The low rates for collector car insurance reflect careful driving and the precautions owners take to protect their investments—but the unforeseen can occur.

Collector car insurers have kept pace with the hobby in their willingness to cover late model, high-performance collector cars, though owners may be required to certify that their vehicles have been maintained in original condition and will be used exclusively for hobby purposes, not for general transportation. Although the rates for late model cars are usually slightly higher than the cost of insuring older cars, collector insurance is still a bargain. By not abusing their policies, hobbyists have kept collector car insurance rates remarkably low and enabled the insurance companies to retain no-deductible comprehensive coverage, a feature that has all but vanished on standard auto policies.

Regardless of rates, an owner's care is always the best insurance. Collector cars are irreplaceable, both from the standpoint of their diminishing supply and the fact that a car you have restored with the sweat of your brow has an intangible value no amount of insurance can cover.

Collector Car Insurance Companies

American Collectors Insurance
P.O. Box 720
214 West Main Street
Moorestown, New Jersey 08057
(This company includes $500 spare parts coverage free.)

The Collector Vehicle Program
James A. Grundy Insurance
501 Office Center Drive
Fort Washington, Pennsylvania 19034
(This company sets no maximum mileage.)

Condon and Skelly
Antique Motor Car Insurance
Route 130 and Berverly-Rancocas Road
P.O. Drawer A
Willingboro, New Jersey 08046
(This company offers reduced rates when more than one collector vehicle is insured.)

J. C. Taylor Antique Auto Insurance
8701 West Chester Pike
Upper Darby, Pennsylvania 19082
(This company offers reduced rates when more than one collector vehicle is insured.)

14
Rust-Proofing You Can Do Yourself

The combination of moisture and untreated metal is the prime cause of rust. Since the undersides of fenders and other body panels are often coated with only a thin layer of paint, or no coating at all, most corrosion damage begins on the inside of car body panels and works out. Areas of the front and rear fenders around the wheel openings are especially prone to rust because dirt, and road salt in wintery regions, collects in crevices trapping and holding moisture against the metal.

Corrosion can be arrested by keeping a car clean, avoiding driving in road salt and providing proper storage, but to prevent rust from developing, the metal has to be sealed against moisture. Paint, of course, coats the outside surface but is not a satisfactory covering for the inside of doors, rocker panels, fenders and other body panel areas that are exposed to moisture through dampness and condensation. There are two ways to treat the metal in these hidden areas. The first is to have a commercial rust-proofing shop coat the metal with a petroleum-based protective coating that is designed to seal out moisture and remain flexible for years.

In order to access the inside surfaces of door pillars, rocker panels and other enclosed structures, the people who operate the rust-proofing equipment drill access holes through which they insert a slender wand that sprays a soft, greaselike coating onto the interior surfaces. To coat door panels, rust-proofing operators remove the upholstery panels. Inside the wheel wells and on the floor pan they spray a tarlike substance that stays pliable, unlike the undercoating found on older cars that dries out and cracks, opening up traps for salt and moisture. In most cases, rust-proofing shops don't guarantee their work on older cars, but when sprayed over unrusted metal the coatings offer the same effective protection as on a new car.

For hobbyists who live in areas not serviced by commercial rust-proofing shops, or who want to do the job themselves, rust-proofing kits are available from auto supply stores, the automotive sections of discount department stores and mail-order

Modern rust-proofing chemicals stay pliable for long-lasting protection.

John Mast at Mast Brothers Rustproofing in Zanesville, Ohio, lifts off the door panel to access the inner metal surfaces.

With the upholstery removed, it's easy to see why rust-proofing is so important. The metal is completely unprotected.

automotive supply companies. The kits contain aerosol spray cans with rust-proofing chemicals designed for both internal and external application, a long slender wand to reach inside enclosed body panels, and plastic plugs to seal the holes that are drilled to insert the spray wand.

With this equipment, hobbyists can duplicate or even surpass the rust-proofing protection of commercial shops. The secret of effective rust-proofing is getting a thorough coating on clean metal. Hobbyists have the advantage here in that they can apply the protective coverings in stages while working on the car. As an example, a friend recently purchased a Mustang Mach 1 with a rust-free body and an engine badly needing a major overhaul. For easy access to the engine and front suspension, both of which he planned to rebuild, Warren removed the front fenders and hood. While these body panels were off the car, he sprayed rust-proofing inside the hood and fender panels and was able to reach areas that would not be accessible when the panels were mounted.

Areas such as the floors and quarter panels that are susceptible to rust but are usually covered can easily be rust-proofed while upholstery and carpet are being replaced. Rubberized undercoating, also available in spray cans, provides effective rust protection for the floor pan. The rust-proofing material supplied with kits for coating panels such as the insides

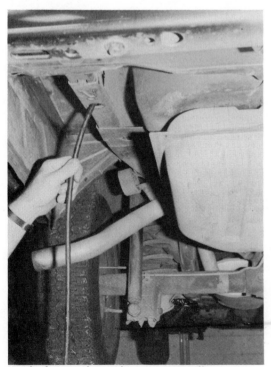

Inside frame channels are especially vulnerable to rust.

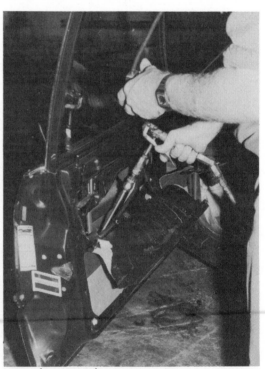

Inner door panels, too, receive a liberal coating.

of doors has a thin consistency and may drip out through the drain holes. If this occurs, leave the doors open while the excess rust-proofing drains out and spread newspapers under the doors on the garage floor to catch the drips. When the dripping stops, make sure that the drain holes are open so that moisture condensing inside the door or water seeping past the windowseal won't settle in the bottom of the doors.

Metal that has been cleaned by sandblasting or chemical derusting should be primed and painted before rust-proofing is applied. To coat the inside areas of hood and trunk panels where a spray gun cannot reach, pour primer through the baffles in the backing panel. Then, with a friend's assistance, rock the panel back and forth until the primer covers the inner surface. Unless zinc-chromate or other rust-resistant primer is used, repeat these steps to coat the metal with paint.

The thicker, tarlike rust-proofing supplied with the kit is used to coat the inside of the fender wells, the underside of the floor and other underbody structures. To prepare these surfaces for rust-proofing, wash inside the wheel wells to remove road dirt and debris, then jack up the car, place jack stands under the axles to support the car's weight and remove the wheels. Spray on the rust-proofing when all metal is thoroughly dry.

In addition to the floor pan, the frame also needs protection from rust. While working underneath the car, be sure to spray rust-proofing inside the rocker panels. The rocker panels are

Fender panels are accessed through holes drilled in the door jambs.

located under the doors and quarter panels. These panels typically rust from the inside out, due to condensation and the fact that the inside metal surfaces may not have been coated at the factory. Rust-proofing can often be sprayed through drain holes in the bottom of the rocker panels. If the panels are sealed, holes will have to be drilled to insert the spray wand. Use the thinner-bodied rust-proofing spray to coat the inside surfaces of the rocker panels and other enclosed areas, including the door and cowl pillars and rear quarter panels. Holes must be drilled to access the insides of body pillars, but inner recesses of the rear quarter panels can usually be reached by removing the taillights and inserting the spray wand through the taillight openings.

Whether you have rust-proofing applied commercially or do the job yourself, protecting body metal from corrosion is an essential step in preserving a collector car.

A heavier-bodied rust-proofing chemical is applied to exterior chassis surfaces.

The finished product has a shiny, freshly painted look.

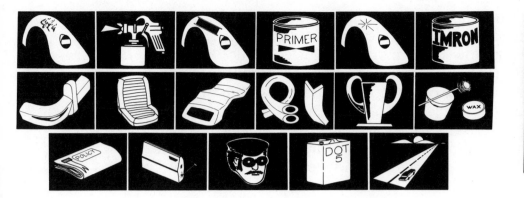

15

Guarding Collector Cars Against Theft

One summer day in 1957, my uncle returned to his car after treating his son to an afternoon with the Yankees, only to discover that he had dropped his keys somewhere in Yankee Stadium. After emptying all his pockets in desperation, he was about ready to give my aunt a call when a stranger who had been watching his predicament offered help. (New Yorkers really are a friendly lot once they're sure you're not going to mug them.) "My car is just like yours," the fellow remarked, "Why don't you try my keys?" Stuck as he was, Uncle Bill still tried to explain that car keys don't interchange, even on similar looking models. "Let's try, anyway," the stranger insisted, "It can't hurt." With that he slipped his key in the lock and in a wink he'd opened the driver's door of Uncle Bill's 1956 Bel Air hardtop. "I've got an extra set of keys, so you can use these to drive home," the samaritan offered.

When Uncle Bill told the story to my father, who worked for Rochester Products, General Motors' lock division, he learned that the odds for finding a matching key set were not as great as he had thought. In those days, GM used a relatively small number of lock and key combinations. The corporation relied on geographic distribution to isolate duplicate sets. In all probability the key match resulted because the stranger hailed from California, not because he drove an identical make and model car. If in the fifties, strangers' keys fit each other's cars, think of the heyday vintage car thieves could have with a master key set.

Collector car thefts do occur. According to the stolen car notices posted monthly in hobby magazines, Corvettes, Mustangs, 1955–57 Chevys are the most frequent, but not exclusive, victims. There are a number of ways to guard a car against theft. Besides stationing a Doberman behind the wheel, you can stall would-be thieves with an assortment of devices that set off a siren or blow the car's horn, block the fuel line, lock the steering, deaden the electrical system or by simply sticking a decal to the window warning that the car is protected by electronic wizardry. Prices for antitheft hardware range from several hundred dollars for state-of-the-art electronic gear to two bits for the decal. None is fully theftproof, and the sticker isn't even foolproof as is proven by the fact that people actually buy them. But by increasing the time it takes to make off with a car, and alerting bystanders in the process, antitheft devices will frustrate all but the most persistent thieves and stymie the joy riders.

Cars most vulnerable to theft are those stored outside or in communal garages, used for touring or general transportation. But even cars that rest securely in locked garages and are driven only for parades and shows are susceptible to damage or destruction that can be prevented by an antitheft device.

The most effective way to keep thieves from entering or tampering with your car is to install an electronic sensing system that sounds a siren or blows the horn (some can be connected to optional airhorns) when an attempt is made to open the car doors, trunk or hood. The sensor systems protect both the car and its contents, such as the battery or engine accessories. When combined with a motion detector, these devices even prevent thieves from making off with wheels and trim accessories. The sensing units can be set off by small voltage drops that occur when the doors, hood or trunk are opened. Motion detectors are operated by a pendulum that swings and makes contact with a wire closing the alarm circuit when the car is moved or jarred.

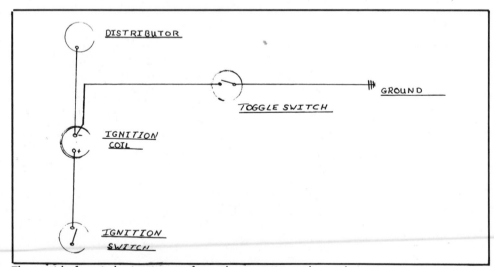

The antitheft switch circuit runs from the negative pole on the coil to ground. The normal ignition circuit isn't affected as long as the antitheft switch is left open.

Although sensing systems give the greatest overall protection, they are somewhat of a nuisance in that they have to be turned on and off each time you enter or leave the car and can be accidentally set off by parking lot attendants and friends.

Several antitheft methods can be used to protect the car itself, though not its contents. One approach is to install a shutoff valve in the fuel line. With the fuel line blocked, even if a thief manages to start the car it will leave him stranded after traveling a short distance. The idea here is to lure the thief into thinking he's making off with the car, then have it quit where he'll be too rattled to hunt for the cause of trouble.

A variety of electronic sensing devices ranging in sophistication and effectiveness are available by mail-order and from auto supply shops. The name and source for one of the premium electronic watchdogs is listed in the supplier section located in the appendix. Fuel shutoffs and other antitheft hardware, including locking lug nuts to prevent wheels from being heisted, are available through mail-order as well as local auto supply shops. Not all antitheft devices have to be purchased. Honey smeared on the radiator threads prevents souvenir hunters from unscrewing motometers or decorative radiator caps from vintage cars.

Often the simplest solutions are the best. If your main concern is stopping a thief from driving away with your car, you can rig a highly effective device for about a $5 investment that many car show judges won't even notice. You'll need a simple single-pole, single-throw (SPST) toggle switch available at nearly

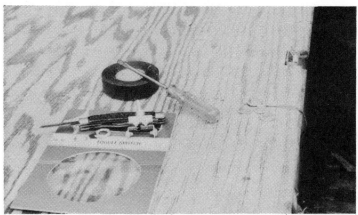

An inexpensive toggle switch, length of wire and electrical tape are all that's needed to give effective antitheft protection.

The ground wire that runs from the coil through the antitheft switch looks to be part of the stock electrical system.

any auto supply and about a six-foot length of 14-gauge automotive electical wire. In most applications, a toggle switch with a one-amp rating will be adequate. The amp rating is usually printed on the plastic switch body. If your car has an amp meter you can determine the exact amp rating for the switch by turning the ignition switch on and noting the amount of discharge. Make sure all electrical accessories, including the dome light, are off when you take this reading. On most cars, the amp meter will show about a one-amp discharge. To install the toggle switch you will need an electric drill, adjustable wrench, pliers, screwdriver, jackknife and preferably a soldering gun.

The toggle switch and wire are used to make a circuit that foils car thieves by grounding the ignition when the switch is closed. Since the toggle switch deadens the ignition circuit by diverting the current to ground before it reaches the points (rather than cutting the hot side of the circuit carrying current to the coil), there is no risk of a short that could drain the battery or, worse, start an electrical fire.

The ground circuit is easy to install. One wire is attached to the toggle switch and the negative or ground pole of the coil on negative-ground electrical systems—the type commonly used on American cars. On positive-ground systems, often found on vintage British cars, this wire is attached to the positive pole of the coil. The other wire connects the toggle switch to a metal ground.

The switch functions by grounding the coil. On this installation the wire runs under the vehicle and is grounded on the frame.

The antitheft switch is mounted behind the seat where it can be easily reached.

If you open the hood and look at the coil, you will most likely see one wire connected to each pole. The hot, positive wire on negative-ground systems goes to the ignition. The negative wire goes to the distributor where it grounds the ignition circuit through the points. When a second wire is attached to the coil's ground pole and connected through the toggle switch to a frame ground, the ignition circuit will bypass the points whenever the toggle switch is closed.

Few thieves will take the time to count the wires hooked to the coil while they're hot wiring a car. With the toggle switch closed and the ignition circuit grounded, if a crook manages to crank over the engine, it will grind away conked-out just as if you had pocketed the distributor rotor. By the time a thief figures he's been foiled, he'll most likely have flooded the carburetor and maybe even run down the battery. At the least he'll have shattered the night stillness or alerted a neighbor—at that point thieves with sense will head for easier pickings.

Installing the ignition-ground circuit is an easy job, even for a novice electrician. The first step is to decide where you want to mount the toggle switch. It should be located out of sight but within easy reach. The photos show the toggle switch mounted in a pickup truck on the raised floor section behind the seat. Although the seat hides the switch from sight, the driver can turn the switch off and on either from a sitting position or when entering and leaving. On a car, the switch could be mounted under the dash or driver's seat, in any convenient yet hidden location.

After deciding where to mount the switch, drill a hole for the threaded shank. Before putting the drill away, check for a

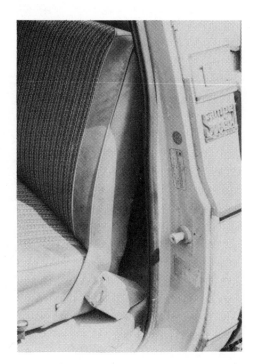

With the seat slid back the antitheft switch is completely hidden from view.

place to attach the end of the wire making the ground connection. The circuit can be grounded by fastening the wire to a bolt on the frame or body sheet metal. If a bolt is not located within easy access, you will have to drill a hole for a small bolt to ground the circuit.

Before mounting the switch, open the hood and locate the coil and the wire that goes from the coil to the distributor. This wire is connected to the ground terminal of the coil where you will attach the wire leading to the toggle switch. To assure a good contact, you should solder a connector to the ends of the wire before attaching them to the coil, switch and ground.

As you route the wire from the coil to the switch location, be careful to keep the wire taut and make sure that it does not contact hot engine parts. Wherever possible, tape the wire to the wiring harness. This will serve a dual function of protecting and concealing the wire. If the wire passes through the firewall, insert it into an existing rubber grommet to avoid drilling a new hole.

The toggle switch has two screws where wires coming from the coil and going to ground are attached. It is usually easier to connect the wires before mounting the switch. The wire from the coil is attached to the "on" side of the switch. It really isn't critical which wire is attached to which pole as long as you remember the on and off toggle positions. Once the wires are connected, you can insert the switch through its hole and secure it in place by tightening the nut that threads onto the shank. To complete the circuit, connect the loose wire to a nearby bolt fastened through the frame or body metal.

The accompanying schematic illustrates the ignition-grounding circuit. After you have installed the switch, you will want to test its effectiveness. Complete the circuit by moving the toggle to the "on" position and attempt to start the car. If

Installing a master disconnect switch prevents wiring shorts from draining the battery and possibly causing a fire.

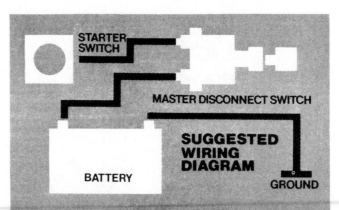

Although this schematic shows the master disconnect switch installed in the "hot" side of the battery, it can also be placed in the ground cable.

the circuit is installed properly, the engine will crank over but won't fire. Now turn the toggle to "off" to break the circuit and try again. The engine will start, just as it did before the circuit was installed. If you turn the toggle "on" with the engine running, the engine will quit, just as if you had turned off the ignition key. In the unlikely event that the switch or the circuit should fail, you can easily restore the car's operation by disconnecting the wire at the coil.

Although vintage cars are less susceptible to theft than newer models, antitheft switches can be installed on these cars to prevent wiring shorts from draining the battery or causing a fire while the car is in storage. Master disconnect switches designed to deaden a car's electrical system are widely advertised in hobby magazines. These switches connect to either the hot or ground cables from the battery. For hobbyists who are reluctant to install any type of antitheft or electrical disconnect switch out of concern that the device will detract from the car's authenticity, one type of master disconnect switch installs directly on a battery pole and the cable it replaces clamps to the switch. This switch can be installed or removed in a few minutes. Simply by turning a knob on the switch, the car's electrical system can be disconnected as effectively as removing a cable from the battery—yet easier and safer, especially for cars whose batteries are located in hard-to-reach spots.

There are a number of alternative methods you can use to protect your car. On cars with electrical fuel pumps, a switch could be installed in the fuel pump circuit, for example. Whatever the approach, an antitheft device should never call attention to itself, except to stop a thief. Two cars belonging to neighbors, a 1965 Impala Super Sport and a Corvette, have been saved from would-be thieves by simple ignition grounding circuits. Once installed, antitheft or electrical disconnect switches should be used. And it's important to make setting the switch a habit, like pocketing the ignition key, when you leave the car.

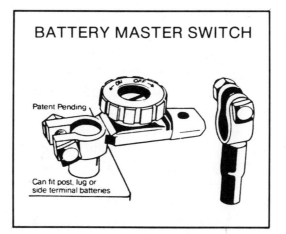

BATTERY MASTER SWITCH

Patent Pending

Can fit post, lug or side terminal batteries

This easy-to-install disconnect switch can be removed for judging.

16
Preserving A Car's Brake System

Hobbyists typically take more care to preserve their car's appearance than its mechanics. After all, with a few thousand miles driving a year, if that much, the mechanical parts should last a lifetime. Actually, limited driving can be more harmful to a car's mechanical innards than high mileage. The cars I have driven sparingly and parked all winter to protect them from the elements have consistently given me more problems than the vehicles I drive every day. Maladies like stuck valves, a frozen clutch and rusted mufflers might have been anticipated; but other quirks like a window crank that spun freely on its shaft when I tried to lower the window after a winter's storage and lights that wouldn't work when I turned on the light switch made me wonder if my parked cars were the favorite haunt of a pack of automotive gremlins.

Looking at the problem a bit more realistically, it is easy to see that moisture was the real villain, except for that pesky window crank. Moisture and its ally, rust. Even when a car is stored inside under a cotton batting cover, humidity and changes in temperature cause condensation to occur. Of course, moisture condenses inside exhaust systems all year round and storage periods simply give the trapped water an uninterrupted chance to eat away at tail pipes and mufflers. Although I've never had a car's brakes fail as a result of corrosion, I do know that standard glycol hydraulic fluid absorbs moisture about as greedily as a dry towel and carries water droplets throughout the brake system, rusting wheel cylinders, brake calipers, master cylinders and brake lines.

Even collectors who live in Arizona or similar dry climates have to contend with brake system corrosion. As proof, the U.S.

Army ran a two-year test on the brake systems of its utility-size vehicles at bases in Arizona, Panama and Alaska to determine, among other things, the moisture absorption rate of polyglycol brake fluid. Although the Arizona test site showed the lowest water contamination levels, the polyglycol fluid in the Arizona-based vehicles contained up to 8.4 percent water at the end of the two-year test.

In addition to causing corrosion, moisture absorbed by polyglycol fluids adversely affects braking performance. Adding water to a glycol fluid base lowers the boiling point of the contaminated fluid to about 250°F, causing the fluid to boil and develop a vapor lock when the brakes are subjected to hard use, as in mountain driving. In cold temperatures, the viscosity of moisture-contaminated polyglycol thickens, causing sluggish brake performance. Until recently there has been no solution to the problems caused by moisture contamination except to flush and refill the brake system periodically, rebuild corroded cylinders and replace rusted lines.

With the introduction of DOT 5 silicone brake fluid, a product developed principally by Dow Corning, brake system corrosion and moisture problems can be eliminated by replacing standard polyglycol with silicone brake fluid. In order to thoroughly drain and refill the brake system with silicone fluid, cylinders or calipers and the master cylinder should be disassembled and cleaned. Brake system parts that are found to be corroded should be rebuilt or replaced.

To save the labor and expense of disassembling brake cylinders that may have just been overhauled, it is possible to

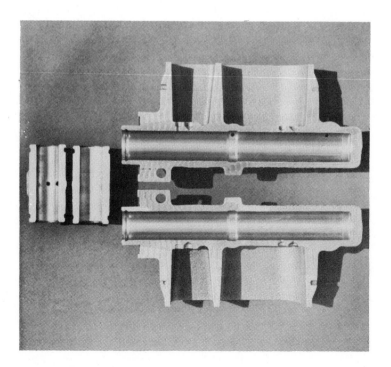

DOT 5 Silicone Brake Fluid protects internal brake system parts from corrosion. The sectioned master cylinder in this photo was taken from a van after 24,106 miles of operation using DOT 5 fluid. The internal lining appears factory new.

gain most of the water-free advantage of silicone brake fluid by flush-filling the brake system with silicone. Since silicone fluid is compatible, though not miscible, with standard polyglycol brake fluid, the glycol residue that remains in the system will not affect the performance of silicone fluid. Flushing and refilling a brake system is basically a straightforward procedure that you can do yourself, even if you have never tackled a brake job more complicated than replacing worn brake shoes. You will need a friend's help, though. While it is possible for one person to bleed a hydraulic brake system, the job is much easier with two.

Before attempting repair or maintenance on a system as vital to a vehicle's safe operation as its brakes, you should have some knowledge of mechanics. Reading the brake section of a service manual before starting out and asking a friend who is familiar with brake systems for help are two ways to avoid costly, perhaps hazardous, mistakes. The basic procedures for flushing a hydraulic brake system are as follows: First siphon or scoop all the old brake fluid from the master cylinder and wipe the chamber or chambers (there are two reservoirs on dual master cylinder systems) with a clean, dry cloth. Next, refill the master cylinder with DOT 5 silicone brake fluid. Allow several minutes for the fluid to settle so that air bubbles can escape, then purge the system of its remaining polyglycol fluid and bleed any air that is trapped in the lines.

Service manuals show various methods for bleeding hydraulic brake systems. General Motors divisions, except Chevrolet, recommend that the air bleeding sequence begin with the left front wheel and progress to the right rear. Chevrolet proceeds from the left rear, while Ford and Chrysler recom-

As part of Dow Chemical's test program, this van was filled with silicone brake fluid immediately after it was purchased in 1976. After three years the van showed no brake fluid leakage.

mend starting from the right rear. Recent Ford manuals warn that the bleeding process will cause the brake warning light to come on, a disconcerting sign that is corrected by repositioning the pressure differentiation valve.

It is wise to study a manual before starting out and take time to study the features of your car's brake system. Service manuals describe two procedures for bleeding hydraulic brake systems: the manual method outlined here and a pressure bleeding process used by brake shops. The pressure method is faster and doesn't require the labor of two mechanics, but it does require a special pressure tank that is not likely to be found in a hobbyist's shop. The manual method is slower but uses common shop tools and accomplishes the same results.

Before beginning the flush-filling process, make sure that the bleeder screws on all four wheels are free. On cars that have had recent brake overhauls or that haven't been exposed to road salt, the screws should loosen easily. If the bleeder screws are rusted and can't be loosened, spray a liberal dose of penetrating oil around the base of the screws, wait a few hours and try again.

Applying heat to the screws can destroy the rubber seal in the wheel cylinder, so if you can't loosen the bleeder screws, you will have to pull off the brake drum and remove the wheel cylinder. From that point you can either replace the cylinder or take it apart and then heat the metal base around the bleeder screws. Once you know that there won't be any major snags in the bleeding process, begin by purging air trapped in the master cylinder. Some master cylinders are equipped with bleeder valves, some are not. The service manual should tell which type is used on your car and should include a drawing or photo locating the bleeder screw. If the master cylinder lacks bleeder screws, loosen the hydraulic line or lines attached to the base of the master cylinder, have your assistant slowly depress the brake pedal until the fluid emerges free of bubbles, then retighten the line.

Bleeding a hydraulic brake system is a simple but slow process of forcing fresh fluid through the lines until all the air bubbles have been expelled. After purging the master cylinder, start at the wheel recommended in the service manual and loosen the bleeder screw (located on the upper portion of the backing plate). Next, slip a section of pliable rubber hose over the bleeder valve and place the other end in a clear, clean glass container partially filled with silicone fluid. As your assistant depresses and releases the brake pedal to force air from the lines, a combination pumping and siphon action occurs. Fluid is pushed through the system when the pedal is depressed and sucked into the system from the jar when the pedal is released. If you tried to bleed the brakes without immersing a hose from the bleeder valves in a jar of fluid, you could pump out gallons of fluid and the system would still be air bound.

As your assistant slowly depresses and releases the brake pedal, the fluid will eventually emerge as pure silicone and show no traces of air bubbles. At that point, close the bleeder screw and proceed to the next wheel, following the bleeding sequence described in the service manual. Brake lines are commonly bled starting with the wheel farthest from the master cylinder and progressing to the nearest. While flushing and bleeding the brake system, continue to refill the master cylinder with silicone fluid as the level drops, to prevent air from being reintroduced into the system. When glycol fluid and entrapped air have been bled from all the brake lines, tighten all the bleeder screws and the job is finished.

Although flush-filling a car's brake system with silicone fluid reduces corrosion, it is impossible to remove all the glycol fluid by this method. A better approach, especially if the brake system needs maintenance anyway, is to dismantle and rebuild the wheel and master cylinders, replace the brake shoes and corroded lines, then refill the reconditioned system with fresh silicone fluid. Once the system is filled with pure silicone fluid you shouldn't have to rebuild these parts again.

As with flush-filling, you will have to bleed the brake lines, using either the pressure method or the manual method described earlier. Even though it appears pure, the fresh silicone fluid that is bled from the lines contains entrapped air, so it can't

Two Army sergeants use a pressure bleeder to convert a Jeep to silicone brake fluid.

be reused. Nearly two quarts of silicone fluid will be required to fill and bleed a dual master cylinder system.

The retail distribution of silicone brake fluid is expanding rapidly. Many of the national auto supply chains, as well as Harley-Davidson dealerships, stock the DOT 5 fluid. Although the silicone fluid costs more than standard DOT 3 polyglycol fluid, collector car repairs are meant to be permanent. When you consider that silicone brake fluid preserves the delicate insides of parts on which the safe operation of your car depends, the extra cost is certainly justified.

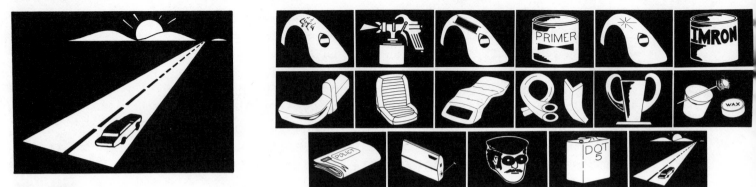

17
End Of The Trail

This book has explained many of the procedures hobbyists can do themselves to refurbish or restore collector vehicles. Along the way a number of suppliers have been mentioned for tools and materials needed to do specific jobs. A more comprehensive list of suppliers is included in the appendix. This chapter departs from the how-to theme that has been followed thus far. It explores the search for parts, tools, restoration supplies, the variety of items necessary to refit and operate vintage cars. In a way, discussing where to locate needed items makes a fitting conclusion to a book on renewing collector cars. Seldom does a restoration or fix-up project end without a new challenge beckoning, and the search for parts, supplies or cars goes on.

There was a time in the early days of the hobby when it looked as though spare parts for vintage cars would disappear as the leftover stock was used up. Incredible as it may sound, a neighbor was persuaded to trade in his twenty-two-year-old, low-mileage, Model A Ford on a new model by a salesman's pitch that before long it would be impossible to buy spark plugs or tires for the old Ford. That was in 1952. Today, except for engine and chassis castings, it is possible to build a new Model A from reproduction parts. Of course, some car parts are in short supply. Bill Cameron, whose comments on alkaline degreasing appeared earlier, went through a search process that would put a private eye to shame in order to equip his stripped and nearly unique 1908 Cameron car. He succeeded and the car made its debut at Hershey in 1982.

In their search for parts many hobbyists overlook the most obvious source: their local auto supply. Like hobbyists, after-market suppliers haven't forsaken collector cars. Stant, Inc., a leading manufacturer of thermostats and automotive caps that fit on radiators, gas tanks and oil filler tubes, maintains a product line that reaches back forty-five years. Although the company's current catalog no longer features motometers or fancy radiator caps (such as those with a Pierce Arrow archer poised in firing position that were once part of the Stant line), the catalog does list radiator caps for Chevrolet and Buick back to 1937, Ford to 1939, Chrysler and Plymouth to 1940. Orphans and foreign makes are included too. The Stant gas cap line includes caps for Essex and turns the calendar back to 1928 for Chevrolet and Studebaker. Tractor and truck collectors will find caps for many of their favorite makes and models listed as well.

Thermostats can stick shut, particularly on cars subject to occasional driving and long periods of storage. Running without a thermostat is one way to make a temporary repair, but it really isn't necessary, since for most cars and trucks new thermostats are parts-counter items. Stant's thermostat line goes back to 1933 for Chevrolet, the early date leader due to the long production run of its rugged, reliable "stove bolt" six. To assure complete and proper installation of the new thermostats, Stant supplies universal gaskets along with its regular gasket line. The universal gaskets are cleverly designed to fit any application and appear stock when the surplus material is trimmed away.

The bright red and yellow Stant displays are easily recognized at service stations and auto supply stores. To request a copy of the company catalog, write to Stant Manufacturing, Connersville, Indiana.

Convertible tops are another item still being produced for collector cars. How much longer replacement tops will stay in

Swap meets are a lively and enjoyable source of old car parts.

production is anybody's guess. It wouldn't seem as though the top makers' business will be growing, unless the remaining convertibles are swept up in a preservation wave. Paints and painting supplies, too, are commonly available, except for nitrocellulose lacquer, which can be ordered from a specialty supplier.

Like old cars, some parts just never pass out of style. Bearings, for instance, have long been standardized equipment. After checking the dimensions of a Model A Ford front-wheel bearing and cross-referencing matching part numbers in an interchange manual, I discovered a range of applications from Maytag washers to International trucks for a part I'd been mail-ordering from a vintage Ford supplier.

While most manufacturers of vintage carburetors are no longer in business, the few that are provide a prime source of carburetor parts. Today the four companies producing carburetors are: Carter; Rochester Products Division of General Motors; Motorcraft, a Ford division; and Holley, now owned by Colt Industries. Rochester Products is probably best known for its fuel injection systems of the late fifties. The GM division is a relative newcomer to carburetor production. No original-equipment Rochester carburetors predate 1950.

Doug Heinmuller, an enterprising car buff and machinist by trade, stocks one of the largest inventories of obsolete carburetor parts. At the closing of Stromberg, once a major carburetor manufacturer, Heinmuller bought out the company's blueprints and back stock. In addition to the Stromberg parts,

Although this stripped-down Model A chassis may not look like much, it carried a rare carburetor, worth nearly the whole assembly's asking price.

While some parts found at flea markets are rough, you can look them over closely before deciding to buy. Sellers will often respond to an offer.

Heinmuller's inventory includes overhaul kits for most classic era carburetors and many others. Heinmuller Restorations, located in Bethlehem, New Hampshire, also rebuilds and restores vintage carburetors.

The best way to scout for parts is to draw up a shopping list. It helps to list needed items under categories like trim, interior, engine, so that you don't overlook parts that may not be needed at the moment, but will be essential later on. Once you have listed your needs, rate them according to priority. This rating can help you stay within your budget and still progress with the project at hand. Sometimes, though, you may have to bend both your priorities and your budget to take advantage of once-offered opportunities, rather than passing by hard-to-find or bargain-priced parts because they came along at the wrong time. You're less likely to make this mistake if, instead of scouting randomly, you are shopping from a list.

Apart from the sources listed so far, two of the most fruitful shopping places for collector car needs are flea markets and ads in hobby magazines. Items available at flea markets depend on the day and the vendors present. In addition, many suppliers advertise in hobby magazines sporadically, so it may take persistence to locate some items. Often you can shortcut the search process by joining a club dedicated to the type of

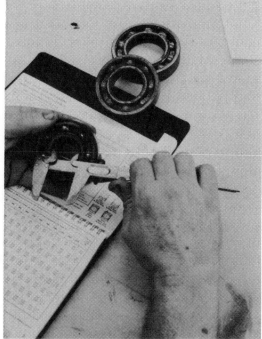

Many of the bearings for antique cars are still in production today. To check for a current part number, measure the old bearing with a set of calipers and cross-reference the bearing by its dimensions in an interchange manual.

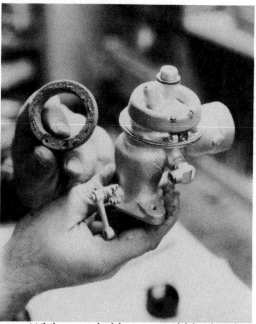

While most hobbyists would be hard pressed to carve a new float for an antique carburetor, to a craftsman like Doug Heinmuller this work is part of the daily routine.

car you are refitting. Club members may be able to suggest suppliers and in some cases club members may have arranged with specialty suppliers to provide hard-to-find items.

Though they're not the collector's haven they once were, junkyards are still a source of mechanical, trim and even upholstery items. A friend has been able to replace nearly all the cracked vinyl door and dash panels on his Mach 1 Mustang by shopping at local junkyards. His success is due to persistence and the good relationship he has built with area junkyard owners.

Refinishing and restoration require tools and hardware not always found locally. H. C. Fastener Company in Alvarado, Texas, is an example of a company specializing in a variety of hardware from cage nuts for fender panels to trim clips and upholstery clips (including those used on old-style canvas tops), as well as assorted tools. The tool inventory includes such useful items as a spatula-shaped device for stuffing headliner into roof channels, door panel removers that won't tear vinyl upholstery, pull rods for straightening those hard-to-get-behind dents and vixen body files, a tool that is now nearly extinct.

Collector cars used many items that are no longer in regular production. These would be virtually impossible to find if specialty suppliers hadn't stepped in to fill the void. Upholstery backing is an example. The plush-looking mohair door panels seen on cars built from the teens through the forties were mounted on tough, water-resistant fiberboard. When car makers switched to molded vinyl upholstery, the sources of fiberboard vanished. The heavy cardboard isn't easy to duplicate. It has to bend around the rear body quarters yet be stiff enough to lie flat on the doors. Cloth upholstery wasn't just glued to cardboard backing, it was sewn on, so replacement panelboard also has to be pliable enough to be stitched without crumbling.

Few hobbyists are equipped to resurface carburetor castings, yet warpage can occur with age, causing poor performance.

To provide a source of pasteboard backing for vintage upholstery kits, Le Baron Bonney, the Amesbury, Massachusetts, Model A and early V-8 upholstery supplier, is producing new panelboard using a laminating process. The company also stocks a wide range of authentic upholstery fabrics, including bolts of new-old-stock material.

At one time vintage tire sizes were so hard to find that hobbyists were forced to switch rims or resort to truck tires in order to outfit older cars. Today, thanks to several tire companies formed principally by hobbyists, tires for collector cars are available in virtually all styles and sizes. The companies that produce and market older-style tires advertise in hobby magazines and sell their wares at large flea markets.

The car hobby attracts an abundance of highly skilled craftsmen who are continually offering new products. Station wagon bodies, in kit form or ready to mount on a chassis and drive away, have been reproduced for the entire Ford woody wagon line. The shops come and go, but each craftsman in turn adds to the preservation of our automotive heritage.

In many cases these craftsmen work in their garages or workshops turning out a variety of items from castings to wheel spokes. Occasionally they advertise in hobby magazines, but more frequently they peddle their stock at flea markets. A few

Jaguar windshields are in plentiful supply at this parts specialist, Welsh Jaguar Enterprises, in Steubenville, Ohio.

years ago at the big Hershey, Pennsylvania, swap meet I met a vendor who was supplementing his retirement income by making wooden wheel spokes for Model T Fords. He told me that when his present stock of wheel spokes was sold, he'd have to hold deliveries until he found another barn. "Another barn?" I asked. "Sure," he replied. "Seasoned oak beams are the only source of dry hardwood stock I can trust to make wheel spokes."

These are the people to call on when you've got a restoration job that requires a specialist's expertise. There's no sense learning on your own parts, especially when they're the only ones you've got. Warren Foster, in Tewksbury, Massachusetts, is a craftsman who spends his spare time rebuilding worn out speedometers and shorted ignition cables for Model A Ford collectors. He doesn't just paint the speedometer housings and glue new number decals on the dials. Instead, he takes each device apart, checks the gears and replates the bezels. When he installs the number decals he makes sure to keep his fingerprints off the polished numeral wheels—otherwise the decals won't stick. Foster gives ignition cables a similar going over. In addition to skill, Foster's quality restoration work requires special tools, contact with a plater who doesn't lose small parts and a locksmith with a stock of Model A key blanks.

Antique radio and plastic steering wheel repairs are other jobs best left to specialists. While it is possible to restore original gauges and other small mechanical parts by learning as you go along, whenever possible you should take apart scrap parts first and seek instructions before starting out. How-to articles in hobby magazines are a good source of tips.

Hobbyists quickly develop the talent of seeing the uncommon in the common. A collector told me recently that he spotted a replacement for his car's missing gearshift knob on a wringer washing machine. Another pointed out that tailgate handles on 1953 Ford wagons are identical matches to inner door han-

As dealers close, car hobby suppliers buy out their stock, assuring a source of vital parts for years to come.

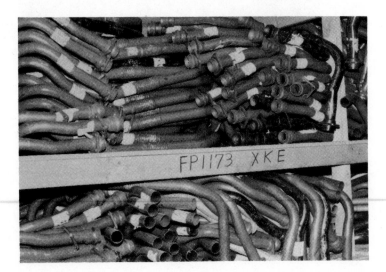

dles on Model A roadsters. Today the 1953 parts are probably the scarcer of the two. Robert Gottlieb, author of *Motor Trend* magazine's "Classic Comments" column, wrote some years ago that after much searching he located a replacement rear end for his Chrysler LeBaron phaeton in a 1937 Dodge pickup. Interchange manuals are invaluable reference aids for matching mechanical parts. These manuals are being reproduced and are advertised in hobby magazines.

Most restoration supplies are really common items. The gas tank sealer advertised in hobby magazines smells just like, and in fact is nothing more than, contact cement used to glue counter tops. It's commonly available from hardware and building supply stores. Hobbyists should avoid the pitfall of thinking that supplies for collector cars have to carry special labels.

The old car hobby isn't meant to be all work and no play. At the end of the fix-up, restoration trail, the hobby offers ongoing opportunities to build new skills as well as share an interest with other enthusiasts. Occasions for enjoying the car hobby abound. Clubs sponsor social events, restoration clinics and other events intended to give hobbyists a chance to meet and mix. Other facets of the hobby include tours, shows, swap meets. All are opportunities to spark friendships that are the car hobby's true bounty. One of the most pleasant experiences any hobby can offer is sharing skills and working with others. When you have practiced and learned the skills described in this book, perhaps you will be generous with your knowledge and experience the rich reward of exchanging your expertise with others.

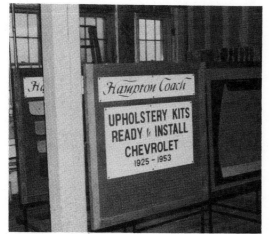

Authentic upholstery kits made by Hampton Coach are a boon to Chevrolet restorers.

Le Baron Bonney has been synonymous with quality Ford upholstery for years. Many hobbyists don't realize that the company also sells a complete line of upholstery fabrics, including hard-to-find, new-old-stock material.

APPENDICES

Routing Rust With A Fiberglass Quick-Patch

Restoration repairs are usually made with permanence in mind. Leather upholstery is replaced with expensive imported hides. Sandblasting or chemical paint and rust removal are commonly used to prepare body surfaces for refinishing. Restorers willingly pay the price for authentic parts and quality service in the belief that a restoration done right only has to be done once. There are occasions, though, when necessity, convenience or expense forces shortcuts.

Car collectors have single-handedly preserved leading and hammer welding, the crafts of metal repair. Rusted metal really has to be replaced with metal to make a permanent repair. But at times, leading and welding really aren't practical. In these situations collectors face a decision. Will I ignore the signs of creeping corrosion, or will I rout the rust with a quick-fix now and make a lasting repair later? Rust damage won't go away on its own, and holes that develop in a body pan, rocker panels or fender wells expose a car's support structures to moisture, dirt and salt, the seeds of rust in snow belt areas.

Welding a metal patch over a hole in the floor pan means removing the carpet and possibly the seats and interior panels. Repairing a small hole takes the same preparation and finishing work as replacing the entire floor pan. Major metalwork is likely to be put off and small holes will grow unless they are sealed, but a fiberglass quick-fix will stem corrosion until permanent repairs are made.

Fiberglass makes metal repair simple because it doesn't require heat. The area that will be covered by the fiberglass patch can be stripped by hand sanding or with a disc grinder. Stubborn surface rust usually found on floor pans is best attacked with a wire brush. A small wire brush clamped in the chuck of an electric drill makes an ideal tool for cleaning tight spots underneath

Fiberglass patches are a handy way to seal holes in underbody metal without welding. The product has only one drawback: It's a mess to work with.

Layering up a patch on a sheet of aluminum foil or waxed paper provides a backing to support the fiberglass cloth. This is an especially handy technique when patching the underside of a car.

Apply the resin with a wooden spreader or old paint brush and build up an ample thickness to soak through several layers of cloth.

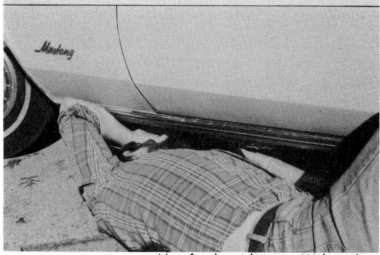

Now for the tricky part. Without the aluminum foil or waxed paper backing the sticky resin adheres to your hands as well as to the work surface.

the car and inside the wheel wells, spots highly prone to rust. The sticky nature of fiberglass doesn't mean that it will adhere to a poorly prepared surface. Seeds of rust that are left underneath will work the patch loose in a short time. After sanding and wire brushing the area that will be covered by fiberglass, wipe the spot with Metal Prep, a dilute phosphoric acid solution, to dissolve the flecks of rust that lie hidden in pits.

Fiberglass isn't difficult to work, but it is messy. The cloth itself unravels easily, catches on fingernails and wads up in snarls as soon as it is coated with resin. Nearly all the mess of working with fiberglass can be avoided if the patch is built up first on a backing of wax paper or kitchen foil, then applied to the car. The process is simple and more effective than laminating successive layers of fiberglass on the car.

Prepare the patch by cutting a piece of wax paper or kitchen foil backing slightly larger than the area the fiberglass has to cover. Next cut several strips of fiberglass cloth for the patch. Instructions for mixing the hardener are listed on the resin can. Follow the proportions and mix a batch that seems more than adequate for the job at hand. (Fiberglass cloth soaks up resin like milk poured over oatmeal.) Smear a layer of activated resin on the foil or wax paper backing with a Popsicle stick or an old brush. Lay one strip of fiberglass cloth in the resin and coat it with a second layer. Spread the next strip of fiberglass over the first and add more resin. Two or three laminations are sufficient for most repairs.

The next step is tricky. Pick up the patch by its backing and apply it to the damaged area. Spread the patch by smoothing out the backing. The critical point here is to keep the fiberglass from slipping off its wax paper or foil support. If that happens, then the gooey resin is likely to snarl the fiberglass cloth, and the whole patch may wind up in a wad on the ground. Hold the patch in place for a few minutes until the resin starts to set.

Special body fillers that contain strands of fiberglass can be used instead of cloth patches to fill small holes. This product is marketed under descriptive product names like Tiger Hair and Stuff-it. Unlike a fiberglass and resin patch, body filler is water-porous, so this material will transmit moisture unless it is sealed.

Fiberglass patches that cover visible surfaces should be coated with filler and smoothed into the surrounding finish. Undercoating will camouflage fiberglass that is applied inside the wheel housings or on the floor pan. Fiberglass patches make sound repairs that will last for years. They may not be authentic, but they will save the metal that is.

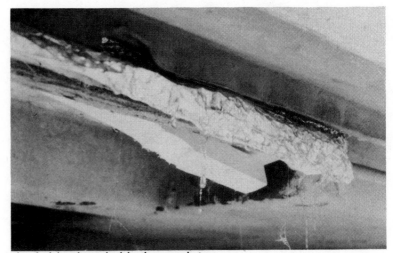

The foil backing holds the patch in place while the resin sets. In this case, a board is used to help support the patch. When the resin hardens, the board and foil can be removed. Only a few drips of resin squeezed past the foil backing.

How To Build A Parts Washer

R. G. LeTourneau, whose creative mind spawned the earth-moving industry, once said, "There are no big jobs, only small machines." This same adage applies to tools. The right tool for the job can turn otherwise impossible tasks into child's play. As hobbyists, we face the dilemma of how to afford all the tools we need. Fully equipping workshops to this degree simply isn't practical. Besides, collecting tools can become a lust, like the medieval land owner who wasn't greedy, he just wanted the property that bordered his own. With some ingenuity, though, we can at least gain access to tools required for specific projects. Here are some suggestions.

Vocational high schools and technical colleges conduct adult education programs that include machine shop classes, auto mechanics, welding and woodworking—each a major area of car restoration. The courses are generally inexpensive and capably taught. Enrolling in a shop course ties together training and access to equipment needed for a project. The tools described in these appendices can be products of just such an approach, coupling learning with practical experience.

Hobbyists could pool equipment and work together on the tough jobs. We carry individualism to an extreme when we feel we have to be completely self-sufficient both in tools and know-how. Besides, working with a friend is generally more pleasurable than working alone. The degreasing chapter described a chemical stripping tank that hobbyist Bill Cameron built to clean his valuable Cameron car. Cameron noted that he shares his degreasing facility with members of his local car club. His action sets an example for all hobbyists.

Some tools get such frequent use that they belong in every well-equipped shop. Every mechanical part that needs rebuilding should be cleaned first. The parts washer described in this chapter is both useful and important for shop safety. Cleaning parts in an open container using a highly volatile solvent such as gasoline is hazardous. The parts washer shown here can be built in a weekend. This tool is inexpensive to build, and once constructed will give invaluable and long service.

The parts washer is basically a thirty-gallon drum, cut into two sections as shown in the plans. The two pieces are hinged together so that the bottom forms a basin and the top becomes a lid that swings shut to cover the solvent bath when the parts washer isn't in use. Braces and a baffle are mounted inside the basin to support a wire mesh that lets parts immerse in solvent while keeping them from lying in the sludge that accumulates in the bottom of the washer. The parts washer stands on sturdy legs cut from channel steel. All the materials, except for the fluid pump, can be purchased from a scrap yard. Since thirty-gallon drums are standard-size containers for products ranging from floor wax to grease and oil, they are often available free from shops, schools, hospitals—nearly any institution. A swimming pool cover pump, bilge pump or any small-capacity submersible pump can be used to circulate the cleaning fluid.

CONSTRUCTION STEPS

Cutting the drum into two sections (see illustrations) with a metal cutting blade fitted into a saber saw is the quickest way to begin. You can cut the drum by hand using a hacksaw, but this is much slower. Wear heavy work gloves when cutting metal and keep a supply of spare saw blades on hand. Cutting the drum with a torch is hazardous for two reasons: Drums that have been used to store volatile fluids may still hold explosive fumes, and a cutting torch leaves rough edges that will have to be ground down for a tight seal between the lid and basin. Before you make the cut, position the drum so that the small drain plug in the cover is located on what will be the left-hand side of the washer's basin section. The plug will allow you to drain the cleaning fluid periodically as sediment and sludge accumulate.

After cutting the drum in two sections, smooth the edges with a file. Next, measure the lid section along the front and sides. Cut a piece of vinyl tubing the same length, slit the tubing and fit it over the front and side edges of the lid. Drill holes at four- to six-inch intervals and pop rivet the tubing to the lid. The tubing is a protection against getting cut or

snagging clothing on the metal edge. It also makes a tight seal when the lid is closed.

The lid attaches to the basin section with strap hinges and is held open when the washer is in use by a twenty-four-inch length of light-duty chain. In this position, the lid serves as a catch-basin for spashed fluid. Adding a handle to the front of the lid makes it easier to open and close.

The rugged channel-steel legs that support the washer are welded to the bottom section of the drum. Tack weld

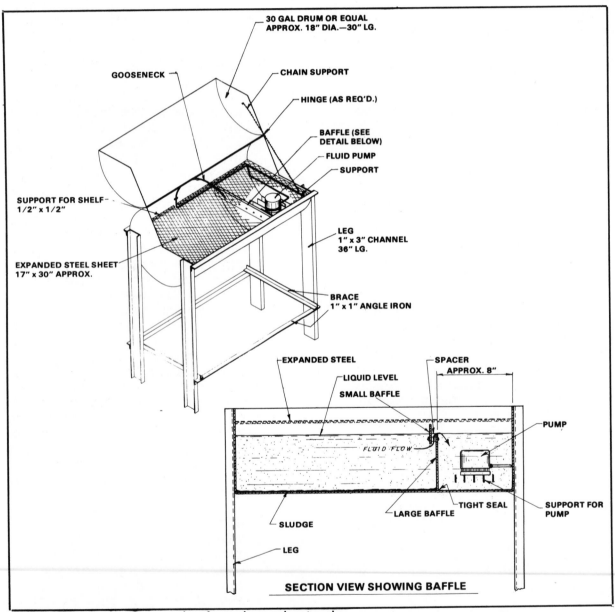

A view of the handy parts washer from above, showing the baffle in close-up detail.

or bolt braces along the front and rear of the basin, first, so that the legs can be welded to the drum's heavy metal lip and the braces. If you attempt to weld the legs to the drum itself, you are likely to burn holes in the thin-gauge metal. This caution applies to arc welding, particularly. Cross braces of one-inch angle-iron can be bolted or welded to the legs to stiffen them and help support the basin.

At this stage, the parts washer can be equipped with the spray feature shown in the plans or finished without the spray nozzle and pump. Using the washer without the spray feature requires a small modification to the plans. The baffle shown in the plans is eliminated and the support braces for the parts rack are attached lower in the basin so that parts can be immersed in cleaning fluid.

To include the spray feature, follow the plans as they are shown. The large baffle that separates the pump reservoir from the fluid chamber is brazed or welded to the sides of the drum. The baffle has to be cut to fit the contour of the drum and the weld should make a good seal keeping sludge from seeping into the pump reservoir. Note that a small baffle is bolted to the top of the large baffle plate. Separating the two baffles with spacers allows fluid to return to the pump reservoir. The small baffle also acts as a support brace for the wash rack. The small submersible pump that operates the spray hose rests on a grid of metal braces fitted against the sides of the drum. The spray nozzle can be made from flexible metal tubing or by coiling a length of welding rod around plastic tubing and attaching one end of the rod to the back of the drum.

USING THE WASHER

It is advisable to avoid using gasoline as a cleaning solvent. Kerosene is an effective solvent which is much less volatile and therefore safer to use. Adding a can of carburetor cleaner to the kerosene in your parts washer will boost its potency. If you remove the wire rack and immerse parts in a degreasing bath, you can substitute a solution containing detergent and mild alkaline chemicals for a petroleum-base solvent. Formulas for safe and effective degreasing solutions are given in the degreasing chapter. Commercial parts-cleaning fluids are more expensive than the generic variety described above, and the nonbiodegradable chemicals in some cleaners require disposal in a chemical land-fill to prevent possible contamination of water supplies.

Depending on the type of pump that is installed, the fluid flow at the spray nozzle may be too great. To decrease the pump rate, remove the impeller housing and trim the impeller blades. Since the blades are usually made of plastic, this job isn't difficult. But it can be tedious because only a small amount should be trimmed at a time. Reassemble the pump and test the flow until the pressure at the nozzle seems right.

Purchase a stiff-bristled parts-cleaning brush to scrub the parts. Remember to wear safety glasses or goggles and rubber gloves when washing parts. To reduce the accumulation of sludge and rapid contamination of the cleaning solvent, first use a putty knife to scrape off heavy grease coatings; then wash the parts. The wire rack can be removed for soaking stubborn coatings. As a safety precaution, close the lid when the parts washer isn't in use. The washer is as simple as a Model T Ford, and during the mechanical stages of restoration it will be one of the handiest devices in your shop.

Building A Hydraulic Press

Tools fall into three categories: those we have; those we would like to have but suspect we'll never own; and those we wish we had every time we tackle a job that requires the special service only these tools provide. Most hobbyists build their tool collections over a period of years. After accumulating the necessary tools, it's time to consider the ones that can make difficult repair jobs pleasurable.

A hydraulic press is not a universal tool like an electric drill or a Skil saw, but it is essential for removing and replacing bearings, gears and bushings, and useful for straightening bent shafts and other parts made of high-tensile steel. Certainly, hobbyists can have a machine shop remove and replace gears, bushings or bearings. But when—as often happens with old cars—rear wheel hubs, for example, have to be cleaned or replaced between removing old bearings and installing new ones, trips to a machine shop that commonly involve waiting until a skilled machinist can break from his work are inconvenient and can be expensive. What happens more frequently is that novices, particularly, try to remove and install bushings or bearings with a hammer and a block of wood. Hobbyists sometimes use this crude method instead of a press either because they aren't aware that tight-fitting parts should be pressed in place—some have never seen a press being used—or they are impatient. Either way, ruined parts are likely to result. In my mind, a hydraulic press is one of the most useful tools a restorer can own. The press described here takes about a weekend to build. After that it's a permanent fixture of the shop and useful to friends as well.

A hydraulic press offers a number of advantages for rebuilding mechanical parts. It applies even force so that broken castings, gouged bearings and bushings become a plague of the past. Using a hammer to replace bearings and bushings can damage the bearing cage or peen over the bushing ends. Bearings with damaged cages should not be used.

If bushing ends are gouged, even slightly, they will have to be filed or reamed before the pins or shafts that are supposed to slide through them will fit. The sharp hammer blows that are required to drive bushings or bearings in place can also break or crack the castings. A press makes easy work of otherwise difficult jobs. For example, driving bearings off transmission shafts without a press is a good way to build a stock of high-quality scrap steel, but a poor way to rebuild a transmission.

Since commercial presses are expensive tools it's difficult to justify the investment in spite of their usefulness. Building a press yourself cuts the cost to a fraction of the factory-built tool's price making it a practical addition to your shop. The plans and instructions presented in this chapter show freestanding and bench-mounted versions of a rugged, versatile hydraulic press. Capacity and the amount of shop space the tool requires are the primary differences between the two models. Each has its advantages.

INSTRUCTIONS FOR BUILDING A
FREESTANDING HYDRAULIC PRESS

The freestanding press is a large-capacity tool capable of press-fitting bearings on long shafts—axles or steering columns for example. Because the freestanding press is heavy and cumbersome to move, the plans and assembly instructions show this press bolted together. Cut-off dimensions and bolt locations are shown in the plans. The eight cuts in the twenty-foot-long channel iron can be made most easily with a power hacksaw or steel-cutting tool that uses an abrasive wheel. Steel yards will cut the channel and angle iron to the required lengths for a nominal fee. Once the steel is cut, the positions of the bolt holes must be carefully measured and marked so that the assembled press will fit together properly and stand true. Before drilling the bolt holes, mark the center of the hole with a punch. A heavy-duty three-eighths or half-inch drill and a supply of sharp

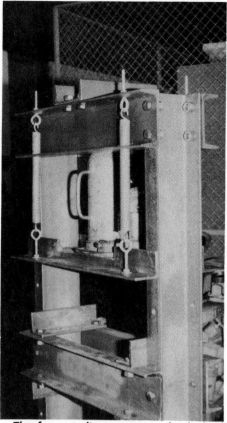

The freestanding press can be bolted together for easy disassembly.

This version of the freestanding press has been assembled by welding.

bits are required to drill the holes. To cut through heavy channel steel, drill the holes with smaller-size bits first, then redrill them to the proper size. Frequently lubricate and cool the drill bit with light oil. When the holes are drilled in one brace or upright, use that piece as a template for the next.

One welding step is required: on the jack-base-plate (part 9). Edges of the jack base (part 4) should be chamfered—or angled forty-five degrees—by grinding to assure a strong weld. The base plate (part 4) is then welded to angle braces (part 5) along both the top and bottom edges. The jack fits inside the two angle braces that form the edges of the four-inch jack-base-plate. When choosing a jack to mount in the press, select a unit that will fit inside the four-inch platform. The entire press structure, including the feet (part 3), upright channels (part 1) and the cross braces (part 8) can be welded together rather than bolted to save the cost of bolts and the effort expended drilling holes. The plans show this press bolted together so that it can be disassembled.

The head channel (part 7) must be carefully centered on the top brace. The hydraulic jack used as the press ram must also be centered. If the jack is positioned askew, the base plate may bind in the uprights or may apply pressure at an angle, possibly causing whatever is being pressed to break or snap out of the press. Note that the work-support-assembly can be moved up and down on the frame channels and is secured by bolts or pins, whichever you decide to use. By repositioning the work-support-assembly, the capacity of the press can be adjusted to fit a particular application.

Return springs are installed to draw the jack and jack-base-plate away from the work when hydraulic pressure is released. Springs of the required size and length can be purchased from hardware and auto supply stores.

After the press is assembled, wipe the steel clean with a cloth soaked in paint thinner or a grease-and-wax-remover solvent used to remove the protective oil coating from new steel.

Materials:

1   4"/1½" CHANNEL — 20'-0 LG.
1   1½"/1¼" ANGLE IRON — 12'-0 LG.
1   1/2"-4" PLATE - 16" LG.
1   8 TON HYDRAULIC HAND JACK
4   EXTENSION SPRINGS — 8" COMP./14" EXT. - (3/4 DIA.)
4   EYEBOLTS — 3/16" DIA × 1 1/2 LG. W/NUTS
32   BOLTS 7/16 D × 3/4 LG
32   NUTS 7/16 SIZE
32   WASHERS 7/16 SIZE
2   PINS - 1/2" DIA. × 5" LG.

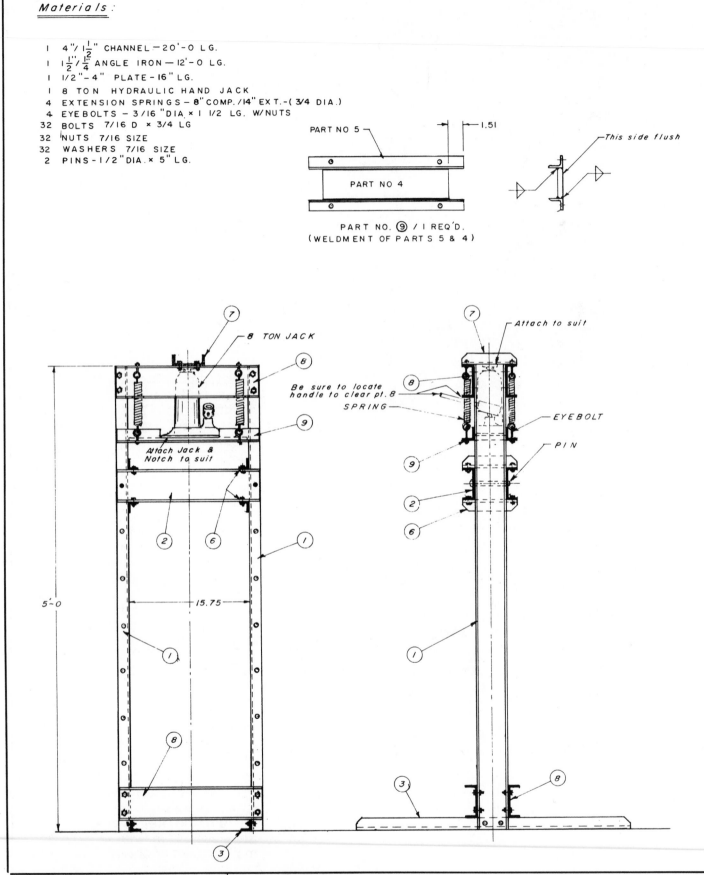

Assembly layout and plans for constructing the full-sized
floor-mounted hydraulic press that is bolted together.

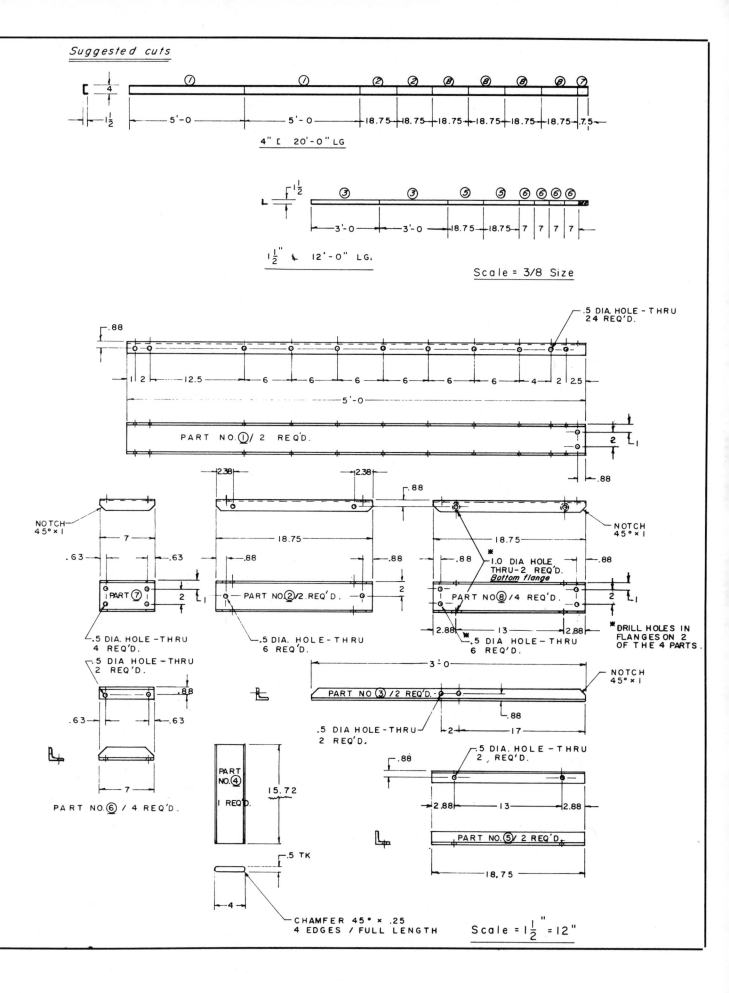

Etch the metal for painting with Metal Prep, a dilute phosphoric acid solution sold by auto supply stores, and the press is ready for painting. Coat the bare metal with zinc chromate or a similar rust-resistant primer. After the primer dries, paint the tool with a durable enamel finish. To assure that the base plate slides freely, spray a coating of silicone or light lubricant oil along the inside of the upright channels.

If you follow the plans and build the press to close tolerances, the finished tool will work as well as a commercial unit costing twice to three times as much.

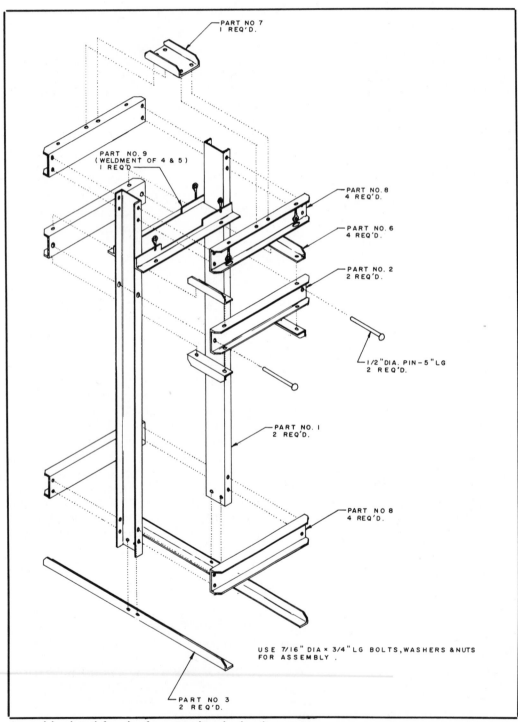

PART NO 7
1 REQ'D.

PART NO. 9
(WELDMENT OF 4 & 5)
1 REQ'D.

PART NO. 8
4 REQ'D.

PART NO. 6
4 REQ'D.

PART NO. 2
2 REQ'D.

1/2" DIA. PIN – 5" LG
2 REQ'D.

PART NO. 1
2 REQ'D.

PART NO 8
4 REQ'D.

USE 7/16" DIA × 3/4" LG BOLTS, WASHERS & NUTS
FOR ASSEMBLY.

PART NO 3
2 REQ'D.

Assembly detail for the free-standing hydraulic press.

INSTRUCTIONS FOR BUILDING A BENCH-MOUNTED HYDRAULIC PRESS

The bench-mounted hydraulic press is a portable tool offering nearly the capacity of the freestanding model. The example shown here features welded construction. Like the freestanding press, it could be bolted together. Since it is smaller and easily portable, welding brings no disad-

This prototype of the bench-mounted press featured in the plans is in the process of assembly.

A finished view of the prototype model. The braces resting on the base brackets are used to support small parts.

vantage and significantly cuts the building time. Either gas or electric arc welding can be used, but arc welding is better suited to thick channel steel. The shorter frame needn't limit the tool's usefulness. Just mount the press over an opening cut in the top of a tool stand and this press will offer nearly the capacity of a floor-mounted model, plus the advantage of portability.

The press dimensions are calculated to eliminate steel waste when stock is purchased in the specified lengths. To build the press, first cut the steel channel and angle stock to the lengths shown in the plans. It is advisable to have the steel yard cut the heavy-gauge channel steel. Cutting the press parts by hand with a hacksaw is a time-consuming job. Slicing the steel with a torch leaves rough edges and uneven lengths, making it difficult to build an effective tool.

Before assembling the press, round the edges and corners of each piece on a grinding wheel. Next, drill in the side supports (part 1) that are required for the adjusting pins and the eye bolts. The holes must be located as shown in the plans. When one side-support has been drilled, it can be used as a template for the other. Holes also need to be drilled in the foot braces (part 6) and the jack base (part 5). Suggestions for drilling holes in heavy steel are given in the instructions for building the freestanding press.

Begin construction by welding the base assembly (parts 8 and 9). Shims must be inserted between the channel and angle pieces before welding, as shown in the plans, so that the guides will slide on the side-supports without binding. The four-inch space separating the base channels (part 4) on the work-support-assembly, allows shafts and other long parts to extend below the press. The hydraulic jack selected for the press should fit between the outside channel braces of the jack-base-assembly, otherwise a notch may have to be cut in one or both channel braces. Cutting a notch will weaken the jack base and should be compensated for by welding a quarter-inch plate to the underside of the jack base.

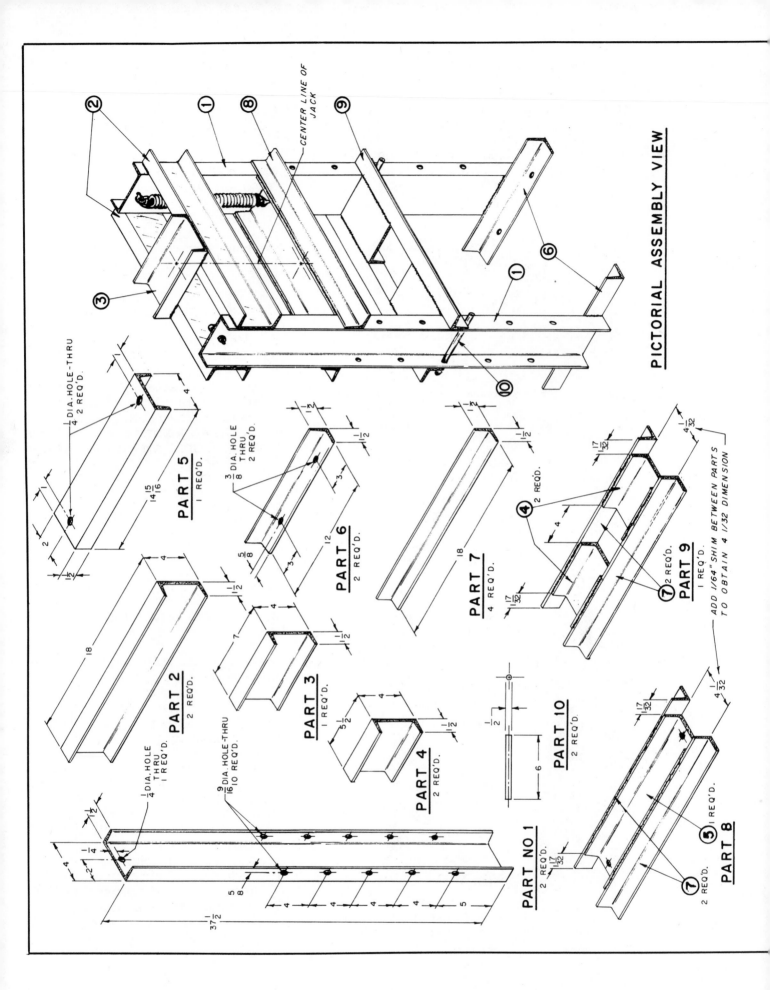

PICTORIAL ASSEMBLY VIEW

CENTER LINE OF JACK

PART 5
1 REQ'D.

PART 6
2 REQ'D.

PART 7
4 REQ'D.

PART 9
1 REQ'D.

PART 2
2 REQ'D.

PART 3
1 REQ'D.

PART 4
2 REQ'D.

PART 10
2 REQ'D.

PART 8
1 REQ'D.

PART NO 1
2 REQ'D.

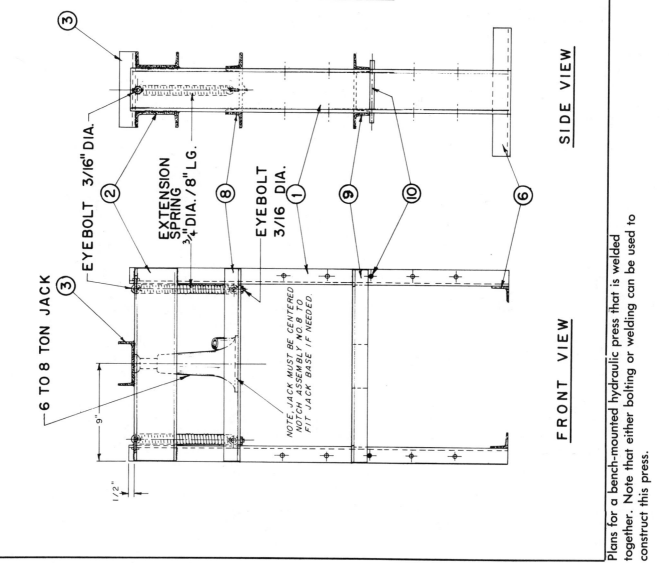

BILL OF MATERIALS

PART	ITEM	REQ'D
1	SIDE SUPPORT	2
2	TOP BRACE	2
3	TOP SUPPORT	1
6	FOOT	2
8	JACK BASE ASS'Y.	1
5	BASE	1
7	GUIDES	2
9	SUPPORT BASE ASS'Y.	1
4	BASE	2
7	GUIDES	2
10	PIN-ADJUSTING	2
PURCH.	6 TO 8 TON JACK	1
PURCH.	EYEBOLT 3/16"D×1½"LG.	4
PURCH.	NUT	4
PURCH.	WASHER	4
PURCH	SPRING-EXTENSION	2
—	3/4"D.×8"LG.	

STEEL: (Parts 1 thru 9)
4" CHANNEL 1 1/2" WIDE – 12'-0" LG.
1 1/2"×1 1/2" ANGLE – 8'-0" LG.

6 TO 8 TON JACK

EYEBOLT 3/16" DIA.

EXTENSION SPRING
3/4"DIA./8"LG.

EYEBOLT 3/16 DIA.

9"

1/2"

NOTE, JACK MUST BE CENTERED
NOTCH ASSEMBLY NO. 8 TO
FIT JACK BASE IF NEEDED.

FRONT VIEW

SIDE VIEW

Plans for a bench-mounted hydraulic press that is welded together. Note that either bolting or welding can be used to construct this press.

Assemble the press frame by welding side-supports to the top braces (part 2). These pieces must join at right angles. To check alignment, clamp a side-support firmly to the top brace and measure the angle with a metal framing square. Note that the plans show the top brace positioned slightly below the top edge of the side-support to provide additional surface area for strong penetrating welds. Weld the parts together along both edges of the side-support and the upper and lower edges of the top brace. After welding one side-support, clamp the other end of the top brace to the second side-support, check the angle, make sure both side-supports overlap the top brace by the same amount and weld the two pieces as before. Repeat the process with the other top brace. Care must be taken while welding the press frame to assure that the side-supports are parallel and that the top braces are aligned. Even small errors will affect the function and safe use of the press.

Two assembly steps remain. Before attaching the top support (part 3), center and clamp two flat washers with a 1½-inch inside diameter hole to the top support, then weld the washers in place. The washers are used to position the jack ram so that the jack can be removed from the press for other uses and quickly centered when it is replaced. Clamp the top support to the top braces making sure that it is centered on the press frame then weld it securely in place. Strong welds are critical to safe use of the press. If you are a novice welder, it is advised that you have a welding shop attach top support, perhaps construct the tool.

If you question whether the welds on the top support are strong enough to hold the full force of the hydraulic ram, bolt the top support to the top braces as a safety precaution.

After sliding the jack-base-assembly and the work-support-assembly into the press frame, weld the foot braces (part 6) to the side-supports. The two foot braces must be centered, clamped at right angles to the side-supports and welded flush with the bottom of the support framework so that the press will stand true. Note that holes should be drilled in both foot braces to mount the press on a workbench or tool stand. With the assembly steps completed, attach the two springs to eye bolts located in holes drilled through the side-supports and to the jack-base-assembly. Dimensions for the springs are given in the plans.

Clean and paint the press frame following the instructions given with the freestanding model. Coat the side-supports with light lubricant so that the jack base will slide easily. Bolt the press frame to a work stand, position the hydraulic jack and the press is ready for use.

In order to use the press to its full capacity, you should assemble a collection of pins, drivers, blocks and plates. To install and remove bushings you will need a collection of steel pins varying in diameter and length. Drivers made of steel tubing are used to install and remove bearings. You will need several lengths of tubing in varying diameters. When you are using the press to install or remove tight-fitting bearings, always select a driver that seats on the inner race. Never attempt to press a bearing on the outer race. You will also need several short lengths of angle iron and channel steel to support various-shape castings and shafts in the press. After using the press in several applications and adding to your collection of accessory blocks and drivers, the press should be essentially complete. Its use isn't limited to pressing bearings, bushings and gears when rebuilding mechanical parts. Both presses are rugged units that can bend or straighten steel and make excellent gluing clamps for woodworking projects.

A number of presses have been built from these plans. I chose the bench-mounted model for my own use. The two designs are similar, yet not identical. Although the instructions call for the large press to be bolted together and the small press constructed by welding, either method could be used to build either tool. The full versatility and usefulness of a hydraulic press will be fully appreciated only when you have built the tool and are using it in your shop.

Building A Jig To Access The Soft Underbelly Of Unit-Bodied Cars

A frame-up restoration in the traditional sense means removing the car's body from the chassis, then restoring the two major components separately from that juncture. The fact that the chassis, sans body, can be accessed most conveniently from the top is the principal reason for separating the two structures. Unit-bodied cars have a distinct disadvantage in this regard. Mechanical components can be removed from the body/chassis structure for overhaul but it is not possible to get "on top" of the situation to replace rusted brake lines, suspension parts and corroded side rails, reinforced rocker panels that unit construction substitutes for frame channels. Hobbyists seldom work in garages equipped with a hydraulic lift, so underbelly repair on unit-bodied cars has to be done by elevating the car on jack stands and working upside down from underneath. This becomes a nearly impossible position to work from when replacing a Porsche floor pan or rocker panels that give lateral support on a Jaguar or Mustang for example.

Readers who are new to the car hobby may wonder what unit-bodied construction is and how to recognize cars that are built according to this design. Although frameless cars gained popularity in the sixties and predominate today, unit-bodied construction first appeared in the thirties with the innovative Chrysler Airflow. Unit-bodied cars do not rest on a separate heavy-gauge frame, but use the body's box-like structure to support the suspension and mechanical components. In this sense, the unit-body design concept is borrowed from the aircraft industry. Designing a body structure that not only envelopes the passenger compartment, but also provides a mounting base for the engine, drivetrain and suspension has enabled manufacturers to build lower, lighter cars. These advantages were offset initially by the difficulty of isolating road

shock and the severe structural damage caused by even minor collisions to unit-bodied cars. Although engineers have been largely successful in surmounting these difficulties, they have not solved the great plague of unit-body construction—rust.

The easiest way to recognize cars built with unit-body construction is to crawl underneath the car at its midpoint and look up at the undercarriage to see whether or not the car has a frame. Another approach is to open the hood and check whether the front frame members continue under the body or if they appear to jut out from the firewall. Popular "pony" cars of the sixties—Mustangs, Cougars, Camaros, Valiants, Chargers and the like—mounted the front suspension on frame ears that were welded to a unit-body. Although "pony" cars made unit-body construction popular, they are by no means the only applications of this design. Lincoln Continentals, sixties vintage, are an example of full-size cars featuring unit-body construction. MGB's, Jaguar E-types and most BMC cars from 1960 onward including the Austin Marina and MG 1100, for example, were built using unit-body methods. The Willys Aero is an example of an early economy car using unit-body construction. Later gas misers, the Falcon and Corvair, also adopted this design and applied it to their pickup models—Ford's Econoline and the Corvair Rampside. Porsche used unit-body construction from the start but VW, its predecessor and cousin, used a unique body/frame design.

Because unit-bodied cars are constructed entirely of light-gauge sheet metal, they are susceptible to corrosion. In addition, this design that uses the body structure to support heavy mechanical components can be severely weakened by rust. Unit-bodied convertibles are a case in point. Convertibles rely on a rigid underpinning to stiffen their flimsy upper structure. For years auto makers mounted convertible bodies on heavy x-member frames. When manufacturers adopted unit-bodied construction in the sixties, the engineers had to design new support structures for the flexible bodies in order to continue building sporty convertibles.

Ford's answer was to buttress its unit-bodied convertibles with two sheet metal boxes extending between the wheel wells. These lateral support braces, called side rails are found in Mustang convertibles, for example. They lie behind the galvanized rocker panels, but are themselves unprotected from rust—and rust they do! It is realistic to expect some side rail corrosion on virtually any Mustang that has been driven regularly on salt-treated winter roads. On badly deteriorated cars, the corrosion damage to these support channels is evidenced by sagging doors and rusted floor sections alongside the rocker panels. Severely corroded Mustang convertibles have actually collapsed when the doors were opened, due to totally rusted side rails.

The problems encountered when installing new side rails on a Mustang convertible illustrate the need for a method to access the soft underbelly of unit-bodied cars. Before new support channels can be installed, the old ones, or what is left, have to be removed. Working underneath a unit body ragtop with a cutting torch to slice out the side rails is a nightmare. You have to gut the interior and elevate the car on jack stands. Once the rusted side rails are cut out (which is necessary before replacements can be installed), the car will fold in the center like a book unless a jack is placed under the stiff transverse brace located just aft of the transmission. Somehow there has to be a better way to restore rusted support members on unit-bodied cars than to jack up the car and work from underneath.

Restorers of 356 series Porsches have contrived a number of ingenious ways to repair floor pan rust, the plague of that unit-bodied car. Some bolt the front and rear of the car to portable stands resembling those used when rebuilding an engine. Like roasting a chicken on a spit, they roll the Porsche first on one side, then the other, even upside down making floor pan replacement, suspension and brake system repair a relatively simple matter. Naturally, the engine, transaxle and battery have to be removed first and the gas tank has to be drained. Others have suspended Porsche bodies, sans engine and transaxle, form overhead hoists and, again, flipped the cars belly-side-up to perform major floor pan surgery.

These methods won't work on Mustangs, Jaguars, Falcons, Chargers and other examples of unit-bodied cars. These cars are heavier than Porsches, which rules out using engine stands to turn the cars over. Secondly, because of differences in body design most other unit-bodied cars lack rugged front and rear mounting points that are required to attach an overhead hoist. However, there is another method for accessing the underbelly of unit-bodied cars which is equally effective and less expensive than portable stands and potentially safer than using either stands or overhead hoists.

Five wheel rims, several lengths of channel steel, a chain hoist or come-along, a section of tow chain and access to an arc welder or welding service are all the ingredients needed to build a jig that will tilt a unit-bodied car on its side for safe, sure underbelly repair. Building a tip-over jig requires skills beyond those of the novice mechanic, but the tool is ideally suited for serious restorers who are rebuilding late-model unit-bodied cars. If you are restoring a unit-body car that needs major metal surgery but feel that building the tip-over jig exceeds your skills, the repair work the car requires probably will also. In this case, the tip-over jig design may be useful to the person hired to do the bodywork.

The tip-over jig has two limitations that should be mentioned. First, because the jig is constructed using wheels that fit a particular car, different jigs may be needed for cars with four or five lug bolts or different bolt patterns. To overcome this limitation the wheels can be drilled for more than one lug pattern. A second, more serious limitation occurs when the tip-over jig is built for cars with

If you have to repair the underside of a car, this is clearly the most convenient angle to position your work.

Rodney Farris of Columbus, Ohio, designed this clever rig especially for restoring unit-bodied cars.

Rodney doesn't take chances, even with his own design. A heavy chain is wrapped around the top support brace to make sure the car can't roll back over.

wire wheels. Since wire wheels are usually designed with knock-off hubs, it is difficult to build the jig using substitute disc wheels. The solution may be to weld hubs from a set of scrap wire wheels in place of the centers of a set of scrap drums. The wheels will never have to be driven on the road, so the hubs don't have to be centered exactly, the only concern is that the welds are strong.

The tip-over jig consists of three parts. Two support braces mounted to the side of the car will rest on the shop floor. Another unit bolts to both wheels on the side of the car that will be elevated. To attach the jig, remove the car's wheels and tires, one side at a time. Bolt the jig to the wheel lugs, then hook a chain hoist to the long support brace connecting the wheels on the side that will be elevated. Raise the car until the support braces on the bottom side rest against the floor. The car should balance against the support braces making this a stable position. To be safe, attach the upper support brace to a solid overhead beam using a length of tow chain. Lifting a unit-bodied car on its side places floor pans, support rails, exhaust and brake systems in easy access and prevents the car from sagging while structural supports are replaced.

It is advisable to remove major mechanical components before raising a unit-bodied vehicle on its side. If the engine and transmission are left in the chassis, their weight puts an added strain on the car and the tip-over jig. Engine oil, coolant and transmission fluid will have to be removed if mechanical components are left in the car. The battery and gas tank have to be drained before tipping any car on its side.

Construction of the tip-over jig is practically as straightforward as its use. The two units that will rest on the floor consist of wheel halves and channel braces welded to spare wheels. The five wheels needed for the tip-over jig are usually available from junk yards. The tip-over jig's design adapts to any unit-bodied car, but in the case of an E-type Jaguar, for example, which features bulging body contours, jigs may have to be altered to extend the support braces away from the body so that the sheet metal isn't crunched when the car is tipped over. As you build the jig, check to make sure that the support braces will clear the body contours. Strong welds are critical on each of the support braces. If you are unsure of your welding skill, have the jig built by a professional welder.

The design of the lower support braces allows the car to raise gently on its side. Construction of these supports begins by cutting a scrap wheel so that it is divided into two semicircles. Each semicircular section is then welded to a spare wheel that fits, or is modified to fit, your car's lug bolt pattern. The wheel-half is welded to the rim of the spare wheel as shown in the accompanying illustration. After making necessary modifications to the spare wheels, weld support braces cut from lengths of 2 × 6-inch channel steel to the half-rim sections. There should be four weld contacts between each brace and the half-rim. Welds at these four points must have deep penetration since these braces will support much of the car's weight. The car's center of gravity will actually rest over the support braces, not the wheels. If the tip-over jig is used on coupes or sedans (body styles that have a higher center of gravity than convertibles), the lower support braces should be reinforced with sections of 2 × 2-inch angle iron similar to the construction used on the upper support.

The single-piece section of the tip-over jig mounts on what will be the car's upper side. Construction of this brace requires accurate measurements so that it will fit the car's wheel lugs. One way to make sure the structure will fit is to mount the spare rims on the car and tack weld the connecting brace. You can then remove the wheels and finish welding the support framework. Strong welds are equally important when building this part of the tip-over apparatus.

The first time you use the tip-over jig be sure the support braces clear the car's sheet metal. The overhead beam that holds the chain hoist used to raise the car must be strong enough to support the car's weight. Light-duty ceiling joists commonly used in garage construction will not support a car's weight. To use the jig in these conditions, you will have to install a carrier beam and reinforce it with floor jacks or posts positioned at either end of the car. Keep the tip-over jig's upper framework securely fastened to the carrier beam during the entire time the car is resting on its side.

Tipping a unit-bodied car on its side conveniently exposes the entire chassis and body floor section for restoration. Before making metal repairs near the gas tank, be sure to remove the tank. Remember that the tank must be drained before attempting to raise the car on its side using the tip-over jig. In order to replace the floors and unit-body support members, you may also need to remove the carpets, possibly even the seats, upholstery panels and trunk mats to prevent these combustible materials from catching fire during welding. Convertibles can be worked on from both sides when they are tipped on their side and this factor greatly facilitates cutting out and welding in new floor panels and frame channels.

When you are finished with body repair, protect the new metal with rust-resistant paint then inspect and replace corroded brake lines and do the same with emergency brake cables. Many mechanical components are easily accessed while the chassis is exposed that will be harder to work on when the car is returned to a horizontal plane.

Restoring unit-bodied cars doesn't have to be a nightmare and it's not, provided the underbelly repair can be made from a convenient working position. For this maneuver, the tip-over jig is ideal.

Support braces welded to the other pair of rims are used to hoist the car over on its side and support it in this vertical position.

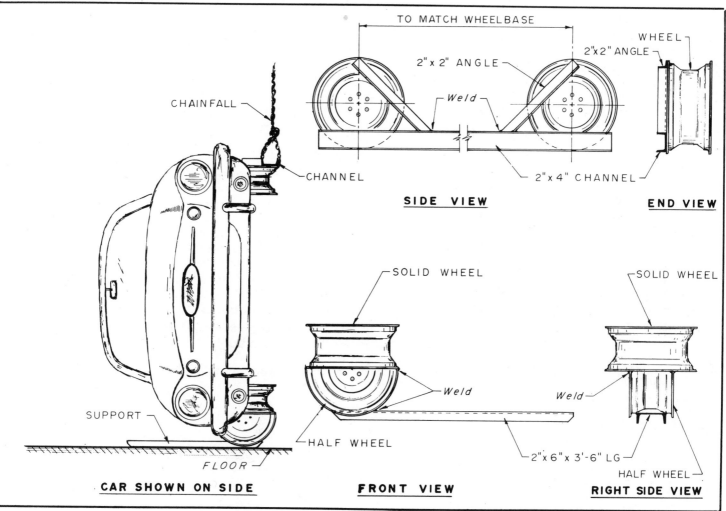

TO MATCH WHEELBASE

CHAINFALL

2" x 2" ANGLE

2" x 2" ANGLE

WHEEL

Weld

CHANNEL

2" x 4" CHANNEL

SIDE VIEW

END VIEW

SOLID WHEEL

SOLID WHEEL

Weld

Weld

SUPPORT

HALF WHEEL

2" x 6" x 3'-6" LG

HALF WHEEL

FLOOR

CAR SHOWN ON SIDE

FRONT VIEW

RIGHT SIDE VIEW

Various views of this ingenious device reveal how simple it really is.

A Researcher's Guide To Automotive Archives

Knowing where to look for information is the first step in successful research. The list of automotive archives that follows was prepared by Howard Applegate and first appeared in the *Journal of the Society of Automotive Historians.*

Current Automotive Companies

American Motors Corporation
Public Information Officer
27777 Franklin Road
Southfield, Michigan 48034
(includes Hudson, Nash and Seaman Body Company)

Chrysler Corporation
Department CIMS 417-24-18
P.O. Box 1919
Detroit, Michigan 48288

Ford Motor Company
Ford Archives
The Edison Institute
Henry Ford Museum
Dearborn, Michigan 48121

Ford Motor Company of Canada Ltd.
The Canadian Road
Oakville, Ontario
Canada L6J E54

Navistar (formerly International Harvester Company)
401 North Michigan Avenue
Chicago, Illinois 60611

Defunct Automotive Companies

Brewster Body Company
New York Public Library
Manuscripts Division
New York, New York 10011

J. G. Brill Body Company
Manuscripts Division
Historical Society of Pennsylvania
1300 Locust Street
Philadelphia, Pennsylvania 19107

Locomobile Company of America
Historical Collections
Bridgeport Public Library
925 Broad Street
Bridgeport, Connecticut 06004

Pierce-Arrow Motor Car Company
Engineering, Transportation Library
University of Michigan
Ann Arbor, Michigan 48109

Reo Motor Car Company
Transportation Library
Michigan State University
East Lansing, Michigan 48823

Studebaker-Packard Archives
Discovery Hall Museum
120 South St. Joseph Street
South Bend, Indiana 46601
(includes Erskine, Rockne and Avanti)

Automotive Supply Companies

Ditzler Automotive Finishes
P.O. Box 5090
Seven Oaks Station
Detroit, Michigan 48235

E I. DuPont de Nemours and Company, Inc.
Archives Department
Wilmington, Delaware 19898

Firestone Tire and Rubber Company
Corporate Research Department
Akron, Ohio 44317

General Tire and Rubber Company
Corporate Communications Department
One General Street
Akron, Ohio 44329

Goodyear Tire and Rubber Company
Archives Department
1144 East Market Street
Akron, Ohio 44316

Museums with Library and Archival Collections

Antique Automobile Club of America
501 West Governor Road
Hershey, Pennsylvania 17033
(library maintained for members of this organization)

Auburn—Cord—Duesenberg Museum
P.O. Box 148
Auburn, Indiana 46706

Automobile Reference Collection
Free Library of Philadelphia
Logan Square
Philadelphia, Pennsylvania 19103

Craven Foundation
760 Lawrence Avenue West
Toronto, Ontario
Canada M6A 1B8

Frederick C. Crawford Museum
10825 East Boulevard
Cleveland, Ohio 44106

Harrah's Automobile Collection
P.O. Box 10
Reno, Nevada 89504

Long Island Automotive Museum
Route 27
Southampton, New York 11968
(includes major collections on Locomobile and Mack)

Los Angeles County Museum of Natural History
Automotive History Collections
900 Exposition Boulevard
Los Angeles, California 90007

Motor Vehicle Manufacturers Association
Library
300 New Center Building
Detroit, Michigan 48202
(includes a photographic reference file)

Museum of Transportation
Library
Museum Wharf
300 Congress Street
Boston, Massachusetts 02110

National Automotive History Collection
Detroit Public Library
5201 Woodward Avenue
Detroit, Michigan 48202

National Motor Museum
Beaulieu
Hampshire, SO4 7ZN England

Pate Museum of Transportation
Library
P.O. Box 711
Fort Worth, Texas 76101

Sloan Museum
1221 East Kearsley
Flint, Michigan 48503
(includes material on Buick and Durant)

Smithsonian Institution
Curator, Automotive Collections
Washington, D.C. 20560

The Society of Automotive Historians, Inc.
c/o the National Automotive History Collection
Detroit Public Library
5201 Woodward Avenue
Detroit, Michigan 48202

A Key To Locating Restoration Supplies

To take some of the leg work out of locating reliable suppliers, three lists are included. The first contains hobby magazines that are excellent sources of ads for services, parts and equipment. The second identifies suppliers whose products are mentioned in this book. The third names additional suppliers of specialty items for collector cars.

Hobby magazines:

Cars & Parts
P.O. Box 482
Sidney, OH 45367
(a monthly publication containing both articles and ads; helpful features include an index to advertisers, a technical information exchange and frequent restoration articles)

Car Exchange
Iola, WI 54990
(a monthly publication containing articles and ads)

Car Collector
P.O. Box 171
Mount Morris, IL 61054

Hemmings Motor News
Box 100
Bennington, VT 05201
(a monthly publication consisting almost entirely of ads; a published flea market)

Old Cars Weekly
Iola, WI 54945
(a weekly newspaper featuring hobby news, articles and ads; special issues spring and fall are devoted to car care)

Special Interest Autos
P.O. Box 196
Bennington, VT 05201

Suppliers referred to in this book:

Automotive Restorations Unlimited
Route 1
Roxboro, NC 27573
(Eliminator polyester primer, also acrylic and nitrocellulose lacquers for all years)

Bathurst, Inc.
801 W. 15th St.
P.O. Box 27
Tyrone, PA 16686
(master disconnect and antitheft switches)

Don Kennett, Inc.
Box 344
Lawrence, MA 01842
(Featherfill polyester primer, also nitrocellulose lacquer for Model A Fords and vintage Chevrolets)

Hampton Coach
70 High St.
Hampton, NH 03842
(ready-to-install upholstery kits for over 80 models of vintage Chevrolets, 1922 to 1953; specializes in recovering sun visors and armrests)

H. C. Fastener
Rt. 2, #27
Alvarado, TX 76009
(trim molding fasteners, rubber bumpers, weather stripping, wiring harness straps, body solder, related tools and supplies)

Heinmuller Restorations
Box 797
Berkley Ave.
Bethlehem, NH 03574
(carburetor overhaul kits and restoration)

Le Baron Bonney
6 Chestnut St.
Amesbury, MA 01913
(rare upholstery fabrics, top coverings, vinyl, leather and carpeting)

Lentin Forese
1646 82nd St.
Brooklyn, NY 11214
(restoration supplies, body tools and painting supplies, including Liquid Ebony, a polishing glaze for enamel finishes)

Metro Moulded Parts
P.O. Box 33130
9571 Foley Blvd.
Minneapolis, MN 55433
(weatherstripping and reproduction rubber supplies)

Snyder's Antique Auto Parts
12925 Woodworth Rd.
New Springfield, OH 44443
(seat springs for Fords plus Model A Ford parts; also a museum of player pianos, old cars and Ford racing engines)

Techne Electronics, Ltd.
916 Commercial St.
Palo Alto, CA 94303
(maker of the Ungo Box, a hi-tech electronic antitheft alarm system)

Additional suppliers of hard-to-get items. This list is intended as a starting point. For items not mentioned here, refer to the hobby magazines, flea markets, club newsletters and fellow hobbyists.

Carburetor rebuilding and supplies:
The Carburetor Shop
Eldon, MO 65026
(vintage carburetor restoration and sales)

Car radio tubes and supplies:
Barry Electronics Corp.
512 Broadway
New York, NY 10012
(radio tubes and electrical supplies)

MHz Electronics
2111 W. Camelback
Phoenix, AZ 85015
(radio tubes)

Madison Electronics Supply
1508 McKinney
Houston, TX 77010
(radio tubes and electrical supplies)

Hubcaps, trim restoration and buffing supplies:
James McConville
4205 W. 129th St., No. 22
Hawthorne, CA 90250
(Chevrolet hubcap skins)

John Young Restoration Services
Westmoreland, NH 03467
(stainless steel restoration)

Tioga Stainless
Apalachin, NY 13732
(buffing supplies)

The Eastwood Co.
P.O. Box 524
Berwyn, PA 19312
(Lumiweld aluminum and pot metal welding rods, buffing supplies, metal repair and restoration tools)

Rubber parts:
Brownlee's Old Time Antique Auto Parts
Lawrenceville, GA 30245
(new-old-stock and reproduction rubber for Ford and Mercury)

Kessler's Antique Cars and Body Shop
Olney, IL 62450
(reproduction rubber parts for Chevrolets 1928–50)

Restoration Specialties and Supply
Windber, PA 15963
(window weatherseal, moldings, trim clips and miscellaneous hardware)

Lynn H. Steele
Route 1
Denver, NC 28037

Upholstery kits and interior supplies:
Bill Hirsch
396 Littleton Ave.
Newark, NJ 07103
(fine imported leather and upholstery fabrics)

Kanter Auto Products
76 Monroe St.
Boonton, NJ 07005
(carpets, convertible tops, upholstery fabrics and seat upholstery kits for "all American makes '32–'60"; nitrocellulose primers and lacquer)

Larry's Thunderbird and Mustang Parts
511 S. Raymond Ave.
Fullerton, CA 92631
(Mustang upholstery kits)

Stan Coleman
320 South St.
Morristown, NJ 07960
(sports car upholstery kits—American and foreign; headliner kits for American and foreign cars)

Wheel rebuilding and restoration:
Dayton Wheel Products
1147 South Broadway
Dayton, OH 45408
(wire wheel spokes and rims, plus wire wheel restoration)

Graber and Sons
3315 Morena Blvd.
San Diego, CA 92117
(specializes in rebuilding wooden wheels)

Wiring harnesses, braiding, shielding and miscellaneous electrical supplies:
Antique Auto Electric
9109 E. Garvey Ave.
Rosemead, CA 91770
(vintage car electrical supplies—West Coast)

Rhode Island Wiring Service
P.O. Box 24H
Kingston, RI 02881
(vintage car electrical supplies—East Coast)

Mallory Electric Corp.
1801 Oregon St.
Carson City, NV 89701
(wiring and electrical supplies)

Buchill Antique Auto Parts
4150 24th Avenue
Port Huron, MI 48060
(wiring diagrams of all American cars since 1915)

Wells Mfg. Corp.
2-26 S. Brooke St.
Fond du Lac, WI 54935
(electrical supplies)

YHZ's Yesterday's Parts
1615 N. Fern
Redlands, CA 92373

Witaker Cable Corp.
2801 Rockcreek Pkwy.
N. Kansas City, MO 64117
(wiring supplies)

Diodes, also called resisters:
Radio Shack
stores located nationwide

Allied Electronics
401 E. 8th Street
Fort Worth, TX 76102

Wood supplies and hardware:
Cincinnati Woodworks
1248 Eastern Ave.
Cincinnati, OH 45202
(replacement wood and supplies for
1941–48 Ford and Mercury woody wagons)

Ed Clarke Restoration Supplies
67 Rockland Ave.
Larchmont, NY 10538
(woody wagon hardware and supplies)

Lasco Design
259 Roosevelt Ave.
Holland, MI 49423
(replacement wood and supplies for
1949–51 Ford and Mercury woody wagons)

Wood Art
10117 2nd Ave. S.
Bloomington, MN 55420
(replacement wood for Ford V-8's)

Lock Repair and Rekeying Service
The Key Shop
114 Crescent Dr.
Akron, OH 44301
(Bonded locksmith with thousands of NOS
locks and keys for older cars to the 1920s.
Will repair and rekey virtually any automotive lock)

Grease Remover
E-C Cleaner
% Carl Holthe
6032 Portland Ave. S.
Minneapolis, MN 55417
(a safe-to-use, non-corrosive, biodegradable cleaner that is ideal for cleaning grease coated metal parts. E-C Cleaner can also be used to remove stains from fabric)

Carbon Monoxide Detector
Ward International
P.O. Box 3628
Granada Hills, CA 91344
(detects carbon monoxide concentrations as small as 200 parts per million. The indicator button is held in a triangular bracket that can be mounted on a workshop wall to warn against dangerously high CO levels)

Rust Neutralizers
Rust neutralizers are a boon for the automotive restorer. They convert red rust to black rust (magnetite), a stabilized oxide that becomes part of the metal substrate and prevents further rusting. The procedure for applying rust neutralizer is to remove loose scale with a wire brush, blow away the scale and dust, and spray or brush on the neutralizer. After the neutralizer has had time to react with the rust, the metal can be primed and painted. With proper application, the result is the same as if the metal had been cleaned to bare steel.

W. L. (Bill) Charonnat
P.O. Box 20663
Castro Valley, CA 94546
(supplies Corroless, which is a base-coat rust-neutralizing primer, applied by brushing or spraying).

H. C. Fastener
Rt. 2, #27
Alvarado, TX 76009
(supplies Fertan, which is a black liquid of watery consistency that is applied by spraying, brushing or wiping on with a rag)

Neutra Rust
(distributed by New York Bronze Co., and sold through auto parts and building supply stores. Neutra Rust is a white liquid that is applied by brushing or spraying).